The Enquiring Teacher
Supporting and Sustaining
Teacher Research.

The Enquiring Teacher
Supporting and Sustaining Teacher Research

Edited by
Jennifer Nias
and
Susan Groundwater-Smith

 The Falmer Press

(A member of the Taylor & Francis Group)
London • New York • Philadelphia

UK   The Falmer Press, Falmer House, Barcombe, Lewes, East Sussex,
      BN8 5DL

USA   The Falmer Press, Taylor & Francis Inc., 242 Cherry Street,
      Philadelphia, PA 19106-1906

First published 1988

Library of Congress Cataloging in Publication Data

The Enquiring Teacher.
  Bibliography: p.
  Includes index.
  1. Action research in education—-Great Britain.
2. Teachers—Training of—Great Britain. 3. Teachers—
In-service training—Great Britain. I. Nias, Jennifer.
II. Groundwater-Smith, Susan.
LB1028.24.E56 1988   371.1′46   88-16376
ISBN 1-85000-295-9
ISBN 1-85000-296-7 (pbk.)

Jacket design by Teresa Dearlove

Typeset in 11/13 Garamond by
Imago Publishing Ltd, Thame, Oxon

*Printed in Great Britain by Taylor & Francis (Printers) Ltd,
Basingstoke*

Contents

Contents

Introduction

Jennifer Nias

Teacher research does not take place in a vacuum. In the context of this book it belongs not just in schools and classrooms but also in all types of institution where enquiry-based teacher education takes place. The chapters in part 1 justify this assertion which is then explored in action in parts 2, 3 and 4. This Introduction presents some definitions and then discusses the implications for teachers who become students on enquiry-based courses, for the schools and colleges in which they teach and for the colleges, polytechnics, universities and teachers' centres which mount and teach the courses. It emphasizes the fact that commitment to such courses is not for the faint-hearted. Involvement in them is a greater risk-taking enterprise than is the delivery and consumption of conventional academic courses.

Throughout this book 'enquiring teachers' is taken to mean those who are students on courses, successful completion of which depends in part on their undertaking one or more enquiries into their own practice or that of their colleagues. Such courses have two main characteristics:

1 Because student enquiries are necessary for the gaining of a credential, they are subject to criticism, from tutors and/or course members. The latter are likely to form part of the course assessment.

2 The process and outcomes of such enquiries are shared with tutors and/or course members, whereas on most conventional courses student writing is a private exchange between student and tutor and is often seen by the latter only in its completed form.

1

At this point it is worth making the distinction between enquiry-based and research-based courses, for not all the former meet the criteria proposed by Stenhouse in his description of research as 'systematic enquiry made public' (Rudduck and Hopkins, 1985). First attempts at gaining greater insight into one's practice by becoming an actively 'reflective practitioner' (Schon, 1983) are often crude and erratic and are seldom shared with more than a small group. Nevertheless, a number of the students engaged in undertaking their own enquiries are using concepts and processes as complex and intellectually demanding as those involved in conventional research. Accordingly, while the editors of, and contributors to, this book recognize the distinction between the two terms, they often use them interchangeably. When a precise meaning is intended, it can be inferred from the context in which it appears.

Behind the decision to give teachers' enquiries a central place in a course which has academic as well as professional currency are epistemological and pedagogical assumptions. These are embedded in the way the course is planned, taught and evaluated but are seldom made explicit. Among the most important of them are:

1 Teachers have the capacity, under appropriate conditions, to undertake valid and reliable enquiries into all aspects of their working lives.

2 However, they do not necessarily possess the analytic and methodological skills to undertake rigorous enquiry. Their courses must therefore provide opportunities for them to acquire these.

3 The topics or issues which they decide to make the subject of enquiry may arise from course content or may contribute to it.

4 Individuals can generate from their enquiries and those of other course members 'practical theories' which may subsequently illuminate or guide their actions.

5 However, their enquiries will not immediately or necessarily lead to action. In other words, professional enquiry is not synonymous with action research, though the two will often be closely related.

6 When students are empowered in these ways to control their own learning and create their own knowledge, status differences between teachers and taught are reduced.

7 Assessment of enquiry-based courses will be problematic because of the absence of public criteria for judging the

quality of performance on them and because of the private nature of much teacher enquiry.

Further, it is likely that:

8 Teachers will need support in undertaking enquiries into their professional lives and practices and in coming to terms with the implications of their findings.

Now it will be clear that courses which embody these assumptions will differ in a number of ways from more traditional library-, lecture- and tutorial-based courses and will, in consequence, affect students, the places in which they undertake their enquiries (normally schools and colleges), their employers (who are also often course-funders) and the providing institutions (from whom all the authors in this book come).

Most obviously, enquiry-based courses make new demands on students. To gather evidence about, to reflect on and perhaps to change one's own professional practice require self-awareness, self-evaluation, self-revelation and probably create self-doubt. Such activities are therefore likely to be threatening because they render individual teachers vulnerable to their own criticism and possibly also to that of course tutors and peers. The deeper this examination by self and others, the greater the need for trust, cooperation and mutual support among school staffs and within the teaching groups.

The need for this kind of support becomes proportionally greater when students' enquiries reveal the case within particular schools for changes in organizational forms or in the practice of others. It is expecting a great deal of teachers to suggest that they should not only modify their own activities but also pit themselves, often single-handed, against the established habits of their colleagues. Yet without action, the insights gained from disciplined enquiry often run into the sands of unquestioned custom. Unless 'enquiring teachers' can effect some changes in their schools there is a danger that, as students, they will become mutually reinforcing but ineffectual reference groups, sharing a critical perspective and a common vocabulary but little commitment to action. So, enquiry-based courses face a three-fold challenge: (i) to encourage in students a constructively critical stance to professional practice; (ii) to help them take appropriate action in response to their enquiries; and (iii) to support them through the consequences of the latter.

All these activities raise issues of confidentiality for students and tutors. For example, the former may be part of a network of information linking schools in the same authority or they may, now or in the future, occupy posts which could affect one another's promotion prospects. Or, the tutors' desire to use and disseminate students' findings may be opposed to the latter's need to protect themselves and their colleagues from further scrutiny. The negotiation between students, schools, local authorities and course-providers of an ethical code covering confidentiality and the right of access is a priority for all who engage in enquiry-based courses.

Such courses may also affect the schools from which students come for less praiseworthy reasons than the generation of legitimate criticism, the desire for change or the stimulation of increased staff involvement. For example, individual teachers occasionally use course assignments deliberately to gather data damaging to their colleagues or heads. Even in less extreme cases, more may be revealed about certain schools than some of their members would wish to be the case. Enquiry may have other consequences too. Interviews sometimes bring to the surface violent feelings which have nothing to do with the subject under discussion but which, having been voiced, can no longer be ignored. Once personal differences among teachers are made explicit or discrepancies in aim are articulated, a school may be permanently divided, even disabled. For the providing institution, involvement in a school and in the lives, feuds and opinions of its staff is temporary and vicarious. But those who make the enquiries have to go on living and working together, harbouring resentments or facing obstacles whose existence has been highlighted by their activity but about which course tutors can do nothing. In other words, work which may have a constructive effect on individual teachers (for example, in raising questions about their curricular aims) may have a potentially destructive effect upon their schools (for example, by encouraging entrenchment and isolationism).

Ethical considerations apart, there are instrumental reasons why enquiry-based courses should be mounted and run with sensitivity towards schools. First, such courses depend heavily upon goodwill. This is particularly the case when students on them are, for example, heads, senior staff or inspectors whose enquiries may seem potentially threatening to teachers. Students normally need the co-operation of others to help in data collection, interpretation and validation. Tutors too may need access to schools in order to judge the accuracy or even the truth of data collected by a student, or to increase their understanding of a particular type of schooling, activities which must be carefully handled if they are not to impair collegial relationships. Then there is the question of academic credibility: the ethnographic research methods used by many 'enquiring teachers' are not understood or accepted by all of their colleagues, especially when the latter have a background in mathematical or scientific research. Lastly, there are the problems raised by the over-use of particular schools. In many traditional teacher education courses the phenomenon of the over-visited school is a familiar one. Its counterpart for enquiry-based courses is the research-saturated school in which several teachers, concurrently or in quick succession, are engaged in probing not just their own activities but also those of their colleagues, causing the latter to feel, in consequence, that they have no peace or privacy. This phenomenon arises partly from the success of enquiry-based courses for, as students share their interests, excitements or findings with their colleagues, the latter are often stimulated into seeking similar involvement for themselves.

The providing institutions are themselves affected by the courses they offer. Most obviously, the latter have to be planned, developed, taught, assessed and evaluated (externally and internally), all of which affect the staff of the institutions and the structures within which they work. However, since these activities are the implicit or explicit focus of most of the chapters in this book, we do not consider them further here. Secondly, enquiry-based courses are resource-hungry. Students need access for data collection to tape-recorders, radio microphones, video and other cameras. New books and periodicals are needed for the library. Tutors, too, often use audio-visual materials for demonstration purposes or to provide course content. They may also need to duplicate large quantities of transcripts or other written data for use in their teaching. Moreover, assignments which call for production of a thick case record of transcripted interview data, field notes, photographs, tape-recordings and the like may impose a substantial financial burden on some students. The conventional essay is in many respects cheaper to research and produce and less demanding of multi-media resources than its successors. Moreover, if in the process of supporting or monitoring student enquiries course tutors visit the latter's schools, the providing institution may face costly transport bills.

Further, enquiry-based courses are often more convenient to teach if students are part-time than if they are full-time, because, for example, part-time students have more instant access to classrooms and schools. However, part-time courses impose tangential strains on institutions used to dealing with the full-time. Students need refreshment and library facilities, buildings have to be heated and kept open. At a time of overall cuts in higher education and often, too, of union restraints, all this can be difficult. In addition, changes are likely to be needed in the administrative and decision-making structures of institutions which mount a considerable number of part-time courses. Internal committee structures may need to be altered, the academic calendar changed, rituals and collective functions modified. It is not easy to make part-time students feel that they are part of the college, polytechnic or university, especially if they are not represented on committees, if the latter meet in the daytime or if facilities for students are limited; in short, if those who manage the institutions do not perceive them as members of it.

Thirdly, such courses require tutors with specific kinds of expertise. The latter must be able to select and teach research methods suitable for use by practitioners and be capable of producing and applying criteria for the assessment of school-based assignments and dissertations, even when these lead into new and perhaps, for them, untried methods of data collection and presentation. Further, they must be prepared to read and research in response to their students' interests and not just their own. Staff in institutions of higher education often possess a highly specialized body of knowledge which may prove insufficient on its own to support and sustain student enquiries. Lastly, tutors must be able, and willing, to find their way round the educational system at large, keeping in touch with the politics of local educational institutions and bureaucracies as well as with classrooms and schools.

The assumptions on which such courses are constructed also have implications for pedagogy. Since it is from their own enquiries and reflections that students derive practical and theoretical insights, tutors cannot teach in didactic or authoritarian ways without creating a conflict between the course's goals and its methods. So, they must be prepared to see their students as intellectual equals, capable of reflecting upon and interpreting their own practices, of abstracting key issues from the latter and generating their own practical theory from their enquiries. Yet students, from habit and out of a personal need for security, will often attempt to press tutors into adopting an authoritarian role. It is not easy to be *primus inter pares*, particularly if one's expertise and authority have for years been underlined by a lecture-dominated pedagogy and by the traditional supervision of teaching practice. Yet the internal logic of enquiry-based courses requires that they develop a pedagogy and therefore a set of social relationships which is student rather than tutor-focussed and through which individual students can control their own learning.

For similar reasons tutors must be ready to develop fresh counselling skills. Of course, anyone involved in the education of adults and particularly adult teachers has always had to be a counsellor. However, research into one's own teaching, workplace and work can touch upon very sensitive areas and cause crises of confidence and identity. For example, the kind of support that course tutors may need to give a student who is undergoing a marriage breakdown is different from that they extend to a headteacher who is slowly becoming aware of how little he/she enjoys the confidence of his/her staff. Similarly, tutors must be capable of creating and sustaining relationships among students which will encourage them to support one another. This in turn suggests that tutors need to understand how groups react and behave and how they can best be used not only to support but also to increase the learning of all participants.

Next, because they are more labour-intensive than traditional courses enquiry-based courses affect the workload of staff. There are three reasons for making this claim. The negotiation of access to schools and particularly to classrooms takes time. It involves visits (for example, to inspectors and schools), the building up of trusting relationships at all levels of school and local educational hierarchies and some ability to familiarize oneself with the individual student's setting. Second, the assignments themselves take more time than essays do to supervise and to mark, since assessment involves scrutinizing audio and video recordings, photographs, fieldwork notes, transcripts of interviews, documentary evidence and the like, as well as the hypotheses which are generated from them. Thirdly, there is a strong tendency for this kind of work to lead to additional demands on staff time. When teachers see that courses can help in the development of individual teachers or whole schools, they will often approach the institution for assistance with, for example, evaluation procedures, curricular reviews or classroom observation. In addition, ex-students seeking to effect changes which arise from their experience of practitioner research may make continuing demands on course tutors for time and moral support.

Moreover, it could be argued that tutors who choose to sponsor and support school-based enquiries ought themselves to be involved in this kind of research. To respect and encourage the development of teachers' own practical theories has within it a tacit imperative that course tutors should do the same. Indeed, one might ask: have we the right to require teachers to undertake activities that we would not ourselves wish to carry out in our own institutions? Furthermore, if course tutors become used to being part of a collegial group in which students question their tutors and each other and take considerable responsibility for their own learning, they may well begin to question their own institutional arrangements, relationships and organization. If we undertook critical enquiry into our own institutions as a direct result of stimulating such activity among teachers, who knows where the changes might stop?

This type of critical questioning may be the more uncomfortable in institutions where traditional paradigms of research are given status. When a group of tutors operating within an orthodox academic programme try to launch a course which is based on the claim that teachers can conduct and interpret their own research, they may run the risk of operating a low status enterprise — with all that implies in terms of resource provision and staff priorities. They and their courses may have to fight for survival if the institutional climate is not favourable towards them or if, for example, external examiners or professional colleagues from other institutions question the propriety and validity of teacher research.

Furthermore, tutors who share a common perspective within an intellectually hostile environment may draw together as a common reference and friendship group. Yet in the process of strengthening and confirming one another they may make themselves more institutionally visible (and thus vulnerable). They may also cut themselves off from contact and communication with other individuals and groups, highlighting their separateness and, in so doing, reducing the likelihood of common action across a broad ideological front. Moreover, in the present economic climate, few small institutions can afford serious internal divisions. Yet their very survival may depend on their capacity to initiate and attract students to fresh courses. When, then, does ideological difference among tutors signal disaster and when is it a sign of hope and rejuvenation?

Indeed, school-based courses are sometimes introduced as part of a bid for local professional support. Yet there are tensions here too. There may be a conflict for both tutors and students between the collaborative nature of their new enterprise and the academic need to assess and put forward for external examination the work of students on it. These are familiar dilemmas and the resolution of them would normally be a problem internal to course management rather than an institutional affair. However, if a course is struggling for survival and recognition, its sponsors are likely to look upon teachers as allies and members of a common reference group and the requirements of examination may cut across this alliance. Moreover, if the identity of the whole institution depends upon its perceived ability to help, encourage and support teachers in schools, then the apparent contradiction between collaboration and judgment may have considerable implications for its credibility.

This is particularly important in the United Kingdom at present because, under the new funding arrangements, many in-service courses depend upon the willingness of central and local government to subsidize or support students on them. Yet course funders are themselves ambivalent towards such courses. On the one hand, some wish to support them because they judge them to combine high intellectual standards with an impact on schools. On the other, enquiry-based courses may be perceived, especially if they are successful, as subversive. Teachers who look systematically and critically at their practice are likely to want to change it and this may bring them into conflict with structures at school level or beyond. Further, fee-providers have little control over what teachers do when they come on such courses. To be sure, this is true of traditional courses too, but it is even more the case when the course content may be generated by the students themselves. Similarly, if enquiry-based courses are seen to encourage teachers in habits of independent thinking with which central government or local authorities are not happy, providing institutions may become, by association, sinister partners in professional subversion. It is additionally important therefore that tutors have the time and social skills to seek out inspectors and education officers, to talk to them and to dispel or allay their anxieties.

Yet to maintain and foster such contacts is not just demanding of time and other resources from the providing institutions. It may also be academically compromising (if, for example, the opportunity arises to give an inspector preferential treatment in competition with others for a place upon a course). Course providers may find themselves compromised in other ways too: what, for example, should tutors do when, under conditions of confidentiality, their students' enquiries reveal educational malpractice in a particular school? In other words, course-providers need to consider with whom they feel they have an implicit contract: is it the schools, individual teachers, their pupils or the latter's parents, the local authorities or central government? Clearly, enquiry-based courses render more complex the relationships between bureaucracies and providing institutions and demand that tutors possess not just tact, sensitivity, integrity and a good memory, but also a high degree of tolerance for tension and ambiguity.

To sum up, the enquiry-based courses which are the focus of discussion in the rest of this book have far-reaching implications for teachers, schools and providing institutions and for the relationships between each of them. For a student, to subject professional practice (be it one's own or that of others) to systematic enquiry and to share the results of this scrutiny with a wider audience than simply a course tutor is to open oneself and one's colleagues to self-doubt and criticism. It is also, in some instances, to put oneself at odds with one's colleagues, to find oneself not only alone in the staff group but also unable to implement the changes to which one's enquiries have pointed. At worst, then, enquiring teachers may be deskilled, disoriented, isolated and rendered impotent by their experience on such courses. Schools too may be opened up to more examination than many of their members want and, as a result, internal differences and divisions may be exacerbated. The need to anticipate and where possible prevent these kinds of damaging consequences means that course-providers must handle their relationships with schools and local authorities with sensitivity, foresight and integrity. Finally, the courses have a three-fold impact on the providing institutions themselves. First, they emphasize the growing interdependence at a personal and at an institutional level between course-providers and course-funders. Second, they require physical resources, are labour-intensive, may dictate staff retraining and suggest new directions for research. They may also lead or lend added point to internal questioning of established pedagogical practices and relationships. Third, they make emotional demands on tutors. Enquiry-based courses are challenging, interesting and rewarding to plan and to run. They bring those responsible for them into a constant and satisfying relationship with the work of the schools and enable them to feel that they are contributing to the development of the profession as a whole. But for these very reasons they require high tolerance for ambiguity, a readiness to live with tension, an understanding of the fact that an institutional boundary which is deliberately made more permeable may also be more easily breached. Further, tutors must understand that if they wish to change the practice of education in schools they are likely also to have to change their own. The chapters in this book reflect the existence of an exciting but a demanding option, one that requires the rethinking of traditional relationships both within institutions and between them.

These chapters also reflect the growing world-wide interest in such courses. The conference in 1986 from which they arose was the third in an international series on *Teaching Enquiry-Based Courses*, sponsored and organized by the Cambridge Institute of Education (the secretarial and administrative staff of which we should like to thank for their unfailing, cheerful and efficient help and support, with the conferences and in the production of this book). The participation of teacher educators from countries such as the United Kingdom, Canada, the United States, the Netherlands, Austria, West Germany and Norway suggests that the field is a burgeoning one. The quality of the chapters indicates that the fruit of this new tradition has deep intellectual roots and is nourished by sturdy growth. The courses reported in this book are hybrids, bred of international cross-fertilization. At a time of despondency in much traditional teacher education, they signal the continuing existence of optimism, variety, vigour and expansion.

References

RUDDUCK, J. and HOPKINS, D. (1985) *Research as a Basis for Teaching*: *Readings from the Work of Lawrence Stenhouse*, London, Heinemann.

SCHON, D. (1983) *The Reflective Practitioner*, London, Temple Smith.

Part 1

Why Enquiry-based Courses?

Enquiry-based courses in teacher education are founded upon well-reasoned and defended arguments. The section which follows articulates the rationale for the provision of enquiry-based courses. This rationale is predicated upon three different, but overlapping, assumptions underlying teacher research (in which teachers are learners, regarding and reflecting upon their own practice). These are: (a) that the focus of the enquiry should be of the learner's choosing; (b) that having perceived the problem (should one exist) the learner should feel moved to change the conditions from which the problem arose; and (c) that the learner will see him/herself as a member of a community of enquirers, rather than as an isolated individual. Letiche, Bell and Rowland draw upon these assumptions in their presentations.

More specifically, Letiche challenges the notion of reducing enquiry, as part of an award-bearing course, to a technical exercise. He couples cognitive action with contextual action and emphasizes the social experience of collaborative learning. He analyzes the interaction between learning by doing, learning to learn and learning via group processes. The curriculum which he proposes for enquiry-based courses has been characterized by Letiche as a negative-curriculum, that is one which is defined by its non-values, by making clear what it is that students are not supposed to do. It is founded upon the notion that there is 'no one privileged approach' to enquiry but recognizes that certain forms and practices are inimicable to practitioner research. Letiche briefly illustrates his argument by drawing upon a medical education case study.

In the second chapter Bell brings our attention to the shift which enquiry-based courses require from the study of received knowledge to the active construction of practitioners' epistemologies. This entails the 'lived experience of an uncertainty about what is worthwhile'. Bell is critical of those protagonists of a particular form of teacher enquiry, i.e. action research, who reduce the research activity to an iconic cycle serving narrow, instrumental interests. He points to the problems in the current pressure for collaboration, for groups to undertake studies, which leaves unexamined the question as to whether group members have any common epistemology. Bell also draws our attention to the products of practitioner research; that is, what is it that the teacher-as-enquirer produces and to what use is it put?

Rowland, too, is concerned with epistemological questions. He examines critically the concept of personal knowledge and asks, 'how does my body of knowledge relate to the knowledge of others?' and 'how does personal knowledge affect practice if it is merely unreflective introspection?' By bringing together reading and personal experience Rowland indicates that a practitioner's body of knowledge is constructed and nurtured in a number of ways.

These three chapters, then, lead us to formulate a rationale for enquiry-based courses as a practice which is itself dynamic and open to critique.

1 Interactive Experiential Learning in Enquiry Courses

Hugo Letiche

There's nothing so practical as a good epistemology.

Introduction

The enquiry-based curriculum for which I shall argue seeks to channel the participants' energy.[1] The students learn to look at their experiences through the eyes of curriculum goals which are non-instrumental in nature. It is as though they become external observers of their own experiences. This is neither a comfortable nor an easy experience. As long as enquiry courses are a pedagogical exception, one can expect that most enrolments will be by highly motivated students willing to take the risks involved in the management of their own learning. Thus, Antioch College's internship curriculum was long able to draw on a willing student body who had consciously chosen an exceptional course of study. Antioch's success led some educators to propagate internships as a solution to the work/university tension. But Dutch universities, with their *required* internships, prove that one cannot rely on this curricular innovation to solve much of anything. What worked well in a situation of self-selection does not achieve comparable results when it is required. Educationists often fall into the trap of generalizing their limited successes. Innovational success, based on a small staff and self-selected students, does not harbor general applicability. When we want students to get rid of the external vantage point (the world as seen by the curriculum) and to observe concretely a here and now, we have to make sure that our pedagogics do not freeze the situation. Learning goals quickly limit the categories of (self-) investigation. The organizational dynamics of the curriculum produce illustrations, models, guidelines and norms of grading. These define what the student has to do, a situation which is inimical to genuine enquiry. This argument is not leading to an equating of enquiry with anarchy. Disciplined professional and cognitive development can be demanded in enquiry course work. What we need is a framework of agreements clarifying what is *not* going to take place.[2] These interdicts clarify the situation wherein one works. Agreements on what one is not going to do are in practice easier to justify, and more simple to arrive at, than are prescriptive rules. And more important still, they do not freeze the categories of thought. Given that individual social responsibility is enquiry learning's most central point of departure, a negative code of research norms can at once act as a necessary procedural statement, and leave ample room for initiative. The mania to equip students with an efficient 'tool kit' leads educators to define behavioral goals, every-which-way. Enquiry becomes so many skills to be mastered according to a pre-set (ideally, highly efficient) research path. Enquiry then, has been operationalized. The intellectual and practical self-management crucial to experiential learning has been sacrificed to a technical approach. Genuine wrestling with a context has been replaced with pre-fab research techniques. Curricular clarity has been bought at the cost of rigidifying learning. 'Proven' teaching techniques, standard lessons, foolproof materials can all now be developed. But we cannot marshal real personal resources in this manner! Enquiry may need facilitation and/or support, but it cannot survive when moulded into a preset curriculum. If students are to attempt to solve practical problems as a learning exercise, they have to be left to get on with it. The educators have to adopt a low profile, as curriculum designers. The rule being developed here is:

> DON'T INTERFERE TOO MUCH IN THE LEARNING PROCESS; DON'T BE AFRAID OF STUDENT INITIATIVE.

The corollary for curriculum development is:

> DEFINE YOUR COURSE'S NON-VALUES; MAKE IT CLEAR WHAT THE STUDENTS AREN'T SUPPOSED TO DO.

I have, along with colleagues at the Rotterdam School of Management, developed enquiry course work, based upon a negative-curriculum, when facilitating student internships and while supervising student research projects.[3] In both situations the stated goal was to encourage experiential learning. In this chapter I shall attempt both to clarify the role of experiential learning in enquiry courses and to examine how a negative-curriculum functions as a basis for enquiry learning. In conclusion, I will defend the thesis that interactive experiential learning defines an epistemology for enquiry course work which needs to be mastered if student work is to be both genuinely independent and subject to high standards of quality. It is important to note that I have limited my attention to issues and problems as they occur in degree granting courses. Since the form of enquiry course work which I know the best is student-based practitioner (action) research the results of this research will be used to illustrate my points. Specifically, I shall offer as both illustration and illumination an account of a graduate student's research and practice wherein the student sought to both describe and prescribe his own actions.

The Nature of Experiential Learning

Experiential learning can be defined as *not* merely abstract: it is the 'learning in which the learner is directly in touch with the realities being studied. Experiential learning typically involves *not* merely observing the phenomena being studied but also doing something with it such as testing the dynamics of the reality to learn more about it, or applying the theory learned to deliver some desired result.'[4] Thus, when we discuss experiential learning we explore a form of interactive knowledge. Not abstraction or observation alone, but cognitive activity coupled to [appropriate] contextual action, is what takes place.

COGNITIVE ACTIVITY + CONTEXTUAL ACTION
= EXPERIENTIAL LEARNING

Fundamentally, in the practice of experiential learning there is a place for the making of an argument, for the raising and testing of hypotheses, and for engaging in the other instruments of rational discourse. Experiential learning must not become an excuse for an educational process, wherein each person's experience is a separate (positive) 'truth,' divorced from broader social and intellectual concerns, or where no prerequisite knowledge is demanded in the research process, which may lead to an impoverishment of research through neglect of methodology and of theory; or wherein there is no hierarchy, sequence, or continuity in learning. Experiential learning bases its 'truth claim' (at least in part) on the intuitive recognition of the givens presented. But this must not lead to the demand that learning be directly accessible or to a demand that expression not be complex. Detailed and concentrated study depends on the use of special research grammars and applied logics. These permit the student to make a buttressed interpretation. Learning not based on preparation which does not make use of investigatory skills, becomes irrelevant, discontinuous, fragmented, lacking in context, impersonal, ahistorical, and trivial. Experiential learning is not merely the passive, unprepared reception of sense data; it depends on active mental participation in 'matters at hand'. It is not the purpose of experiential learning to increase impulsive reaction at the cost of thoughtful response; the manipulative stimulation of anti-intellectual 'spontaneism' is inimical to enquiry.

Experiential learning is based upon the study of contextually grounded givens. The interpretative labor of describing these 'meaningfully' is immensely active. By thinking through this activity, one encounters the hermeneutic process. I have tried to capture this line of development in a paradigm that is at once self-reflective (methodological knowledge) and socially dynamic (new ways of seeing/dealing with the 'world').

At least three different combinations of *cognitive activity* and *contextual interaction* have been proposed as sub-sets to experiential learning. Experiential learning is not identifiable with one prescribed technique; it is made up of a dynamic tension between the differing elements. The learning strategies of experiential learning do not stress either/or options, but the complementary utilization of a variety of approaches: learning by doing; learning how to learn; and learning through experiential group processes.

In considering learning by doing the emphasis is on a direct encounter with experience. 'Progressive education,' beginning in the twenties [the moving forward, step by step, to an improved use of individual powers, in order to be able to meet human needs], and 'radical education,' in the sixties [spiritual growth, through social exchange, directed towards individual ethical insight], both stressed learning by doing. The argument for *learning by doing* begins by denouncing the reduction in schools of learners into a passive mass of disinterested 'listeners'; when motivated to learn, students will individualize themselves by doing things.

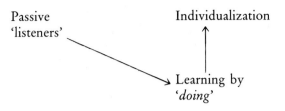

If we pursue the analysis of the rhetorical opposites used in the argument, we discover:

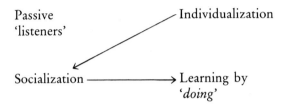

If we begin with the 'individualizing' effect that the stress on personal powers and needs has, we can rightfully criticize the evident lack of attention to the positive value (and cultural significance) of learning through social exchange. Everyday experience and material reality need to be acknowledged as a necessary background to all learning. The criticism of one-sided individualism, leads to an emphasis on socialization. This standpoint translates into a programme of *learning by doing*, wherein the learner is introduced to cooperative learning. Learning is not realized by the mere collecting of sense data; bare physical stimuli only become significant when mitigated by social experience. Modern knowledge is a result of human beings' efforts to meet their social and physical needs. Knowledge must not be taught as so many empty symbols without meaning for the learner. Knowledge needs to become the learner's ongoing reconstruction of reality based upon a dialogue between particular needs and shared aims.

Attention to the students' readiness to learn, to motives and to constructive ingenuity is, in theory, all well and good; but how does one plan or evaluate course work grounded in the learner-context? How can one distinguish between genuine circumstantial commitment and the slavish following of imposed rules? Criteria for the 'living through' of situations are difficult to define. What is it to 'have an experience'? What is the difference between mere sense perception, and experiencing? Does the instructor pre-structure the learning-field to stimulate experiential development? Should one provide so much order that meaning is inevitably to be found; or should there be a realistic threat of failure, wherein learning may not take place? What is the relationship between the 'instructor' [facilitator] and the 'learner'? How can one evaluate learning-through-practice? How does one know that any learning actually took place? If the learner *'experiences'*, what right does the instructor have to evaluate that experience? Can we qualitatively differentiate between different learning results, practices, approaches? What do we [can we] know about situational learning processes?

This brings us to learning how to learn. Students often want to know *how* to learn, and not just how to evaluate the information that they are shown in textbooks and lectures: not just finished ideas, but an insight into the invention and discovery of thought is demanded. The teacher has to develop some systematic way of investigating problem-solving, theoretical reflection, and applied research. Skills such as those of: problem discovery and formulation; the organization and processing of information; idea generation; and the evaluation of ideas meet the bill.[5] The critical issue is: *What happens when people learn?* Which cognitive processes or thinking skills underlie learning? What problem-solving and goal-directed strategies are applicable?

When faced by adult learners with the question: *'Learning, how do you do it?'* a sophisticated answer is necessary. A cookbook approach will not be convincing. Alternative sources are to be found in the studies of professionals' heuristic procedures,[6] and/or in research into thinking strategies.[7] The prevailing research emphasis is on learning styles and learning aptitudes. The themes of learning styles and of lifelong learning have been widely explored.[8] But the partial nature of any single learning heuristic has been well established:

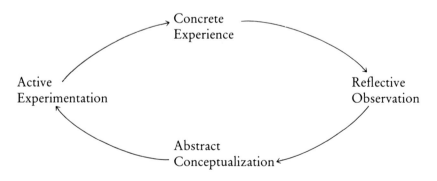

Kolb instructs the learner not to get stuck in one heuristic approach, however comfortable it may seem. It is just by passing through all the phases of the experiential learning cycle that one moves effectively from theory to practice and back again. Professional performance and cognitive comprehension are complementary. Concrete social involvement and the increase in our stock of knowledge are mutually supportive.

Vygotsky clarifies the social/cultural background to learning. His insight into the development of 'higher psychic processes' offers a promising start for further research into the pre-conditions (social and individual) for learning. He has demonstrated that the self-reflective ability self-consciously to thematize one's use of heuristic devices depends on collective intellectual development and is a codeterminant of future activity. Thus the emphasis is upon the social context in which learning occurs. It is my contention that we should consciously strive to participate in a working community where the mind is stimulated to be inventive and the sensibility is encouraged to be exact.

Already such conditions exist, for instance, the Tavistock social skills movement brings learning from personal experience to the attention of the student. In a relatively unstructured environment, the individual is often trained to be more 'open' in interpersonal communication. The relationship between outer-directed social demands and inner-directed needs is usually highlighted. This area of research has centered on personal psychology and on training methodologies. Issues include: 'What is personal development/growth?'; 'What are effective training didactics, and why is this so?'; 'What are the dynamics of the relationship individual-group-trainer?'. A considerable amount of research has attempted to demonstrate the value of this sort of learning.[9]

Thus, the three aspects of experiential learning each contain a specific form of cognitive activity and of contextual action:

Learning by Doing

Cognitive Activity	*Contextual Action*
Identify, analyze, offer criticism of modern social aims and definitions of physical needs.	Cooperative, pragmatic activity in the cause of social evolutionism.

Learning to Learn

Cognitive Activity	*Contextual Action*
Development of thinking skills/insight into heuristic strategies.	Learn practitioner skills, integration work/learning.

Learning via Experiential Group Processes

Cognitive Activity	*Contextual Action*
Insight into personal and group interaction	Increased openness, flexibility, understanding of the other, self-exploration.

The interaction of the three approaches can achieve a learning process rich in experiential value, and heuristically powerful enough to make enquiry successful. In the next section I will compare the strengths and limits of the established experiential learning cycles to those of the multi-faceted learning strategy based on the triad described above.

Learning Paradigms and Experiential Learning

Let us accept, for the sake of argument, that learning paradigms fall into two major categories: stimulus-response and field theories,[10] alternatively called associationist/behaviorist and organismic theories;[11] or mechanistic and organismic models of development.[12] Cleavage among them runs along the following line: are learning principles derived from elementary processes or are learning events described as human activity? In the latter model, learning is event. Research 'will tend to emphasize the significance of the role of experience in facilitating or inhibiting the course of development ....'[13] This research pursues learning as becoming, as discovery, and as change. 'Enquiry is directed toward the discovery of principles of organization, towards the explanation of the nature and relation of parts and wholes, structures and functions....'[14] This dynamic learning activity demands to be analyzed in a non-linear manner; a systems approach seems the most appropriate. To adapt Ackoff's description of a system: a learning system would have to display three properties (i) the properties or behavior of each element of the set have to have an effect on the properties and/or behavior of the set as a whole; (ii) no part can have an independent effect on the whole and each is affected by at least one other part; and (iii) the elements cannot be organized into independent sub-groups — all sub-groups interact and each affects the performance of the whole.[15] Learning thus is a process whose *phases* are a part of a larger, interrelated system.

Kolb, for example, has been the instigator of much contemporary interest in *experiential learning*. He seems to describe learning as a system, as 'a complete package with exercises and theory ... allowing the student to go through all phases of the experiential learning process'.[16] His enquiry cycle is as follows:

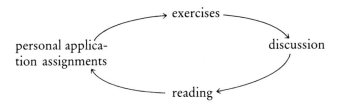

Chickering has modified and amplified the cycle thus:[17]

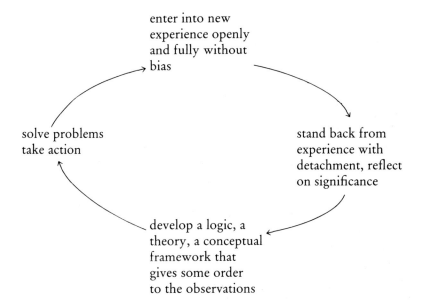

Neither form of the learning cycle really meets Ackoff's three criteria. My objections to Chickering's scheme center on the contention that his various elements do not really form a system as described in condition (iii). The whole [*learning*] is viewed structurally, whereby it remains divided into its parts. It is not viewed functionally, whereby the parts would be perceived as an indivisible whole. The learner proceeds progressively from the one stage to the other as if climbing a ladder. A hierarchy of knowledge is implied: beginning with naive openness, passing via detachment and conceptualization, and arriving at practical action. Initial openness may lead to reflection, but how does reflection make initial openness possible? The elements in the system may have an incremental effect on problem-solving, but how do they influence each other? The progression is sequential, the synthetic mode of thinking wherein each element is understood in a larger system is not realized. This is an analytical model of learning in which the explanation of the whole is derived from the explanations of the parts. The effect of setting the learning cycle up as an analytic model is that it becomes a procedure-to-be-followed instead of becoming a system which contains heuristic guidelines to help learning take place.

Kolb's descriptions of the learning cycle appear to be somewhat paradoxical. On the one hand he has integrated his learning cycle into a broader learning philosophy, but on the other hand that unity is not to be found in the concrete exercises proposed in his organizational psychology course. In his theoretical writings Kolb stresses that the effective learner has to master all four learning stances.[18]

Kolb's concept seems less reified than was Chickering's, thanks to the inclusion of the goal: long-range integrative growth leads towards a more open person-world interaction. But the learning cycle remains, from a philosophical perspective, a very idealistic proposition. The only development that is mentioned centers on the self and its mental self-realization; sometimes in a more reflective, and otherwise in a more applied, stance. The chief benefits of thought are not shown to lie in shared achievement, in immediate experiential cooperation, or in situational ethical clarity. Society seems to be defined as a collection of learners. Via the learning cycle the individual transcends the partialities and limitations of his/her learning strategy and ascends to a more integrated form of learning. The products of learning — measured in achievements and/or past actions — only seem relevant insofar as they have contributed to individual growth. Kolb seems to strive more for totalization than for activity. The mental growth is ultimately to reach an integrated, inclusive form of insight wherein the mind cognitively and affectively seizes all the most essential qualities of reality.

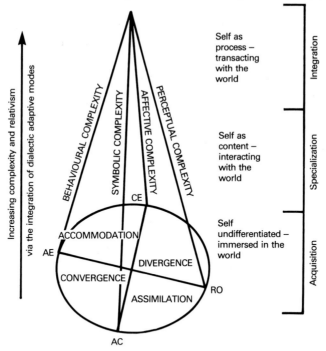

The experiential learning theory of growth and development[19]

In contrast to Kolb I wish to argue for an interactive learning paradigm. I agree with Kolb that the products of individual learning are not the crucial point. Life is not some sort of gigantic school quiz, wherein one has to constantly give back the 'right answers'. The products of lots of thought are never 'consumed', or made use of in any concrete manner. But, by engaging in thought one enters into an intense interaction with one's context. Learning presupposes a fundamental commitment to participation; to learn one has to interact intensely with surroundings. In learning one translates, somehow, natural life into description which may or may not be prescriptive in nature. This is not a mere process of translation; the principles of choice are crucial. At issue is: 'What aspects of "natural reality" are worth translating into some sort of learning process and why?' Each of Kolb's four learning styles has a different answer to that question: for the one it is direct description in natural language that counts; for another it is reflective observation; or it is the development of theory; or it is preparation for practical action. But Kolb's learning taxonomy threatens to reduce the signified [the description of circumstance] into a peripheral factor. He steps over too many crucial matters: is every circumstance somehow [*a priori*] describable? What is the relationship of the description to its object, of the signified to the signifier? Are the descriptions cultural objects, in contradistinction to natural objects? Should one describe reality more from the inside or from outside?

For a learning model to give answers to these questions it will have to focus more on the whole of the learning process than Kolb does — the interpretative power of his model lies too much in the description of the various parts i.e. the different learning styles of the assimilator, accommodator, converger, diverger. Kolb has not focussed enough on the whole, the interrelated, the system. He doesn't answer the question: 'How do the aspects of learning fit and work together?' Of course learning can be divided into parts, but the various aspects when viewed functionally ought to coalesce.

The model of interactive learning that will be proposed here takes the following form:

LEARNING BY DOING

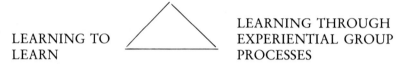

LEARNING TO LEARN

LEARNING THROUGH EXPERIENTIAL GROUP PROCESSES

For the interactive learning paradigm genuinely to be a systems approach to learning it will have to meet the three criteria of Ackoff. Does the model in fact do this?

1 The properties or behavior of the varied forms of learning each have an effect on the properties and behavior of the other forms.

2 The properties and behavior of each part, and of how they affect learning as a whole, depend on the properties and behavior of at least one other element in the set. Thus, each type of learning presupposes at least one other type of learning.

3 Every possible sub-group of two or more learning styles possesses the two aforementioned properties. The system cannot be divided into independent sub-systems.[20]

The first question then becomes 'Does each form of experiential learning influence its two compatriots?' Or, to recast the question, will change/development in one activity influence, inevitably, performance in the others? *Learning by doing* only occurs when the subject organizes sense perceptions and events into a cogent whole. An 'experience' is the result — it is the sign — which 'intellect' or 'mind' leaves behind on the plane of meaning to show that 'man is capable of restoring consciously ... the union of sense, need, impulse, and action'.[21] Experiencing is only fully possible when the individual is conscious of its structure. Thus, learning by doing depends for its fulfilment on a growing insight into learning heuristics. Its achievement depends on the success of a form of learning to learn. Furthermore, learning by doing seeks the reintegration of 'scholarship' within daily life; and of theory with everyday events, doings, sufferings. It is when the person has been struck by an emotion of disharmony, of being unsettled, that he/she is provoked to grow and expand by developing new insights, skills, practices. There will either be development rooted in vital adaption or passive accommodation. The originating 'unrest' comes, most often, from the self-other relationship. Its solution determines the individual's future 'openness' to interaction. Thus, learning originates in, and provokes change in, experiential group interaction.

Learning to learn cannot exist unto itself — it is based on research into basic thinking processes such as decision-making, creativity, remembering. It examines what practitioners really do and how they could do it better. The investigation of problem-solving skills presupposes a group of 'doers' whose efforts can be analyzed. Learning to learn is understood, here, to center on the process of cognition. Its objective is to make the individual's cognitive actions more conscious, and the society's formative role in the development of thought more evident. The power and possibility of, at least partially, choosing one's own intellectual processes is the goal. Awareness into one's way of seeing — into one's manner of defining situations — is an important result. The recognition that how I see others, and react to them, is significantly dependent on my own definitions, is only actualized when concretely experienced in here-and-now group processes.

Each form of learning does in fact presuppose the other two forms; each is interdependent with the other two. *Learning by doing* is based upon the learner being able to differentiate between mere sense data and having an experience. Thus a heuristic insight into learning (learning to learn) is necessary. Furthermore, learning is shown to take place through cooperative activity wherein the quality of the interactive relationship (experience of group processes) is crucial to the end result. *Learning to learn* can best be described as an artisanal activity. By seeing how practitioners cope with problems one discovers the heuristic rules needed to proceed. This is obviously an approach wherein *learning by doing* and *learning in interaction with others* are both present. *Learning through experiential group processes* takes (most often) the form of group dynamic exercises, wherein the relationship task/process is explored. The emphasis is often on the social consequences of doing and/or on the individual's own focus of learning. Learning as a cognitive activity and as social action is personalized — the role of the 'I', and of the 'self', in relation to 'others' within the learning process is explored.

Is it impossible to pair any two forms of learning and let them function independently, irrespective of the third? *Learning by doing* coupled to *learning to learn* misses a field of activity wherein the results can become relevant and effective. Only in the direct experience of 'others' is the learner confronted with the essential social/cultural reality of learning. Activity [defined as action, plus self-insight into the means of action] can only be realized in relationship to concrete social reality. *Learning through experiential group processes* confronts the individual with the intersubjective 'nitty-gritty' of circumstantial activity. Without adequate social psychological contextualizing learning remains mentalistic or idealistic.

The combination *learning by doing* and *learning through experiential group processes* threatens to become 'spontaneistic' at the cost of self-understanding. Awareness of one's own intellectual processes offers ability and freedom of choice. *Learning to learn* and *learning through experiential group processes* tend to reproduce the poles of the Cartesian dualism that is so characteristic of Western thought. The former learning approach can deteriorate into 'rationalism' and the latter into 'blind subjectivism'. By coupling them, without retaining *learning by doing* as a field for interaction, one destabilizes thought. The result will be a form of mental schizophrenia, wherein the individual flip-flops between the extremes of 'intellectualism' and 'emotionalism'.

Can then the interactive learning paradigm make it over the hurdles that concrete research practice will place before it? When the learner confronts circumstance, what happens? As I have already argued, experiential learning gains in exactitude and creative possibility by defining its non-values. The crucial interdict that has emerged in the preceding investigation is: **Do not base your experiential learning on a learning cycle.**

The three themes which make up the interactive learning paradigm do not form a neat model. While they are not mutually exclusive, there are significant differences. *Learning by doing* is an educational concept. Research in this field has focussed on concepts such as connoisseurship (Eisner), enquiry (Bruner and Schwab), having an experience/group investigation (Dewey), non-directive teaching (Rogers and Page). Experimentation in didactics predominates. *Learning how to learn* is a cognitive, psychological theme. Most learning psychology has focussed on laboratory research, leaving field research underdeveloped. Applied learning psychology has not developed easily. Psychologists reproach educational practitioners for being unscientific; practitioners reproach psychologists that experimentation has not led to improved methods. Kolb, Piaget and Vygotsky have managed to straddle the psychology/teaching fence. Knowles, Ausubel, Schon and Stenhouse have contributed to the known repertoire of learning techniques without being able to offer a satisfactory learning or social psychological explanation for their practice. Training has remained a field apart, with strong links to clinical psychology.

In the late sixties the 'radical educational movement' sought to link training and education; 'awareness training', 'personal development' and 'self-discovery' resulted. In the eighties a renewed emphasis on cognitive development has emerged, wherein training is used in conjunction with *learning how to learn*. Each element possesses a focus of its own, and is in some facets complementary to the others. The attractiveness of the paradigm is that it remains dynamic each pole exerts its own pull on the learning situation without being able to dominate. The triad defines a creative instability wherein a variety of learning activities can develop. The interactional learning paradigm provides guidelines; it makes demands of practitioners. The basic rule is: Take each of the three poles into account. The paradigm cannot easily be reified. It demands that the learning process be attended to, without prescribing a definite procedure or pre-defining the learner's position.

The **result** of interactive learning would be a description of actions undertaken wherein one has attempted to do justice to the three facets of the model. Am I in fact claiming that experiential/interactive learning should produce contextually grounded descriptions as their learning result? If I distinguish between explanation (causality), formalization (rational analysis/logical constructs), interpretation (hermeneutics) and description, then I immediately sense that my objectives lie in the realm of description. But I note that I cannot define description very well. I have to leave description itself behind, and avail myself of other levels of abstraction in order to formulate any definition. To some degree I can indicate what description is *not*, that is explanation and formalization, though I am convinced that description is impossible without hermeneutic supports. I am willing to claim that description entails a direct rendering of the imminence of persons/things/institutions. A description is a projection of a subject who objectifies a world; thus it takes place along the cutting edge of subjectivity and objectivity. Several problems for description that we have already mentioned are: can we assume *a priori* that everything is describable; what is the relationship between the object of description and the description; what is the relative value of the insider's and outsider's perspective? The answers to these issues lie in the relationship between the researcher and the researched. Humanistic social sciences have asserted the superiority of the 'dialogue'. The argument runs: the subject, i.e. the researcher, confronts in traditional experimental/behavioral research an inimical opposite of 'non-identity' and 'exteriority'. This encounter with a seemingly non-human object which repulses all efforts at identification does not lead to the development of a 'human science', in the sense of a knowledge rooted in intersubjectivity. In response one seeks intersubjectivity, or dialogue, as an alternative basis for knowledge. In an 'I'/'Thou' relationship, between the research and the researched, one finds a radically human basis for research.

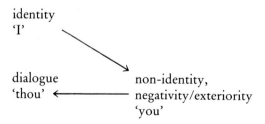

When the production of knowledge is based on the identification of the two logically separate categories, 'identity' and 'dialogue', one gets closure without opposition. There is no outside or exteriority, just union in the sought after *rapprochement*. If we schematize more fully the rhetorical possibilities we discover the alternatives:

S 1	S 2
identity	alterity
'I'	'he/she'

S −2	S −1
dialogue	non-identity
'thou'	negativity/exteriority
	'you'

The pattern we have already followed is:

(A) S 1 to S −1, leading to S −2

Let us try:

(B) S 1 to S −1, leading to S 2, and

(C) S −2 to S 2, leading to S 1.

In (B) the proposition reads: the researcher confronts the 'other' and is unable to penetrate this alien factor; empathy cannot be achieved with the research 'object'. The researcher therefore moves off towards a reflective or more detached position. Description is generated when the object outside oneself [the '**he/she**'] is attended to. The '**he/she**' has none of the familiarity of the '**I**' or '**thou**'. A correspondence is established between the researcher and the reader. The closed researcher/researched relationship is broken open. The potential reader is put onto equal footing with the direct participants. Description ceases to be, what 'we' ('I'/'thou') share, and becomes 'what there is to see that was worth experiencing'. Why it was 'worth experiencing' and what cognitive means one needed to experience it are now realistic points of discussion. The researcher is an experiencing agent who has every reason to be self-conscious about his/her activity. The goal of the 'I'/'thou' correspondence is to be at one with the subject matter/the object of knowledge — all alterity is banished. The researcher reaches for a holistic perception of the individual/other, as well as the person/circumstance, relationship. By thematizing the 'he/she', circumstantial partiality and subjective distance are reiterated. The description is acknowledged to be a deliberate cognitive effort. There may be a complex learning process of cooperation, self-reflection, and interaction that went into one's research, but the description is not intended to be designed to transcend the subject-subject or subject-object differentiation. There is neither totalization in the researcher/researched relationship, nor exhaustivity in the description; the knowledge is partial and contextual.

The remaining line of argument, scheme C, mirrors a process of self-discovery. The logic begins with an 'identity' which is in communication with the socially adapted 'other', but which is confronted with the insight that this 'self' is not really one's own [a problem of authenticity]. The discovery of a 'self' which turns out to be foreign from oneself reveals the existence of alienation, the possibility of freedom, and the problem of indeterminance. Thereby a step towards existential insight has become possible. What is described in scheme C is an identity crisis, which ideally resolves itself through the achievement of a strengthened personal core. While logic C is important to the processes of learning through experiential group process, logic B predominates in interactive learning.

Interactive Experiential Learning and Enquiry Courses

Enquiry courses are threatened on one side by vacuous formalism and on the other by conceptless realism. The former depends on experimental objectivity, and the latter on participatory observation, to legitimize its activity. The one loses itself in dependent and independent variables, unable to adapt itself to practicalities; the other sticks too close to the object studied, unable to produce any new insights. Neither the one nor other statement of methodological intent clarifies the purpose or goal of practical investigation. Practitioner research has always been plagued by a crisis in its rhetorical stance. How can one study social existence while remaining within it? The practitioner is inevitably both the subject and object within his or her research focus. It is difficult to master this duality: to grasp a logic wherein one is cause and effect, subject and object, existentially involved and structurally limited.

The brunt of my work is centered on pedagogics and on the social psychological investigation of learning. My effort to get research and instruction in *learning by doing* in *learning how to learn* and in *learning through experiential group processes* in balance with one another has taken place while supervising student research projects. In that context the insight that the various aspects to experiential learning are complementary, and not competitive, has been able to grow. But for many the commensurability of the three stances still has to be demonstrated. I have been able with my research students to initiate a fundamental discussion wherein experiential learning has come a bit closer to achieving an epistemological clarity grounded in our concrete usage. Experiential learning poses the problems of the social sciences in a different manner than does positivism or psychological humanism. It actively endeavours to grasp the complex dualities of experience/experienced, discourse/discussant, circumstance/innovation.

I am personally committed to the combination of doing research and supervising student work in this field. It is only by discussing one's own and students' ongoing research that one is consistent and effective. Investigation of experiential learning is at an exploratory stage. The process factor in the subject matter makes it didactically self-defeating to present experiential learning as a 'linear truth.' A large dose of process thinking is needed to work with this material. Course work lets us pose and investigate the relevant learning problems. To ensure that relevance one has to grapple with concrete learning problems, one's own and/or one's students'.

To clarify the theoretical description, a short resumé of a graduate student's research within the Interactive Learning Paradigm is now offered to both illustrate and illuminate the concepts. The research was done by a graduate student who had just received his first teaching appointment, a temporary one. He had been selected in January 1985 from some ten candidates for a half-year teaching assistantship to be assigned to the course 'Communication skills' in the University Medical School. The course was organized by a senior tutor, and taught by three teaching assistants. The other assistants had received one-year appointments in September 1984. The medical students were in their third and fourth year of study. The course is goal centered on 'listening with empathy'. The planned exercises and the choices for the reading list zeroed in on the doctor/patient relationship. The graduate student obtained the job because he had an extensive background in health care. He had been a nurse in a psychiatric hospital before beginning his university study of 'pedagogics and psychology'. His nursing training had included an initial and advanced course at a Polytechnic. A second motive for the interviewers to give him the job was that he had made an independent and responsible impression.

The student's theoretical interest had been slowly gravitating towards psychoanalysis, and the Lacanian School. Ideas which stress autonomy and self-reliance appealed to him. His career plans centered on teaching and/or consulting. He had a strong preference to do things in his own way, at his own pace, and to judge himself by his own standards. In his nursing career he had found the hospital organization to be restrictive of personnel's creativity and intrusive towards the patients' privacy.

Upon receiving the appointment he was introduced to the programme by the tutor and the fellow TAs. He was told that the medical students felt a strong resistance to the course. Their training was technical with an emphasis on causal thinking — this alienated them from the process goals of the course. The medical students thought that everything psychological was weird and threatening. In response to this student opposition, the senior tutor had prepared a course script wherein the exercises and learning goals were set forth, week-by-week. The course lasted six weeks, one morning or afternoon per week. The new TA was to start work in a fortnight. He would have two groups per cycle of six weeks, teaching altogether three cycles.

In the first phase of his research the teacher/research inventorized his expectations and set out on the following research cycle:

Medical students are socialized in a manner
antithetical to developing skills in empathy.

Response: argue the case. Make it
clear that *you* need these skills.

First action step: explain what
students can expect from me,
and what I EXPECT OF THEM.
Lecture: importance of conversation
skills for general practitioner

Evaluation: I've
approached this in
a self-defeating
manner; I've got to
rethink the course.

Monitoring: Record
interaction on tape.
Keep notes of my
impressions.

Rethinking/reflecting: I'm teaching
them skills, just as if this were any
other medical course!

The teacher/researcher had discovered that he needed better to clarify his goals. His original plan: To study the resistance to empathy amongst medical students, had been overtaken by events. His own proselytizing had proven to be an important barrier against the development of an empathetic discourse.

The student/researcher was thus confronted with the weakness of his content definition. He had begun to do research, to collect data, to describe his teaching of the 'Communication course' with the assumption that his practical focus on 'student resistance' was self-evident. But the situation had rejected that interpretation. He had penetrated into the social relations of the 'Communications course' and had discovered that the interactions did not follow the expected pattern. Description of social life was proving to be unsettling! What should he now do: Create a new hypothesis; to explain which phenomena? His original theme had been based on the oppositions of: openness/resistance, staff/students, emotion/rationality, dialogue/diagnosis. But the explanatory power of all the oppositions had failed him when his own teaching style turned out to be a crucial learning blockage. He decided to try temporarily to drop his dualistic assumptions — to bracket his expectations of who is what — and to try to describe teaching a 'Communication course' as best he could.

But he had lost his conceptual landmarks. Without some sort of hermeneutic structure description becomes everything and nothing. What would he describe, and why? He decided he would better define the quality demands which he would place on the research. If he could define a meta-language of research for himself, he could wait and see what would emerge in the teaching practice. A research meta-language would tell him what not to forget without determining the content of research.

The interactive learning paradigm became his research meta-language. Thus, he took on the obligation to monitor his practice on all three experiential learning levels. He would have to ask himself: What is learned here by doing, how could it be improved, what is my role in it? He'd have to define: How are these students learning to learn; How am I learning to learn through this teaching? And he'd have to develop and evaluate the experiential group processes in the classroom, as produced by the exercises, prompted by his style of teaching, and influenced by the interactions within the teaching corps and student body.

Once he abandoned the initial hypothesis, alternative action strategies proved plentiful. The interactive paradigm was important as a research heuristic. It freed him from being tied down to defining numerous research goals. The demand that the action steps also be research phases in the forced him to see each action as a research hypothesis. His attitude was now: I'm describing my actions with the use of the quality controls I have committed myself to. He had found a way to do description.

New action steps included: (i) He would formulate a self-critique of his initial defensiveness; (ii) discuss it with his colleagues; and (iii) explore curricular alternatives with them and in the class-room. His most important methodological problem was: What should I describe? There is no dearth of technical literature on qualitative research methods. One can avail oneself of (i) analytic memos; (ii) diaries; (iii) profiles; (iv) document analysis; (v) photo-graphic evidence; (vi) tape/video recordings and transcripts; (vii) make use of 'outside' observers; (viii) interviews; (ix) run-ning commentary; (x) shadow study; (xi) checklists, questionnaires, inventories.[22] All these techniques will generate description of the research objective in 'A course in conversation skills for GPs'. The problem is not too little potential data, but too much. The choice of focus can be put outside the explicit boundaries of the research by choosing a 'pragmatic' focus. A goal such as improving student participation (or even authenticity) in the conversation skills course can be set, and common sense definitions of 'improve' are to be opera-tionalized. In such a research strategy there is no agreement on what one will not do. Any reasonable concept to 'improve' is potentially valid.

The teacher/researcher had encountered the negative effect which having a plan can produce. He had attacked the assumed prob-lem (medical student resistance) so forcefully that his presence over-whelmed spontaneous interaction. The chosen theme, empathy in the doctor/patient relationship, had simply been snowed under. But when he introduced his new theme, trainer inflexibility caused by the fear of not achieving course learning goals, he met with colleague resistance. He was told that the problem simply did not exist! He had begun with the theme of student resistance and now he felt himself confronted with lecturer denial! The TAs and the senior tutor rejected point blank his interpretation of his in-class problem. They repeated that the trainer has to meet the resistances of the students not *vice versa*. The course goals are, they insisted, jeopardized by student reluctance to face up to self-confrontation, not by any staff reluctance. The teacher/researcher wrote-up these crucial inter-changes in detail. He described what everyone said, their manner of expression and the implicit affective undertones. He also took note of his own emotions and associations.

His next action step was to return to the classroom and to discuss his felt problem with the students. Instead of telling them what had to be done, he asked what they would find purposeful within the stated goals. What should the 'Communication course' be in their opinion? This cooperative approach opened the way to redefining how the course should be run. Issues such as 'How the general practitioner reacts to discovering incest within a family of patients' and 'What does one do with feelings of sexual arousal towards patients?' came forward.

The teacher/researcher had no hypothesis anymore, no definition of 'improvement'. He was out to describe his teaching situation as best he could, which meant to him taking heed of the three learning approaches. His only commitment was to describe his context. He was attentive to what had happened to himself and to the students in the course. He had explored speech as shared sentiment and as a means of categorization. Should the doctor or the patient steer the conversation? What is the role of the lecturer, and of the students, in the course? Who controls which interaction, and how? Does the doctor understand the communication structure upon which his diagnosis is based? Does this insight strengthen or weaken his diagnostic insight? Is he sufficiently aware of the tension-begetting influences of modern medical technology? What is the students' way of existing with their medical knowledge? Are they at ease with what one experiences with patients; do they accept what is avoided in the contact? What do they want of their self-image as doctors, what don't they want to know about themselves? The research generated a broad, speculative, thorough description of the course and the connected issues. From the sharpened descriptions grew actions; actions which had been prudently informed rather than actions generated in unreflective haste.

Conclusion

In conclusion let me return once more to the concept of negative-curriculum. The interactive learning model warns the researcher not to forget the complexity of experiential investigation. It asserts that there is no one privileged approach to circumstance. It is an investigatory heuristic to be used so that prematurely achieved closure, or unwanted limitations to scope, will not take place. Interactive experiential learning does not attempt directly to transcend description. It is not a method, in the sense of calling for a regularly prescribed research arrangement; nor is it a collection of techniques. It is a meta-language that endeavours to create quality criteria for research without becoming a fore-structure that pre-determines content. These criteria form an epistemological statement which tries not to say what knowledge is, but to indicate that there is a complex play of interrelationships between *learning by doing, learning to learn* and *learning through experiential group processes* with which one can render a context describable and upon which one can act. The interactive learning model is a process of exploring and experimenting that is characterized by a demanding emphasis on the training, knowledge and talent of the practitioner. As a teaching/ research device the model emphasizes not only how to do research, but also the potential efficaciousness of doing it. Interactive learning is capable of not only generating accurate description, but also of raising creative hypotheses which lead to new practice.

References

1 I wish to express my gratitude to Professor Claude Faucheux for his support in developing these ideas.
2 The idea of negative values had been developed in organizational psychology by Professor Henk van Dongen.
3 See LETICHE, H. (1986) 'Facilitation fallacies', paper given at CARN, March (published in *CARN Bulletin* 1986) for a description of earlier work, done at the Nutsseminarium, University of Amsterdam.
4 KEETON, M.T. and TATE, P.J. (1978) *Learning by Experience*, San Francisco, CA, Jossey-Bass.
5 CRUTCHFIELD, R.S. (1972) 'Nurturing cognitive skills of productive thinking' in SILBERMAN, M.L. *et al.* (Eds) *The Psychology of Open Teaching and Learning*, Boston, MA, Little Brown, pp. 192–5.
6 SCHON, D. (1983) *The Reflective Practitioner*, New York, Basic Books.
7 KOLB, D.A. and FRY, R. (1975) 'Towards an applied theory of experiential learning' in COOPER, C. (Ed.) *Theories of Group Processes*, New York, Wiley, pp. 33–57; KOLB, D.A. *et al.* (1984a) *Organizational Psychology, An Experiential Approach to Organizational Behavior*, Englewood Cliffs, NJ, Prentice Hall; VYGOTSKY, L.S. (1962) *Thought and Language*, Cambridge, MA, MIT Press; VYGOTSKY, L.S. (1978) *Mind in Society*, Cambridge, MA, Harvard Press.
8 KNOWLES, M. (1973) *The Adult Learner: A Neglected Species*, Houston, TX, Gulf Publishing.
9 CAMPBELL, J.P. and DUNNETTE, M.D. (1986) 'Effectiveness of T-group experiences in managerial training and development', *Psychological Bulletin*, pp. 73–104; and HORNSTEIN, H.A. *et al.* (1971) 'Some conceptual issues in individual and group-oriented strategies of intervention into organizations', *Journal of Applied Behavioral Science*, pp. 567–77.
10 KINGSLEY, H.L. and GARRY, R. (1957) *The Nature and Condition of Learning*, Englewood Cliffs, NJ, Prentice Hall, p. 83.
11 TABA, H. (1962) *Curriculum Development Theory and Practice*, New York, Harcourt Brace, p. 80.

12 KNOWLES, M. (1973) *op. cit.*, pp. 16–17.
13 REESE, H.W. and OVERTON, W.F. (1970) 'Models of development and theories of development' in GOULET, L.R. and BATES, P.B. (Eds) *Life-Span Development Psychology*, New York, Academic Press, p. 134.
14 *Ibid*, pp. 133–4.
15 ACKOFF, R.L. (1983) 'The systems revolution' in LOCKETT, M. and SPEAR, R. (Eds) *Organizations as Systems*, Milton Keynes, Open University Press.
16 KOLB, D. (1984a) *op. cit.*, p. xiv.
17 CHICKERING, A. (1977) *Experience and Learning*, New Rochelle, Change Publication, p. 18.
18 KOLB, D. (1984b) *Experiential Learning*, Englewood Cliffs, NJ, Prentice Hall.
19 Figure reproduced from KOLB, D. *ibid*.
20 ACKOFF, R.L. (1983) *op. cit.*
21 DEWEY, J. (1958) *Art as Experience*, New York, Capricorn Books, p. 25.
22 ELLIOTT, J. (1981) 'Action-research: A framework for self-evaluation in schools', *TIQL Working Paper No 1*, pp. 4–12.

2 Action Inquiry

Gordon H. Bell

If we accept that an award-bearing course represents a form of action in which members of an institution attempt to control what counts as knowledge, how does that situation affect 'enquiry-based' courses? In an important sense, enquiry leads where it will. The idea of linking enquiry to 'courses' or 'academic years' and similar devices distorts the overriding criterion of the pursuit of truth. To this extent, joining a course to engage in enquiry might be regarded as a motivated form of irrationality. Put in these terms, the very act of becoming a course member carries with it the means of becoming an agent of one's own domination.

It may be that the pathologies of enquiry embedded in such a process have been tolerated for so long because the type of investigation brought about under these conditions has limited ethical significance. This perhaps explains why the dominant mode of pedagogy has traditionally centred on the pursuit of scholarly enquiry in which the study of texts by individuals is favoured as against (say) the collaborative study of an existing practice by participants. A course process grounded in scholarship ensures a retreat into one type of evidence, namely written evidence which is studied in isolation from the situations described.

Perhaps by way of recognition of the gap thus created between knowledge and its application, some institutional authorities have sanctioned an empirical base to enquiry. The theory of a course brought about under this regime ensures that reality is observed but not changed except in the interests of the enquiry. The definition of knowledge shifts from the study of texts to the study of 'data'. But here what counts as data and acceptable reflection upon it, is restricted so as to cast the enquirer in a role which has much in common with linguistic philosophers where the mode of enquiry is celebrated as 'leaving everything as it is'. Once again, the course process ensures that it has limited ethical significance because of an assumed gap between the gathering of 'facts' and the world of 'values'. By adopting certain techniques in collecting 'data' so as to dehumanize the observer, and by applying further techniques in processing these data so as to convert human judgment to numerical calculation, the value neutrality of the outcomes is said to be safeguarded. Even if such a claim could be sustained, it would be a hollow victory in terms of education or professional development for I shall assume that what education is about, other than schooling or training, is the lived experience of an uncertainty about what is worthwhile. The engagement necessary to enter upon such an enterprise will crucially depend upon an ability to sustain ethical discourse, for insofar as what counts as knowledge is socially located if not socially determined, then ethics matter.

The drift of this type of argument has had its effects upon some awarding bodies who have produced variants of the scholarly and empirical forms of enquiry-base. The selection of texts to be studied can be made more or less socially 'responsible', so long as they are not too socially responsive. Observers of school and classroom realities can involve more or less 'participation', so long as this is not too democratic. The subject of investigation can be rendered more or less 'practical' provided the outcomes are measured against academic criteria. Thus what remains constant within varying degrees of acceptance of the idea that an ethics of discourse is one criterion of a mode of enquiry, is a formalized hierarchy arranged in a sense Foucault describes as 'archaeological' in which entering upon an archive of awards supposedly warrants nearness to truth.[1]

These then are some of the issues that confront designers of enquiry-based courses where decisions have finally to be taken about method and how the twin problems of the development and ownership of knowledge are to be resolved. The concept of action inquiry arose as an outcome of such a debate.

The Theory of a Course by Action Inquiry

Clearly, courses with a commitment to enquiry need not necessarily concern themselves with whether their process has ethical significance. Not all courses are educational in this specific sense; they may train or instruct, reproduce skills or develop materials and techniques independent of human interest. But insofar as the education of teachers is connected with the development and transmission of knowledge in which human interests are central, then the relation between the ethics of the course process and its subject matter is a crucial determinant of worthwhileness. On this question, it can be argued that a basic assumption of a course designed for professionals is that it be grounded in practice in such a way as to open its principles and procedures to the possibility of improvement. Insofar as the funding of such courses is expressly provided to support the continuing education and training of teachers, it follows that the boundaries of what might otherwise count as 'practice' be focussed on schools.

On these considerations alone, we have ruled out much of what has traditionally passed as pedagogical enquiry. For we have indicated that text-based investigation is not sufficient, and that subject matter peripheral to schools as centres for the acquisition of knowledge and experience, though desirable, is neither necessary nor sufficient. On the grounds of what it is to be a professional, teachers need to be involved not only in transmitting knowledge but in developing knowledge of this as a practice. It follows that teaching itself needs to be put on a practitioner research basis.[2]

Prior to addressing the problem of method, i.e. by what mode of enquiry such research should proceed, there is the issue of prevailing modes of discourse influencing both the definition of practice and its means of investigation. Educational theory and practice have long been dominated by a dependency on knowledge as authority; whether this has stemmed from academics, inspectors, professional researchers, politicians or teachers themselves. In a situation where little has customarily been expected of teachers to contribute to a critique of this body of expert opinion, a structure of communication has arisen which largely excludes them. In this way, teachers have been disenfranchized from knowledge of their own practice.[3]

This situation has favoured the evaluation of courses in terms of an individual's expansion of experience at the expense of the complementary concept of practical professional knowledge. The issue then at stake is whether the course award accredits personal growth or professional development. Characteristically this distinction is not generally made. Professional development is often taken to mean both personal and professional growth. But in the context of enquiry-based courses, what kind of 'research' is it that has personal referents only? A necessary condition of a professional enquiry is evidence in a form that is accessible to scrutiny and developed through a process that can dependably contribute both to the development of the profession and the improvement of schools. A key criterion of the evidence arising from such studies is the extent to which it is possible to appraise the nature and scope of agreement in judgments about matters of worthwhileness. Reports evaluated in terms of personal professional growth may or may not provide access to such judgments.

The implications of these arguments for course designers are that they provide four main starting points: better links between research and the improvement of schools, a shift in the location of support for the study of practice from college-based to school-based activities, closer attention to the problem of transferring practical knowledge from one practitioner to another, and greater scope for the supported self study of practical problems in teaching.

What form of enquiry will help achieve these goals? The short answer is, 'research that will help the practitioner'.[4] This phrase, taken from the writings of Kurt Lewin, introduces what is rapidly becoming an orthodoxy in defining the basis on which teachers may research their practice. 'Action research', originating in the work of Lewin and his associates, has been interpreted in various ways as the main vehicle for building effectively upon the starting points outlined above. A general consensus is forming around the view that as the basis of this type of enquiry is everyday problems experienced by teachers aiming to deepen teachers' understanding through a process of planned and evaluated change, teaching will be revitalized and the resulting restructuring of the curriculum will enhance the quality of pupil learning.

But action research as a sole definition of the enquiry base has its limitations; some structural, some contingent upon the way in which the new orthodoxy has developed. The central issue here is whether the principle of reflection on practice has its quality assured by adopting this mode of enquiry rather than another. The problems here are concerned with the dogmatism evident in the idea that one must change one's teaching in order to investigate it, that intervening with a view to improvement is a justified action, assuming that research cycles over time are appropriately comparable, and that the only form of worthwhile reflection is that which arises through testing one's own theories in action. These concerns can be focussed by considering the fact finding stage of the action research cycle. In relation to such facts as have been gleaned, a plan of action has to be framed. But not only is the methodology unclear (a military metaphor of 'reconnaissance' is used by Lewin to describe this stage) the main problem is not knowing in advance what would count as a relevant consideration. Using this procedure, one can only make a more or less educated guess at the implications of acting upon the subject of investigation, and this poses difficulties about where to draw the line in framing an action plan.

But there is a deeper issue about the nature of practical problems in education and the conditions of access to them. Not all concerns worthy of study are located in the practice of individual teachers. Policy issues in particular, (say) child abuse or special educational needs, are not amenable to coherent analysis on the basis of individual uncoordinated enquiry. 'Collaborative forms of action research begs the question as to whether it is the same empirical problem being studied by individual action, whether co-ordinated or not. A generic label applied to a group does not ensure a common epistemology. The collaborative development of theory grounded in a common database would perhaps meet such conditions, but the extent of collaboration needed poses severe practical problems in general and ethical barriers in particular where inter-professional perspectives may be necessary. If we suppose that such objections are matters of procedure rather than principle, there is still the issue of dogmatism evident in the requirement that one must intervene directly in the problem situation as a condition of dialogue.

Several further problems arise from this precondition. It may well be the case that intervening directly is either not possible because the boundaries of the problem are not fully in the control of the practitioner, or else it would be untimely to act within the period available for investigation. This is particularly problematic for an award-bearing course which operates to a limited timetable and especially where this is full-time. More importantly the rules of discourse introduced through the technology of the action research cycle are biased towards one form of action and one form of reflexivity based upon it. In advance of a fuller analysis, we may reasonably assume that whatever is meant by the development of practical professional knowledge we may expect it to be multiple rather than uniform.

One aspect of this multidimensional structure may be assessed by considering the frameworks for dialogue necessary in validating accounts of 'good' practice based upon the studies of action researchers. Here critique is valued from many different perspectives and not those solely derived from statements grounded in the data of planned and evaluated change. Indeed from the point of view of meeting the criterion of 'systematic enquiry made public' built into the concept of research, unjustified restriction on a partnership in dialogue, whether with other course members or with participants in the practice being studied, poses difficulties for management of the course and/or maintenance of its rationale. Tailoring this dialogue to a timetable or to coordinated cycles of action may well distort the practice being studied and the processes of improvement otherwise available. Unless course members are organized in teams and these teams are managed to meet the epistemological conditions necessary to develop practical knowledge, it is suggested that a course process grounded solely in action research is in danger of degenerating into more or less satisfying forms of socializing. Meanwhile, the opportunities available for utilizing the professional knowledge and experience of course members and other invited participants will be arbitrarily reduced.

Action research, then, as an enquiry base offers the advantage of being a means by which practical professional knowledge can be developed through projected improvements in teaching and learning being tested by practitioners. The lived experience of what is pedagogically worthwhile is subjected to rational critique. But the ethics of discourse thereby created has a rule governed structure that limits the coherence of that experience when undertaken individually, and offers restricted conditions of access to interactive research and development when pursued in a collaborative form.

If we accept that the technology of action research cycles can create a form of discourse in which reflection on action is central but can restrict the possibilities for improving a practice or a participant's mode of thinking about it, then the question arises as to how both action and enquiry can be extended in a way that preserves the benefits of action research whilst reducing the costs.

On the grounds that discourse about improving practice needs to be framed yet open, systematic yet responsive, active yet participative, ways need to be found for expanding the forms of experiential learning open to course members. This means increasing access to modes of critique on action and reflection, and rethinking the frameworks of reporting so as to maximize the transfer of such knowledge and experience as has been gained through the course process both between participants and across providing institutions.

If this is considered to be a tall order, it merely confirms how small the present order is. The prevailing influences on action research-based enquiry courses tend to glorify process at the expense of product, ignore means of maximizing knowledge transfer especially across institutions, and understate the relation between policy makers and practitioner researchers. Making public is presently a curiously private affair, bewitched by a politics of sponsorship linked to powers to define. Under the baleful influence of a mode of scholarly communication that has so far largely only been complained about in terms of its poor potential for increasing the gross national product, few voices are heard for empowering teachers to develop knowledge of their own practice, whether this be links between schools and industry or improving their own performance.

Insofar as such issues are addressed by providing institutions, the current orthodoxy is to talk about action research as being reported in the framework of a 'case study'. This highly ambiguous term, with its associated unclarity as to how its procedures should be interpreted so as to meet award-granting standards, may nevertheless offer a clue as to how some of the restrictions presently embedded in action research-based courses can be removed. If case study is viewed not simply as one means of reporting action research, but a complementary mode of reflection and action on professional experience, the resulting basis for investigating practical problems will be significantly extended. Moreover, if case study as an independent mode of enquiry is systematically linked to action research, then many of the limitations identified previously may be overcome. It is this latter framework for investigating pedagogical issues that I shall refer to as 'action inquiry'.

Space does not permit any fuller justification of this framework for developing practical professional knowledge except perhaps to indicate that whereas action research develops practical intelligence through the learned manipulation of interactions between teacher and taught, practitioner case study develops practical insight by investigating those issues that are not amenable to the observation of planned change. At the interface of these two modes of reflection and action exists what has been termed 'action learning'.[5] This form of reflection and action arises directly from the assumptions of both case study and action research and represents the hidden curriculum of enquiry-based courses. The effective management of this process is not only a central condition of quality assurance in any enquiry-based course for professionals, it provides the means of linking action research to case study. Engaging in action inquiry thus combines practical intelligence with practical insight in developing professional knowledge and experience. The course process is grounded not only in trial and error change but in actions to improve judgment through the development of prudence. On the one hand there is an enquiry emphasis on the explanation of interventions designed to improve a practice, and on the other an interpretation of a practice in action.[6]

The Practice of a Course by Action Inquiry

It was against this background that the enquiry base of an award-bearing course was first defined, validated and approved. The main aim of the course was to provide an opportunity for practising teachers to make a contribution to a body of practical knowledge of teaching and school improvement. Course members undertook supported self studies of practical problems arising in their own practice by focussing on the pedagogical and curricular issues using action research and case study methods. Either method could be used at any time, but the linkage between these modes of enquiry is strategic and is determined by the course member in a framework of dialogue between other course members, participants in the practice being studied, and with tutors, consultants and other practitioner researchers. The hope was to develop an interactive network comprised of these groups to provide a forum for collaborative validation. The tangible products of this activity were reports in a format that could be made readily accessible to other practitioners.[7]

Evaluation of the course took a variety of forms: internal through the use of group evaluation techniques, questionnaires and formal meetings; external through a visiting examiner and HMI; and independent through commissioning a teachers' centre warden and LEA adviser to become participant observers and provide formative feedback. The remainder of this contribution provides a brief summary of the main points to emerge from this evaluation to date.

The first year of the course culminated in a feasibility study to test out a proposal for action inquiry as developed through prior discussion and a survey of knowledge and experience. Evaluation issues to emerge at the end of the first year revealed a potential gap between a course member's ability to implement effective change in their practice and their capacity to render this knowledge and experience accessible in written form. In particular, the issue of excelling in course reports in a way that may not be reflected in school-based change raised the spectre of a discrepancy between skills of reporting and performance in teaching. The question then arises as to how any professional enquiry-based course can ensure that the final asssessment of performance reflects a course member's competence in both theory and practice, whilst avoiding the situation of assessment requirements inhibiting practical professional development.

The problem of determining appropriate criteria of assessment to underpin the course process is a matter for ongoing debate. In this case, the criteria used were derived from an account of the logic of naturalistic enquiry, namely, credibility, transferability, dependability, and confirmability.[8] But it was felt that perhaps not all of these criteria were equally applicable to every part of the course. Indeed, an elaboration of these criteria may well be called for in the light of further analysis of a distinction between action inquiry and naturalistic inquiry.

What did the course members themselves think about the course at the end of the first year? Using a group evaluation technique, the question was put as to what they considered to be strengths and weaknesses of the course.[9] Nineteen items were identified as strengths:

(a) raises expectations and experiences;
(b) meeting other professionals;
(c) interaction between course members;
(d) pursuing relevant issues;
(e) techniques for evaluation;
(f) clarifying ideas;
(g) improving practice;
(h) transfer of evaluation techniques;
(i) in-depth study of curricular area;
(j) valuable background philosophies condensed;
(k) variety of projects;
(l) awareness of latest information;
(m) improving skills in data gathering;
(n) expertise passed to other colleagues;
(o) questioning own teaching performance;
(p) common weaknesses shared;
(q) work in classroom context;
(r) teacher-based research;
(s) making time to pinpoint ideas.

A prioritized voting procedure placed these items in rank order of felt importance:

1 improved practice;
2 in-depth study of curricular area;
3 clarifying own ideas;
4 interaction between course members.

Eighteen items were identified as weaknesses:

(a) time demand great;
(b) timing in school year;
(c) relevance of some material;
(d) sequence of course elements;
(e) time for tutorials;
(f) lack of contact for discussion with other course members;
(g) initial advice on topics;
(h) capitalizing on expertise;
(i) short notice of future plans;
(j) practical research in early stages;
(k) interference with teaching;
(l) credibility of the award against competing alternatives;
(m) time wasted travelling;
(n) guilt feelings about teaching suffering;
(o) inaccessibility of library;
(p) access to specialist help;
(q) guidance in presentation;
(r) isolation from sources of course support.

The voting procedure prioritized these items as follows;

1 timing in school year;
2 time demand great;
3 (tied items) practical research in early stages and interference with teaching.

If one takes the evaluation of this first year as a whole, from an LEA perspective the importance of practical improvements in schools and classrooms was paramount; from an HMI perspective the ability of the LEA to capitalize on the expertise and resources of course members at the end of the course was emphasized; from an external examiner perspective the difficulty of assessing benefits of various kinds and not just the 'practical' was highlighted; from a course leader viewpoint the problem of raised expectations about available resources for self-supported study was a matter of concern.

The second year is largely concerned with refining and developing the issues to emerge from the feasibility study and ensuring that both case study and action research have been used as a means of penetrating the depth implications of the practice being investigated. The final stage has been interpreted as a debriefing process in which course members, having built up in a systematic way access to each other's professional judgment, can share the outcomes of their action inquiries and explore ways of validating their recommendations. In short, critical method was linked more intensively with investigative method than had occurred previously.[10]

The course process had hoped in this way to democratize dialogue, for example, from the course leader to the course members, from individuals to pairs, from small groups to the whole group, from insiders to outsiders. The planned use of two residential conferences was recognized to be highly influential in facilitating such dialogue and in developing group confidence and cohesion. However, the immediate priority in developing enquiry-based courses must surely lie in improved networking so as to support schools in undertaking curriculum development and to act as a resource to future courses whether in this institution or others. A system of microcomputer databases may assist the development of a means of communication which will be more functional than the present forms of educational discourse and a small-scale project is currently underway to test this idea.[11] The main aim is to democratize further the knowledge base developed by course members through their professional studies by making their personal skills in action inquiry available to other teachers with like interests. This then raises the issue of institutional cooperation following the formal closure of a course.[12]

An indication of the depth of interest may be gained from questionnaire data gathered from course members at the end of their penultimate term. They were highly supportive of the course experience, especially on such issues as appropriate teaching methods, the extent to which personal/professional experience had been utilized, the usefulness of professional exchange between teachers of different age ranges or specialisms, and the freedom to express opinion. The group were more diverse in their views on the extent of direct guidance needed, the ability to work collaboratively with other course members outside formal sessions, and whether there was sufficient variety of presentation. A strongly negative consensus formed around the notion of having more formal sessions, for example, lectures.

Concerning course content, they rated highly the professional relevance of topics chosen for discussion, the stimulus provided through recommended reading, the course guidelines assisting in focussing enquiry, and the extent to which the data collected had helped reflection on professional concerns. Opinion was more equally divided on the degree of difficulty experienced in keeping data, and on whether more written assignments were preferred.

As to the course outcomes, course members were strongly positive about their feelings of increased confidence in their ability to evaluate and develop the curriculum, their understanding of the criteria for rational presentation of a case, the degree of clarity about the concept of the curriculum, and about their perceived ability to succeed in assisting curriculum development in their own or in other schools. They were strongly convinced about the potential of research-based teaching and the degree of encouragement offered through the course for looking critically at their own teaching. A negative consensus formed round the question of independent study. A majority of course members felt that they had not been 'reasonably supported' in doing this. Whether the reasons are course-related or more personal and/or domestic is not clear. In-school time allowance had been given for action inquiry, but opinion was divided on whether this was sufficient.

Asked to identify up to five important concepts introduced through the course, members showed a measure of agreement in several areas: confidence in ability to maintain self study, the management of change, practitioner research, evaluation of practice, the value of rational discussion and debate, the relevance of up-to-date research, critical thinking, the practical aspects of classroom research, and the value of personal research in a school context.

Concerning the reasons for success and failure of tutor-led sessions, course members explained relative failure in terms of tutors issuing handouts that were read out rather than talked through; not being totally prepared; content being too complicated; no real knowledge of specialist area under discussion; restricted understanding of course guidelines; a group situation not being conducive to learning — including the degree of course member alertness, and insufficient acknowledgement of professional experience.

When a tutor-led session had gone well, course members explained this in terms of positive forward suggestions being made, 'pointing in the right direction' to improve the quality of work, a variety of approaches being used with no jargon, and debate being led with a sense of purpose. A measure of agreement emerged in the areas of using peer experience, allowing group discussion and listening to opinion, offering relevant material of direct interest at the right time, and knowing the needs of the group well enough to make appropriate suggestions. A clear consensus was evident on such matters as 'knowing what they are talking about', preparing well, and providing clear presentations and handouts.

Space does not permit further interpretation of these responses except to note that there are interesting comparisons to be drawn between the listed items from year 1 to year 2, in particular, the guilt complex notion, the character of possible interference effects on teaching, self perceptions of increased credibility and access, and the nature of report writing in an award-bearing course.

Overall, this preliminary evaluation points to group member satisfaction about the course process on a number of dimensions of crucial importance in improving the quality of teaching and pupil learning. This judgment is confirmed by independent observers but the data leave less clear the extent to which actual improvement in practice had occurred beyond the immediate circumstances of individual classrooms and outside the confines of the individual problems studied. In short, the degree of change in teaching style, the transference effects on thinking about the wider curriculum, the extent to which research-based teaching is a temporary system or more continuous, and the extent of influence on whole school policies are all matters for further evaluation.

Summary

The concept of action inquiry attempts to create a framework for dialogue on practical professional concerns which is responsive both to the preferred learning styles of practitioners and to the felt needs of schools. As an enquiry base for INSET its central purpose is to support research-based teaching with a view to improving practice and to transferring practical professional knowledge and experience. In this form of research the study of change is preferred to the study of texts, the study of cases of professional action is preferred to the study of experimental samples, and the focus of enquiry is on practical issues as distinct from theoretical issues. The conduct of the investigation is controlled by course members themselves in a collaborative framework of dialogue validated by colleagues and co-professionals. The way ahead must therefore be not only by continuous improvement in the design and delivery of courses but also by trying to match those factors conducive to professional growth within a course to conditions of service outside it. The main priority for course management lies in the direction of helping schools to develop knowledge of their own practice.[13]

Notes

1   FOUCAULT, M. (1974) *The Archaeology of Knowledge*, London, Tavistock.
2   RUDDUCK, J. and HOPKINS, D. (1985) *Research as a Basis for Teaching: Readings from the Work of Lawrence Stenhouse*, London, Heinemann.
3   BELL, G.H. (1985) 'INSET: Five types of collaboration and consultancy', *School Organization*, 5, 3.
4   LEWIN, K. (1946) 'Action research and minority problems', *Journal of Social Issues*, 2, pp. 34–46.
5   REVANS, R. (1982) *Action Learning*, London, Chartwell Bratt.
6   BELL, G.H. (1985) 'Can schools develop knowledge of their practice?', *School Organization*, 5, 2.
7   Sheffield City Polytechnic, Department of Education, Diploma in Curriculum Development (School Focussed); BELL, G.H. (1984) 'Supporting school development', *Dialogue in Education*, 1, 1.
8   GUBA, E.G. and LINCOLN, Y.S. (1982) 'Epistemological and methodological bases of naturalistic inquiry', *Educational Communication and Technology Journal*, 30, 4.
9   O'NEIL, M.J. (1981) 'Nominal group technique: An evaluation data collection process', *Evaluation Newsletter*.
10   These issues have been tackled through uses of the concept of a 'critical community' within the course process of the Certificate in Educational Action Inquiry (Course Leader: Peter Ovens), Manchester Polytechnic, Faculty of Community Studies and Education.
11   DENNIS, S. (1987) *Practitioner Research and Microcomputers*, University of Sheffield and Sheffield City Polytechnic (mimeo).
12   BELL, G.H. (1983) 'Information technology and teacher research. Working paper 9', *Schools Council Teacher Pupil Interaction and Quality of Learning Project*, Cambridge Institute of Education.
13   This is a version of a paper first presented to a conference 'Developing Enquiry-based courses' at Newnham College, Cambridge, 15–20 September 1986. I am indebted to the course members of the Diploma in Curriculum Development for their comments and support and to the advisory staff of Humberside and Sheffield LEAs for their help in resolving the many issues of design and delivery that are not recorded here.

3   My Body of Knowledge

Stephen Rowland

Introduction

I learnt my body of knowledge, not someone else's.

We were sitting in a seminar room at the University, reviewing the previous term's 'Classroom enquiry' course, when Margaret, one of the course participants, made this statement. The course in question was one of a series of part-time courses which made up University of Sheffield Division of Education's MEd programme. Her comment made me stop and think. It forms the starting point to my reflections about my provision of the course and its relationship to the participants' professional development. On the one hand I felt delighted that Margaret felt so positively about her own learning. On the other hand it raised so many questions about the work we had been doing. For example:

- How does the 'my body of knowledge' relate to the knowledge of others? Wasn't the 'course' supposed to be about sharing in the knowledge of other participants as well?
- How does this relate to the external knowledge as represented in research literature?
- How can such learning effect change in the classroom if we never get outside our own body of knowledge and view things from a different perspective?
- Is this learning of one's own body of knowledge part of a continuing process, or is it a result of a brief period of reflection and introspection, a kind of therapeutic interlude?

In reflecting upon the course I shall consider these four themes because I think their exploration is important if we are to empower teachers to make their own enquiries into the learning which they facilitate. These themes also raise fundamental questions about how I understand the nature of academic pursuit. But first, I need to describe the course itself.

The Classroom Enquiry Course

The course sessions, run during the spring term 1986, were held after school, for about two hours, on ten occasions during the term. There were eight course members excluding myself, the course tutor. They were in their first or second year of the three-year part-time MEd and taught in a very wide range of institutions from a primary special school to a college of higher education.

The aims and outline of the course were described in the course handbook from which the teachers chose their options:

> This course aims to develop skills of observation and interpretation of children's learning by integrating the roles of teacher and researcher. Course participants will be expected to observe, in detail, activities in their classrooms and present samples of children's work and descriptions of their activity for discussion amongst the group. The approach will be interdisciplinary, drawing upon a range of curriculum areas with a focus upon the thinking which underlies the children's activity. We shall also consider the implications of this for teaching and promoting educational change.

For the first session of the course I prepared a document which repeated these aims, suggested a provisional course structure and outlined the form of the coursework and its criteria for assessment. For the course structure I suggested how the sessions might develop from a period of exploring an area for enquiry, focussing down, developing observations, considering issues emerging from these, and so on, through to a final course evaluation. There were to be a few suggested readings, but it was clear that the main form of the sessions would be considering the individual enquiries as they developed and discussing the more general methodological and practical questions of enquiry.

Each teacher's enquiry was to be recorded in a project file and some guidance was given as to what kind of material might be relevant: descriptive accounts, samples of children's work, reflective writing, and so on. The course assessment was to be on the basis of the project file, and the criteria used were made explicit:

1 Your ability to reflect on your observations through your writing.
2 Your preparedness to take risks in interpreting pupils' work.
3 Evidence that your enquiry relates to your experience as a teacher.
4 The success of your file in communicating your thinking during the course.

Most of the other courses on the taught MEd programme are assessed by means of a course essay or assignment. Since I could not therefore assume that the participants were used to working in the kind of research mode that I envisaged, I felt it was necessary to be quite explicit about my expectations. Criterion 2 above, concerning risk, in particular needed some discussion. It appeared to be greeted by a combination of surprise and relief by teachers who had come to believe that research necessarily involved a search for certainty and the minimization of risk in interpreting data. I had in mind the comments of Eisner (1978) that:

> Doing qualitative evaluation . . . the enquirer puts himself or herself on the line whenever something is written and shared. Unlike the application of standardized tests . . . the individual doing qualitative evaluation has a personal stake in the work that is being done.

My experience has been that teachers, in their writing (though not in their conversation), are reticent to take the risk involved in putting themselves on the line, and that it was therefore helpful to make this an explicit expectation in their writing.

The introduction of these ideas to the participants in the first session of the course set the broad framework of a course whose procedures were to be quite open-ended. I took what I considered to be a low profile role in facilitating the teachers' enquiries and providing a context for these to be shared.

The data I shall now draw upon to reflect upon the course consist of the course notes I made in preparation for and during the sessions, the project files of the teachers (each of which included a section evaluating their work on the course), and notes made at the meeting the following term at which participants and a University colleague joined me to review the course. The themes I want to pursue are those suggested above: the problem of sharing our work; the role and function of research literature; the effects on classroom practice; and enquiry as an on-going process.

Sharing Our Work

When I came to read the project files I was impressed by the value of much of the work presented, the insights that had been gained and the understanding that was demonstrated. It was apparent, however, that while the teachers felt that they had learned a great deal from the course, they felt that they had not learned much from each other's work. Some of the reasons for this were beyond our control, such as illness and industrial action which affected much of the work. Other factors related more to the problem of developing what Kemmis (1980) called a 'critical community' within the space of ten two-hour sessions. As Margaret said in our discussion on the course:

> We provided each other with occasional enlightening comments but we were extremely polite and kind. . . . Everybody was terribly nice about my ideas.

Partly this is a matter of time, but given these constraints it is important to try different forms of organizing discussion in an attempt to cultivate the kind of trust which is required if people are to take the risk both of exposing themselves and of providing and receiving critical feedback. Most of our discussions centred upon the work of individuals and were held within the full group of (on average) seven or eight people. Since such a discussion might take three quarters of an hour, each person was only able to share their work on three or four occasions during the course. This meant that people did not become familiar enough with the issues with which each was involved and were therefore not often in a position to offer enlightening criticism. Two useful suggestions were made for overcoming this difficulty:

> *Sue*: In retrospect I think it would have been more value to work in small groups or even pairs with the occasional group discussion.
>
> *Rob*: It might be more useful experientially and administra-

tively to locate the sharing-criticizing activities in the schools of those teachers involved, thus making the whole enquiry more school-based ... releasing further time for more specifically directed activities in the course sessions.

Both of these suggestions are very useful, and I shall no doubt make use of them when I plan the next course. They perhaps suggest, however, that a clear distinction can be drawn between the activity of sharing each other's work and 'more directed' activities. In individual or paired supervision work, it is natural enough to move onto, for example, more general methodological themes when these are appropriate to the investigations being pursued. What is more difficult is to tie in such discussion to the enquiries of seven or eight people each of whom is progressing at a different rate. My problem here is the same (but not so extreme) as the classroom teacher's problem of teaching from the interests of individual children. Here, even if the problem of organization and control can be overcome, there is the danger that, without sufficient opportunity for feedback from tutor or peers, the children's work will become too individualistic. The problem is one of intervening at the appropriate moment.

For some teachers, although the course itself did not provide sufficient opportunity to share their work, it did introduce them to the idea which was then developed with staff at school. This would seem to further emphasize the value of basing enquiry more firmly in the school.

Another difficulty in sharing the work appeared to be the lack of an appropriate unifying element. Although the two main preliminary reading texts, Armstrong (1980) and Rowland (1984), provided a common approach to me, as course tutor, they clearly did not provide a common knowledge base to those who had not already embarked on this kind of study.

> *Margaret*: We could have shared a vocabulary if we had more of a knowledge base.
> *Sue*: Given the range and background interests and types of experience of the MEd group I found difficulty in establishing a unifying element.

Reading through the project files it was clear to me that, by the end of the course, we did indeed share a good deal of common language and understanding. If a shared knowledge base is essential in order to develop a critical community, is it possible to ensure that such understanding is developed prior to or in the early stages of the course? Is this not where the course must direct itself to a more considered study of the 'research literature'? Should that not provide the 'unifying element'? This takes us on to the second theme which I want to consider.

The Research Literature

It would be nice and tidy to imagine that, in putting on a course, all I have to do to ensure that there is a common knowledge base at the outset is to prepare a list of preliminary readings. Since these would outline the 'field' and perhaps the 'language' of investigation as well as the basic knowledge, we should all know where we are, have some idea of where we are going, and a few clues about how we shall get there. Such a view, however, is inclined to overlook the very personal and creative nature of reading. The meaning of a text for one person is different from its meaning for another. It will be dependent upon the context of the reader, the history of their ideas, recent experiences and so on. On a course such as this, with teachers from a wide range of backgrounds, it seems unreasonable to expect that a few well chosen texts could provide this common base.

Furthermore, there appears to be a particular difficulty with preliminary reading in a course of this nature, which is explicitly based upon direct experience. Such a list seems to be giving the message that, in order to provide a knowledge base, we can rely upon second-hand experience through reading, but in order to build upon that base during the course, direct experience is necessary.

Here is how Sue expressed this frustration:

> Preliminary to the classroom enquiry option I attempted to read the two set books on the preliminary reading list but found this a difficult if not impossible task. I reworked my way through parts of the whole but found the emphasis on description totally alienating. Throughout the course, as well as reading around the area, I persisted with the two books and still had difficulty. Towards the end of the course when I read the epilogue of *The Enquiring Classroom* I suddenly found it made sense and I had sufficient understanding to receive what was being said. Many of the points echoed my own recent experience and for the first time really made sense. I had needed to share the experience rather than receive it second-hand.

The problem here could be simply that the preliminary texts were badly chosen, or that the research field lacks sufficient definition to make a selection of texts easy. I think that this teacher, however, is saying something more significant than that. It concerns the relationship between understanding gained through reading and understanding gained through reflection upon experience. For her it was the experience which provided 'sufficient understanding to receive what was being said'. It was where the text 'echoed' experience that sense could be made of it. To put this another way, understanding has to be grounded in experience and not texts, even though the latter may help to illuminate that experience.

There were rather different reasons why Jamie thought reading more appropriate in the later stages of enquiry:

> It was only after completing my research that I went to the literature. I would normally have approached the literature first but I was interested to make my own findings first without relying too much on previous investigations.

I think this reflects a desire for authenticity in enquiry. Jamie did in fact go on to consider several other works related to his own investigation, and these enabled him to place his own ideas within a wider context, thus giving added meaning to them. But the step he has taken is to say: 'I'm O.K. My ideas are significant. I'll see what the others have to say later.' Such an approach does not reflect arrogance, but a concern to assert the validity of one's own experience. This attitude is, I believe, admirable amongst a teaching profession which is continually having its ability to make educational judgments undermined by hostile political forces. It is, perhaps, a step in what Polanyi (1958) calls the programme of self-identification:

> I believe that the function of philosophical reflection consists of bringing to light, and affirming as my own, the beliefs implied in such of my thoughts and practices as I believe to be valid; that I must aim at discovering what I truly believe in and at formulating the convictions which I find myself holding; that I must conquer my self doubt, so as to retain a firm hold on this programme of self-identification.

There is a danger that more traditional forms of educational study and research literature, in their constant appeal to the authority of published work, encourage the very kind of self-doubt which Polanyi's philosophical reflection is aimed to conquer. There is nothing like an educational text, followed by a long list of bibliographic notes and references, for making the teacher feel an outsider to the world of academic research. Too many experiences like that can put one off reading educational work altogether, let alone writing it. The baby is then thrown out with the bath water. Or the alternative danger is that the teacher, as student, learns to play an academic game of quoting as many references as possible. The authority of the work is then seen to be based upon the extent of the quoted references, rather than upon the clarity and rigour of the argument. Graham was very conscious that he was not playing this game. But this caused him problems:

> Another problem the compilation of my enquiry file has caused me, and is still causing me, is as a result of spending three years at college then a further three years part time at the university doing a BEd. I am conditioned therefore into constantly referring to the 'authorities'. In this enquiry file I have not done that. This is because of the way it has developed . . . .

One teacher summarized the role of research literature for her in this course by saying that we were 'looking at ourselves rather than the research literature'. From the experience of the course and of those who have gone on to continue the process of enquiry through independent studies and dissertations, the need to read 'research literature' does emerge, and can become a vital source of further development. Whether 'looking at ourselves' is an adequate focus for a course for this sort would depend largely upon how the participants understand the effects of such reflection. This is what I want to turn to now.

The Effects

While the context of the individual enquiries was the classroom, the focus of them was not normally defined in terms of a problem for which a changed pattern of teaching was to be developed. Participants were encouraged to focus on anything which particularly interested them or caught their imagination. The range of areas studied was wide and included the exploration of 3D work with very young children, language development activities for children with special needs and various kinds of problem solving approaches.

With this wide variety of studies, the effects of the enquiry were often specific to the individual. For example, Graham reported that:

> It has changed my way of dealing with creative writing ... I *never* now begin by picking up my red pen and working through the work with it. But I do read it through with the child and discuss it with them.

But behind this quite identifiable change in teaching tactics lies a changed understanding of children's writing. Graham also writes that he is now inclined to view it as a product 'for appreciation' rather than as a practice in the techniques of writing and spelling. This change towards seeing children's language as expressing significant ideas was reflected in different ways in several of the enquiries, each time accompanied by a change of teacher tactics. For example, Margaret wrote:

> I finished the enquiry with a determination to assume that every child has a hidden treasure, and it is my job as teacher to enable that child to find it.

But, as Margaret went on to report, this is a time consuming process which can only be undertaken by spending longer periods with individual children:

> This meant seeing him less frequently — I marked his books less often, and he did fewer English exercises. I gave up quantity for quality, and this practice has since been extended to all the rest of the children; I am now less likely to interrupt an important discussion with a child in the service of the great teaching god of keeping busy.

This concern for discovering the meaning in the children's language and action reflects the convergence between the process of enquiry and the process of teaching. For it is by paying careful attention to the children that we are able to collect our 'research data'. This is also a strategy which enables us, as teachers, to intervene appropriately in their learning. The effect of giving this kind of attention was explained by Bob in relation to children's problem solving.

> By consciously 'homing in' on small groups of pupils, and almost blotting out the rest of the class, I have become far more aware of the importance of listening to my pupils, and coaxing out their ideas and strategies for solving problems.

So often in the past I have heard but not listened — without listening one cannot act as a resource or a catalyst because whatever one says surely takes the form of dictation or pronouncement rather than genuine interest, and is often no more than a form of assessment to the child.

All of the reported changes appear to reflect a shift in the teachers' thinking towards what might be described as a more child centred approach to learning. Such a shift, I would argue (Rowland, 1985), is not coincidental, but reflects a research perspective which is itself integrated with a particular pedagogical stance which places the learner, rather then a body of knowledge, at the centre of the curriculum.

Enquiry as an Ongoing Process

It may be that this course provided teachers with an unusual opportunity to reflect upon their own practice and beliefs. It would be misleading, however, to evaluate the changes reported as if they were due solely to what took place while they were conducting their investigations. Learning is not only the result of what we do, but also of how we give meaning to what we have done. For any individual, the course must be seen in terms of the prior experiences which have, perhaps, been given added meaning by reflection during the course. Equally, however, future events will alter the significance of what took place during the enquiry. All we can say with certainty about the educational value of an experience is: 'We'll have to wait and see.'

Many of the course members did see their own enquiry in terms of a longer term development. For some, this is to be represented formally by pursuing further enquiries either in independent study options (rather than choosing a taught course) within the MEd programme or through their own research for their dissertation. For others, such as Margaret, the manner in which the enquiry process continues is not part of a formal course of study or research, but integrated into everyday teaching:

The enquiry thus continues, and this report becomes part of the teaching and learning process.

Several of the teachers, in their enquiry files, said that their enquiry led them to learn about their own as well as about the children's learning:

Bob writes:

> From conducting my classroom enquiry I have come to a
> number of conclusions about learning, not only children's
> learning but also my own, for indeed I have learnt a great
> deal about myself, as well as my pupils.

This relationship between our awareness of our own learning
and the learning of others seems to be a reciprocal one. By observing children (or other adults) learning I am reminded of my own
past and present experience of learning and new understandings of
that experience are suggested to me. On the other hand, it is my
thoughts about my own learning which help me to make sense of
the learning activity of others whom I observe.

Learning about oneself is, in a sense, a therapeutic experience.
Not in the sense that one starts with a 'problem' for which help is
sought, but that it requires a kind of self searching which can be
painful as well as illuminating. That such a process is necessarily
part of a continuum of ongoing experience is expressed by Sue like
this:

> I have found the process of classroom enquiry very illu-
> minating because it was as much about my own learning
> experience as that of the children so exposing my preoccu-
> pations and inadequacies. The need to be open to the experi-
> ence seemed rather like taking religious orders as one almost
> had to lose a sense of self to strip away all the fixed notions
> built up over the years! The process has been a very three
> dimensional experience and not unlike the process I go
> through when doing my own art work, where I have come
> to realize that one specific piece of work or period of time is
> not a conclusive, exclusive picture of the sum of the parts —
> merely part of a continuum.

My own enquiry on this course, one expression of which is this
chapter, is certainly part of such an ongoing process. Its value for
me lies not only in the extent to which I may have provided an
opportunity for others to reflect upon their own practice and beliefs. It depends equally upon the ways in which their developing
awareness has helped me to reconsider my own preoccupations and
inadequacies as a collaborator in our learning.

References

ARMSTRONG, M. (1980) *Closely Observed Children*, London, Writers and Readers.

EISNER, E.W. (1978) 'Foreword' in WILLIS, G. (Ed.) *Qualitative Evaluation*, California, McCutcheon, p. xv.

KEMMIS, S. (1980) *Research in Action Research*, Geelong, Deakin University.

POLANYI, M. (1958) *Personal Knowledge*, London, Routledge and Kegan Paul, p. 267.

ROWLAND, S. (1984) *The Enquiring Classroom*, Lewes, Falmer Press.

ROWLAND, S. (1985) 'Classroom enquiry: An approach to understanding children's learning', *Teachers Studying Children's Learning*, Leicestershire Education Committee, 4, pp. 2–7.

ROWLAND, S. (1986) 'Something you grow into', *British Journal of In-Service Education*, 12, summer, pp. 81–5.

Part 2

Pre-service Teacher Education: Some Dilemmas and Resolutions

In a recently published critique of teacher education (Popkewitz, 1987) a number of writers argued that many teacher education programmes, both pre-service and in-service, have failed to provide conditions for critical debate which will lead to students reconceptualizing and transforming their understandings of taken-for-granted practice. They argue that by devoting significant proportions of courses to the inculcation of skills and the acquiring of established bodies of knowledge the cultural reproduction cycle not only continues but is strengthened.

Each of the accounts which follow represents a practical example of a conscious attempt to penetrate those structural forms which serve utilitarian interests. Singly each one is a modest proposal, collectively they allow us to conceive of the possibility of a radically different teacher education programme arising from and feeding back into the discourses associated with a critical view of schooling.

The difficulties for the learners in the pre-service situation are most particularly associated with their perceived lack of status in both the teacher education institution and the schools in which they may be placed for 'practical' work. The courses described here have sought for ways which will, not withstanding, allow learners both to collect sensitive information and the opportunities, collaboratively, to comb it for understanding.

Smith and Sachs provide us with a well-supported rationale for students undertaking 'end-on' teaching courses of only one year to engage in creating ethnographic accounts of youth culture. They cite a course for which they were responsible which allows students to explore unfamiliar cultures in microsettings as a grounding for discussion of the political and social forces affecting youth culture.

The work of Isaac and Ashcroft has been predicated upon the notion 'a theory of the action rather than a theory into action'. They have devised a problem-solving model which enquires in real time into real problems. Structured around Berlaks' *Dilemmas of Schooling* (1981) each unit of the course focusses upon one dilemma.

The chapter presents a case study of enquiries, conducted by pre-service teacher education students, centred upon the financing of nursery schools and youth training scheme programmes and involving the interrogation of witnesses.

Groundwater-Smith addresses the problem of the extent to which the pre-service student may gain sufficient access to data in schools and argues that, notwithstanding the obstacles, the learner may become an active enquirer when dealing with case record materials. The study outlines a course which provides opportunities to research case records in ways which reveal the coherence between the intended and operational curriculum and the sociohistorical spaces within which curricula evolve. The process is designed to be a collaborative one and also insists upon the learners exploring and examining their own ideologies.

While the earlier chapters in this section deal with innovatory practices, Robottom's account is concerned with identifying the complexities and contradictions arising out of reconceptualizing pre-service teacher education. He points to the hierarchical division of labour, particularly in an emerging institution, in putting policy into practice. He sets out the historical development of a BA (Ed) course at Deakin University, Australia, which rigidly separated the academic preparation of students from their teaching practice. A revised version redistributed the time spent in the University and the school classroom and the nature of the activities with which the students engaged. Robottom reveals the extent to which students themselves were captives of conservative research paradigms and emphasizes the difficulties involved in attempting to penetrate their views.

A problem which continues to thread its way through the pre-service teacher education debate is the value of the apprenticeship model whereby neophyte teachers are attached to skilled practitioners to learn the craft of teaching. Beyer and Zeichner (1987) argue that field-based teacher education contributes to 'utilitarian teaching perspectives in which teaching is separated from its ethical, political and moral roots . . .' (p. 315). Altrichter's chapter, which concludes this section, proposes an enquiry-based course which while based on an apprenticeship model does not interpret this notion in narrowing and confining ways. The early phases of an innovation are portrayed in which cooperating teachers researched features of their own practice thereby identifying issues which concerned them. These experiences then acted as the core for a teacher education programme, with students taking on research commissions alongside the teachers. In this way teachers revealed their own uncertainties about their practice and welcomed students as co-researchers.

Certainly none of these responses reflects the practice of mainstream teacher education, but they do indicate in positive and creative ways the possibility for change.

References

BEYER, L.E. and ZEICHNER, K. (1987) 'Teacher education in cultural context: Beyond reproduction' in POPKEWITZ, T. (Ed.) *Critical Studies in Teacher Education: Its Folklore, Theory and Practice*, Lewes, Falmer Press, pp. 298–334.

POPKEWITZ, T. (Ed.) (1987) *Critical Studies in Teacher Education: Its Folklore, Theory and Practice*, Lewes, Falmer Press.

4 It Really Made Me Stop and Think: Ethnography in Pre-service Teacher Education

Richard Smith and Judyth Sachs

Educational Ethnography

There is now a long history of ethnographic work in schools. This work occurs in many forms, represented by anthropological studies and sociological approaches. The ethnographic approach has also influenced educational research and ways of thinking about teachers, students and classrooms.

A major difference between the two traditions lies in the uses to which ethnography is put. On the one hand, ethnography, the *sine qua non* of the anthropological tradition, has centred on education as cultural transmission (Funnell and Smith, 1981). On the other hand, ethnography in the sociology of education developed around the inadequacies of positivistic educational research techniques. The latter tradition, drawing on the interpretive models of symbolic interactionism, social phenomenology and ethnomethodology, demonstrated the diversity and complexity of teacher/student experience and activities (Hammersley, 1985; Woods, 1986), and provided an alternative to mechanistic and psychologistic description of schools.

In both traditions the ethnographer's claim is that school (or any other) life is best represented by the researcher as only one who has known it first hand can (Marcus and Cushman, 1982). Ethnographic realism generated from face-to-face interactions in everyday life situations and anchored in the views of the other rather than the researcher, is characterized by the use of illuminative portrayals of school life. In stark contrast to positivistic analyses of school affairs, ethnographies provide a rich store of detail that allows for a vicarious experience on the part of the reader.

Both traditions exhibit similar inadequacies in the relative emphases given to methodology and data analysis and to theoretical issues. Educational ethnographies of the first tradition have been criticized for their uncritical use of cultural transmission models which rely on psychological assumptions. Part of the failure in this tradition to link inter-psychic social and cultural perspectives with intra-psychic processes of learning (Tindall, 1976) has been traced to the Boasian ideals of privileging methodology and data collection rather than theory in the research process (Ianni, 1976; Burton, 1978; Burnett, 1979) which has characterized the mainstream discipline. Similarly in the second tradition, ethnographers have seriously engaged with the problems of meaning in the production of authentic accounts rather than with theoretical schemes for analysis (Hammersley, 1980). This focus has led Woods (1984) to criticize school ethnographies for being consumed with the 'area of data analysis' rather than with theory development, and Hammersley (1985) argues that 'interpretive ethnography' is condemned to rely on vague and untested ideas (p. 245). Further, Pollard (1984) notes that recent reviews of the field indicate the failure of ethnographic work in schools to achieve cumulative theoretical growth and coherence in the sociology of education (p. 179). Both approaches, by neglecting macro-sociological and theoretical issues, are in danger of becoming atheoretical and losing credibility in the educational research (Dockrell and Hamilton, 1980) and policy areas (Foster, 1975; Pollard, 1984).

Ethnography in Teacher Education

While the ethnographic work surveyed above, notwithstanding its weaknesses, provides many insights into areas of school and organizational life, ethnographers have been less interested in teacher education as a research area. Atkinson and Delamont (1985) point out that 'there is a marked absence of published ethnographies focussed on teacher socialization as a process' (p. 310). School ethnographies have provided input into discussions of teacher education and ethnographers and teacher educators have made claims about the efficacy of ethnographic techniques for teacher education programs. Woods (1985) for example argues that ethnography could be used to induce reflectiveness and to encourage 'observational skills' in pre-service teacher education students, but he sees in-service education as the more appropriate place for it

(p. 51). Bolster (1983) sees 'interactionist' ethnography as appropriate for generating knowledge that is useful and interesting to teachers, and as a strategy for teacher development at the in-service level. A more optimistic assessment of ethnography at the pre-service level is provided by Gitlin and Teitelbaum (1983) who claim that small-scale ethnographies 'can enable these future teachers to become more sensitive to the process of schooling in a far more fruitful way then is usually the case in teacher education programs' (p. 226).

They go on to describe two teacher education programs at the universities of Utah and Wisconsin in which ethnography is an integral part of developing reflective, questioning, investigative and flexible teachers (*ibid.*, p. 233). This is important. Gitlin and Teitelbaum make the point that ethnography is used towards these ends in the two reported programs. It is not an end in itself, dedicated to the production of scholarly papers directed at a narrow range of academic peers. It is rather part of a pedagogical strategy, which includes a critical campus-based seminar (Zeichner, 1981), thought to be helpful in creating the discursive practices of reflective teachers. In this way, the Wisconsin 'enquiry approach' to teacher education (Zeichner and Teitelbaum, 1982) integrates school experience and macro-contextualized ethnographies of schools. Pollard (1984) maintains that the micro/macro-level links of this kind are necessary if ethnography is to serve critical ends, namely the linking of classroom activity with wider social, political and economic conditions (pp. 188–9). He is less enthralled however with the use of ethnography as a 'means' of improving professional competence in teacher education programs if that means focussing exclusively on the micro-level.

Whatever the focus, the efficacy of ethnography for pre-service and in-service teacher education programs has not yet been demonstrated (*ibid.*, p. 192). It is then of some interest to evaluate the impact of an ethnographic exercise on pre-service teacher education students. The remainder of this account is directed at that task.

The Context of the Study

The teacher education program to which we refer is a two-semester 'end-on' Diploma in Education course undertaken by graduates as a preparation for secondary teaching. The program is conventional. That is, each student must undertake two specialist curriculum studies professional courses, two foundations courses based on psychology and sociology respectively, and two blocks of practice teaching together with some other professional preparation. It is in the latter School and Society (SAS) foundations course that the ethnography to be discussed is located.

The SAS course runs across two semesters. The course is designed around a teaching practicum in each semester when students are off-campus for five weeks at a time. Because the students (some 200 in 1986) bring disparate disciplinary backgrounds to the program, the SAS course has a doubly difficult task: it needs both to introduce students to the fundamental concepts in the course and to take account of the different forms of enquiry which they have met thus far.

The course is designed so that it introduces and elaborates key social science concepts to students in some twelve professional specialist areas including mathematics, 'hard' sciences, economics, languages and the like; and so that it provides meaningful access for all students to areas such as the sociology of the school and youth sub-cultures. Part of this dilemma for faculty is that of selecting powerful concepts which help organize the reading material and which sensitize students to the contextual embeddedness of educational practices. One such concept is that of 'culture' which, along with 'social structure', is introduced early in semester one as a major organizing framework. For this reason the ethnography exercise is introduced in the early part of the course.

The ethnography is attached to the 'culture' concept so that the concept, the technique for carrying out a 'mini-ethnography', fieldwork and the ethnographic text are all completed in five weeks. Clearly, the idea of ethnography as an extended fieldwork experience is radically altered in such a regime. In addition, the Queensland ethnographic exercise is based on highly stylized procedures for eliciting cultural knowledge adopted from the cognitive anthropology paradigm exemplified in the work of Frake (1962), Goodenough (1981), and Spradley and McCurdy (1972). Within such a theoretical perspective, students are encouraged to work with a few informants to the extent that they are able to construct at least one taxonomy, to provide a componential definition of terms within the taxonomy, and to discuss their data in relation to the theory of culture contained in the teaching program and readings. Students are encouraged, and coached, in seminar work dealing with interview and questioning techniques (for example, Levine *et al.*, 1980) to select sites about which they are unknowledgeable, to visit the 'scene' on a number of occasions, to elicit 'folk' categories and to develop some cultural competency (Keesing, 1974) in the culture of the informants. Because of a range of difficulties concerned with 200 students entering state and private schools during the early part of the school year, the ethnography is not specifically pitched at 'studying' schools. Consequently not all students elect to study specifically 'educational' scenes (for example, teachers, students, school-leavers, etc.) but instead study, for instance, bike-gangs, Jehovah's Witnesses, punk and skin-head youth sub-cultures, break-dancers and kitchen 'crews' at outlets of the MacDonald's hamburger chain.

Some Theoretical Constraints

The ethnography has been designed by faculty with three ends in view. First, the exercise is premised on the notion that meaning is derived from 'lived experience' (Schutz, 1971) and a fruitful way to learn *about* the idea of 'culture' is to 'learn' a strange culture. In practice of course students learn fragments of informants' culture(s). But even a truncated experience of recreating the informants' culture(s) satisfies the criterion if it enriches a student's knowledge *of* the culture concept. Second, because fieldwork experiences involve interpretive work in face-to-face relationships and the ambiguous status of fieldworker, they are likely to lead to a significant measure of self-discovery (Crick, 1978). The encounter with a stranger is a way of becoming conscious of what is taken for granted in one's own conceptual and emotional frameworks. The ethnography is in this sense a way of creating the conditions for discussion about teacher and student knowledge, the modes in which curriculum knowledge is encoded and decoded, the explorations of such modes and their social effects. Third, the ethnography provides documentary evidence for students that cultural heterogeneity is a feature of society. There are two dimensions to this insight. On the one hand, it provides an experiential basis for a critical discussion of a commonly held functionalist view that 'society' and 'Australian culture' are monolithic. On the other hand, it raises the apparent contradiction that 'individual' informants have 'private' cultures, yet live in networks of social relationships in which meanings are often widely but unequally dispersed. This understanding of 'culture' is developed in later parts of the SAS course dealing with general issues of an ideological nature (for example, Apple and Weis, 1985; Wexler, 1982; Giroux, 1983; Green, 1986).

Two questions about the ethnography are of interest to us:

(i) What is the student reaction to it as a pedagogical strategy; and

(ii) What are its perceived effects/lack of effects on students?

To help answer these questions the following research program was undertaken.

Research Procedures

First, during the period when students were undertaking their ethnographies, a group (fifteen) of them were interviewed informally about the exercise. On the basis of this interview and faculty input, a survey form consisting of twelve Likert-scale items was constructed. These items were directed at the impact of the exercise on theoretical understandings of the culture concept, the logistical problems of completing it and the efficacy of the preparation for it provided by course teaching and reading. In addition, the survey attempted to gauge student commitment to the Diploma in Education program and to the SAS course. This dimension was suggested by the authors' experiences in the program over ten years and by the work of Murdock and Phelps (1973) and Rowe (1983). The survey was completed by 53 per cent (sixty-one women, forty-four men) of the student group at the conclusion of the exercise. The items were analyzed and cross-tabulated in four groups, 'theory', 'logistics', 'preparation' and 'commitment' respectively.

Second, students provided comments about the exercise on the survey form. These were collated and found to reinforce the structure of the survey form. Third, a month later, after the first high school teaching practicum, twenty-two students were interviewed about the ethnography by the authors. Data from each of these techniques are included in the discussion which follows. Space does not permit a full reporting of the results; these may be obtained by referring to Smith and Sachs (1986).

Some Results of the Survey and Interviews

In general terms, the exercise was well received by students. The results of the survey, the written comments made by students and the interviews indicate a high level of acceptance, on their part, of the ethnography as a worthwhile pre-service teacher education activity. Their major concerns were the procedures used to introduce the exercise and the course preparation for doing it.

A great deal of the variance came about as a result of the curriculum studies of the students. Social science and mathematics students were least happy with the preparation provided by the course. The major concern of both of these groups of students was that the formal lecture which tied methodological guidance with theoretical concepts was scheduled too late in the preparatory sequence. As such it was not very 'useful' in the lead-up to the exercise. This was exacerbated by some inconsistencies between the printed course outline and the advice given in the major methodological lecture. Specifically, the outline directed students to the study of 'educational' issues while the lecturer (one of the authors) suggested going beyond educational 'scenes'. For some students, already involved with informants, this caused anxiety insofar as they were not sure that what they were doing was in fact appropriate.

Further, some of the social science students, already cognizant with sociological approaches to culture, found the explanations of the concept restrictive. In the view of a few such students, ethnoscience approaches are 'at least questionable'. In contrast, the view of a number of mathematics and science students was that they lacked a sufficient theoretical depth to 'really come to grips with what was asked of us.' Questioning techniques were identified as a problem in this sense because the theory emphasizes the perspective of the informant. Even if this is understood, the framing of questions within the structure of 'structural' and 'attribute' question forms is a difficult task. Further, these students found difficulties in organizing a mass of interview data, especially those who had tape-recorded their interviews (see Bolster, 1983).

The best general descriptor of the initial reaction to the exercise by many students is that of anxiety. This is summed up by a student with an economics background who when interviewed described her reaction as 'Shit, what's an ethnography?' Other comments reinforcing this response included 'the lead-up to the actual doing of it was unclear' and 'it was too open-ended at first.'

It will be recalled that the students as a group possessed disparate disciplinary backgrounds, and many of them, particularly the math/science students, are, for all intents and purposes, quite unaware of sociological concepts and approaches. The reported confusion and anxiety about the exercise are under these circumstances predictable. Students in the science/math areas suggested that 'all that early stuff on culture went over our heads.' Others were mystified by the purpose of the exercise exemplified by 'what's this got to do with us as teachers (of math/science)?' Still others found the write-up of a 'literary' document very threatening, reflecting the demands of scholarly work in scientific disciplines. This was summed up in the laconic way by a math student: 'Good practice for illiterate maths/science Dip Eds in stringing more than two sentences together.'

In spite of these difficulties students reported that 'everyone was talking about their experiences' in the period when the exercise was underway. The anxiety paradoxically brought students together. Those who 'hadn't done their homework' and those who had, students reported, spent time informally discussing their fieldwork and techniques. The level of interest generated by nearly 200 separate ethnographic projects under way at the same time was apparently a notable feature of the exercise, but one which passed unnoticed, even by the faculty involved in SAS, who were more likely to hear negative comments about the 'irrelevance of SAS'.

The logistics of undertaking the exercise reflected idiosyncratic responses rather than those which could be characterized by disciplinary background.

We concluded that, for most students, undertaking the exercise did not present serious logistical difficulties but for individual students, this was not the case. Some students reported feelings of 'culture-shock' when confronted by cultural forms which were far from their own experience and which restricted their ability to complete the task. Some found the demands of repeated returns to informants very time-consuming and in a few cases physically and emotionally draining. Not all students are without family and other responsibilities which constrain the amount of time available for such an exercise. Others, as we have indicated, experienced difficulties in coping with what was for them an ill-defined and amorphous task couched in mystifying jargon. For them, the amount of time and effort invested was daunting; in one reported case, over eight hours in the field. Nonetheless, the majority of students did not experience great difficulties in this area.

From logistics we turn to the impact of the experience upon the awareness of one's own and others' knowledge and values under-lying the culture and related concepts, theories and the development of knowledge and skills that a teacher might use in schools.

Self and Others

All but a few of the students we interviewed were convinced that the ethnography has heightened their awareness of their own taken-for-granted knowledge and the perspectives of others. Some of their comments are illustrative. For example, the exercise 'shows you where you're coming from'; the ethnographic experience is 'an awareness thing. It really made me stop and think'; 'It just opened my eyes completely because I interviewed people I had no idea of.' For one student who had spoken to us about the strangeness of her informants' lives, the ethnography sensitized her 'not to be shocked by others' beliefs and attitudes.' In relation to others, the task 'showed me a different perspective, different ways of organizing the world'; 'It emphasized to me that people have different attitudes and that perspectives differ and why.' By way of drawing the ideas of self and other together a student described her early school leaver informants in this way, 'It made my experience (of school) like a different planet.' Another who studied unemployed youth reported that the exercise 'changed my whole outlook on what teaching would be like. My schooling was much different. When I got there (i.e. to practice teaching school — RS/JS) I was always thinking about and trying to relate what they'd (informants) said.'

These comments seem to us to exemplify a necessary process in the comparison of cultures specified by Boon (1983, p. ix). He argues that different cultures are integrated systems of differences, and to understand a particular culture, 'displacement' from it must be possible. The ethnographic exercise has clearly facilitated this process for many of the students in our sample.

Transfer of Ethnographic Skills to Teaching

The interviews indicated that the expectation of a transfer of skills from the exercise to classrooms was not fulfilled. Students could not recall having consciously used the questioning techniques of the exercise for example in their teaching situations. While a few students reported in comments on the survey form that they expected to use ethnographic techniques in school projects, the later interviews showed this to be over-optimistic. The constraints of being a 'student teacher' in somebody else's classroom apparently take precedence over such expectations. Nevertheless some social science students commented that the techniques had been 'filed away' and would be used when they became fully-fledged teachers.

Theoretical Understandings of the Culture Concept

The most positive and negative comments in the interviews and on the survey forms were directed at theoretical understandings. These ranged from 'it's a complete waste of time' to highly supportive comments about the way in which the exercise illuminated the theoretical concepts; 'ethnography has a lot to offer. It provides a good transition from theory to practice', and importantly, 'I enjoyed doing this very much. It was fun.'

One comment made in the interviews, that 'the ethnography itself was a pointless waste of time', is worth exploring. This student, a physicist, in fact gained a high grade for his work and was supportive of the effects of the exercise on his own self-awareness and awareness of other cultures. His comment was directed at the positive outcomes accruing from the process of doing the field-work and he considered the 'write-up' a waste of time. Thus,

> (It was) a useful exercise though the product at the end wasn't the paper itself but the experience of talking to people and getting familiar with concepts of ethnography, culture and society.

In relation to the intentions of the exercise, it was successful for him for 'what I got out of it'. Part of his concern may be captured by the comment of another science student, 'I hate writing essays, being wishy-washy. That's the comment the science people make.' Nevertheless, this student by objecting to the 'validity of the (written) ethnography' makes the telling point discussed earlier: the written product is not a research document. It has little, if any, integrity beyond the exercise in which it was constructed. The overall justification of producing a document is now under consideration by the authors but awaits another occasion for its discussion.

Giroux's (1983) concern about the connection between the

culture theory and wider social issues was canvassed by the authors in the interviews. Two responses are reported in order to address the micro/macro-links that concern Giroux and Pollard.

The first is that of a student who studied an urban youth sub-culture and who underwent his first high school practice teaching session in a working-class neighbourhood. He reported that his ethnographic field-work was immediately relevant in his teaching role. He described in detail the differences between an 'academic' geography class and a 'low stream' science class at year 10 level, which he described as being 'different societies'. He was able to recount fine-grained cultural differences between the behaviours of the students and in the ways they were 'processed' by the school. He indicated that his sensitivity to these issues led immediately to him asking why these differences were there in the same school. He reported thinking about 'the intensity of it all, it's too daunting' as he tried to see beyond the specifics of the school situation. He looked to the remainder of the SAS course to help him unravel some of the wider issues he had already experienced from a perspective which he attributed to the ethnography.

The second example is that of an English student who felt that her knowledge of the culture concept had provided a framework for analyzing educational issues. While she frankly admitted that her own ethnography of flight stewardesses was a micro-study, she saw numerous ways in which gender and work-situation were related and could be generalized. That she did not make those leaps in her write-up was, she claimed, a function of the time restraints on the exercise. In any case, she reported, 'the rest of the (SAS) course doesn't let you lose sight of the wider issues.'

This seems to be a crucial point in our view. The articulation of the ethnographic exercise and on-campus course work is where the potential of ethnography as a critical referent is given value. It is not simply the nature of the ethnography or the content of the course-work that matters but their mutual reinforcement. Of course, teacher educators, including sociologists who teach foundations courses, have little control over the decoding of exercises like the ethnography and course content and the use made of them by students. At best, a course such as SAS can structure the conditions in which relational thinking and critical consciousness about education-in-context can be developed. For the student quoted above, the course creates situations which necessarily demand relational thinking.

Concluding Remarks

This account has made the case that ethnography is an effective strategy for developing theoretical insights in pre-service teacher education students. While recognizing the dangers of focussing on concepts such as culture in isolation, the data from this study suggest that ethnography has considerable appeal for teacher education students and given a suitable course-work shell, has a strong impact on the ways in which they form their 'educational' perspectives. The discussion has also indicated that the acceptance, and the effects, of ethnography are subject to the academic background of students, particularly the science/math-humanities/social science split. The Queensland experiences has underlined the importance of taking these background factors seriously in the lead-up preparatory course-work to the exercise to ensure that the task is well understood across its different dimensions. Finally, the chapter indicates that ethnography for pre-service teacher education students need not necessarily focus on schools to be an effective sensitizing exercise if the intention of it is to develop critical insights into education and society. Indeed, there may well be good reasons for avoiding such common-sensically well known sites.

References

APPLE, M. and WEIS, L. (1985) 'Ideology and schooling: The relationship between class and culture', *Education and Society*, 3, 1, pp. 45–63.

ATKINSON, P. and DELAMONT, S. (1985) 'Socialisation into teaching: The research which lost its way', *British Journal of Sociology of Education*, 6, 3, pp. 307–22.

BOLSTER, A. (1983) 'Toward a more effective model of research on teaching', *Harvard Educational Review*, 53, 3, pp. 294–308.

BOON, J. (1983) *Other Tribes, Other Scribes: Symbolic Anthropology in the Comparative Study of Cultures, Histories, Religions and Texts*, Cambridge, Cambridge University Press.

BURNETT, J. (1979) 'Anthropology in relation to education', *American Behavioural Scientist*, 23, 2, pp. 237–70.

BURTON, A. (1978) 'Anthropology of the young', *Anthropology and Education Quarterly*, 9, 1, pp. 54–70.

CRICK, M. (1978) 'Anthropological field research, meaning creation and knowledge construction' in SCHWIMMER, E. (Ed.) *The Yearbook of Symbolic Anthropology*, London, Hurst and Co, pp. 15–37.

DOCKRELL, W. and HAMILTON, D. (Eds) (1980) *Rethinking Educational Research*, London, Hodder and Stoughton.

FOSTER, P. (1975) 'Reflections on the Waigani seminar', in BRAMMALL, J.

and MAY, R. (Eds) *Education in Melanesia*, Canberra, Australian National University/University of Papua New Guinea, pp. 515–21.

FRAKE, C. (1962) 'The ethnographic study of cognitive systems' in GLADWIN, T. and STURTEVANT, W. (Eds) *Anthropology and Human Behaviour*, Washington, Anthropological Behavior, Society of Washington, pp. 72–85.

FUNNELL, R. and SMITH, R. (1981) 'Search for a theory of cultural transmission in an anthropology of education: Notes on Spindler and Gearing', *Anthropology and Education Quarterly*, 12, 4, pp. 275–300.

GIROUX, H. (1983) 'Critical pedagogy, cultural politics and the discourse of experience', *Journal of Education*, 167, 2, pp. 22–41.

GITLIN, A. and TEITELBAUM, K. (1983) 'Linking theory and practice: The use of ethnographic methodology by prospective teachers', *Journal of Education for Teaching*, 9, 3, pp. 225–34.

GOODENOUGH, W. (1981) *Culture, Language and Society*, 2nd edition, Menlo Park, CA, Benjamin Cummings.

GREEN, B. (1986) 'Reading reproduction theory: On the ideology-and-education debate', *Discourse*, 6, 2, pp. 1–31.

HAMMERSLEY, M. (1980) 'Classroom ethnography', *Educational Analysis*, 2, 2, pp. 47–74.

HAMMERSLEY, M. (1985) 'From ethnography to theory: A programme and paradigm in the sociology of education', *Sociology*, 19, 2, pp. 244–59.

HAMMERSLEY, M. and WOODS, P. (Eds) (1976) *The Process of Schooling*, London, Routledge and Kegan Paul.

IANNI, F. (1976) 'Anthropology and educational research: A report on Federal agency programs, policies, and issues', *Anthropology and Education Quarterly*, 7, pp. 3–11.

KEESING, R. (1974) 'Theories of culture', *Annual Review of Anthropology*, 3, pp. 14–97.

LEVINE, H., GALLIMORE, R., WEISNER, T. and TURNER, J. (1980) 'Teaching participant-observation research methods: A skills building approach', *Anthropology and Education Quarterly*, 11, 1, pp. 38–54.

MARCUS, G. and CUSHMAN, D. (1982) 'Ethnographies as texts' in SIEGEL, B., BEALS, A. and TYLER, S. (Eds) *Annual Review of Anthropology*, 11, pp. 25–69.

MURDOCK, G. and PHELPS, G. (1973) *Mass Media and the Secondary School*, London, Macmillan.

POLLARD, A. (1984) 'Ethnography and social policy for classroom practice', in BARTON, L. and WALKER, S. (Eds) *Social Crisis and Educational Research*, London, Croom Helm, pp. 171–99.

ROWE, K. (1983) *Mass Media and Adolescent Schooling: Conflict or Co-existence?* Stockholm, Almquist and Wiksell.

SCHUTZ, A. (1971) 'The stranger: an essay on social psychology', in COSIN, B.R., DALE, I.R., ESLAND, G.M., SWIFT, D.F. (Eds) *School and Society: A Sociological Reader*, London, Routledge and Kegan Paul, pp. 32–38.

SMITH, R. and SACHS, J. (1986) 'Ethnography in Pre-service teacher education: A case study', paper presented at the annual conference of the Sociology Association of Australia and New Zealand, Armidale, 9–12 July.

SPRADLEY, J. and McCURDY, D. (1972) *The Cultural Experience: Ethnography in Complex Society*, Chicago, Science Research Associates.

TINDALL, B. (1976) 'Theory in the study of cultural transmission', in SIEGEL, B. (Ed.) *Annual Review of Anthropology*, Palo Alto, CA, Annual Reviews, pp. 195–208.

WEXLER, P. (1982) 'Ideology and education: from critique to class action,' *Interchange*, 13, pp. 53–78.

WOODS, P. (1984) 'Ethnography and theory construction in educational research', in BURGESS, R. (Ed.) *Field Methods in the Study of Education*, Lewes, Falmer Press.

WOODS, P. (1985) 'Sociology, ethnography and teacher practice', *Teaching and Teacher Education*, 1, 1, pp. 51–62.

WOODS, P. (1986) *Inside Schools: Ethnography in Educational Research*, London, Routledge and Kegan Paul.

ZEICHNER, K. (1980) 'Myths and realities: Field-based experiences in pre-service teacher education', *Journal of Teacher Education*, 31, 16, pp. 45–55.

ZEICHNER, K. (1981) 'Reflective teaching and field-based experience in teacher education', *Interchange*, 12, pp. 1–22.

ZEICHNER, K. and TEITELBAUM, K. (1982) 'Personalized and inquiry-oriented teacher education: An analysis of two approaches to the development of curriculum by field-based experiences', *Journal of Education for Teaching*, 8, pp. 95–117.

5 A Leap into the Practical: A BEd (Hons) Programme

John Isaac and Kate Ashcroft

Teachers and their education are currently significant because of the pressures to improve schools. Traditionally the content of teacher education has been the focus of debate. However, if, as Schon (1983) suggests, qualifying teachers need to be reflective practitioners, the successful development of future teachers may depend on the learning experience of the qualifying programme rather than the content.

Experience does seem to support the view of Zeichner and Teitelbaum (1982) that once survival skills have become the objective of the student, critical thinking in the teacher is inhibited. The programme being described in this chapter attempts to provide experiences that encourage the student to acquire the skills that are thought to be needed for the teacher to learn through enquiry. It was assumed that enquiry or question-asking is related to problem-solving. This became the focus of the course because the premise on which the course team based the early thinking about the work was that teachers in primary schools needed to be able to solve problems and to cooperate both with each other and with the children.

The problem-solving model arose from the experience of the tutors in their classroom teacher days and from the work of a number of writers (Smith and Geoffrey, 1968; Gauthier, 1963; Reid, 1975; Schon, 1983). The type of problem that seemed relevant was suggested by Gauthier (1963) and developed by Reid (1975) into a number of characteristics of practical problems. This work reinforced a feeling that some of the 'scientific' approaches to the issues of the classroom and learning had not proved useful because the problems were not of the order that would make such thinking helpful. The ex-primary teachers in the team reacted with recognition to the Gauthier idea that 'the sphere of the practical is necessarily the sphere of the uncertain; this is the condition of significant action'. One must look before one leaps but one must still leap' (Gauthier, 1963).

Another influence on the thinking of the team was the way, described by Argyris and Schon (1974), in which 'espoused theory' may or may not become 'theory in use'. It seemed clear that many years of attempting to teach theory to novitiates and then getting them to apply it in the school and the classroom had not been very successful. Although the student teachers could write about theory, in many cases it was apparently unusable in the classroom. Possibly the most critical change in conditions between the use of espoused theory in the study situation and in the world of the classroom is the time element. Students, and indeed teachers, seem to say 'Stop the world I want to get off.' As Argyris points out, the classroom keeps going,

> This requires developing one's own continuing theory of practice under real time conditions. It means that the professional must learn to develop micro-theories of action that, when organized into patterns, represent an effective theory of practice. (Argyris and Schon, 1974)

As a result of the discussions of the team involved in the course design the programme which was evolved has an enquiry-based approach which aims to incorporate the experience of work going on in real time and on real tasks, although it often takes place in the lecture and seminar room. The traditional higher education format of lectures and learning from books and papers also takes place but the main emphasis is on direct experience.

An undergraduate course incorporating approaches that can be seen as related to the preparation of teachers, who later will enquire and be self-critical, presents some difficulties in higher education, especially in the area of assessment and relations with the external examiner.

For enquiry to take place it is necessary that the issues raised are real ones and ones for which there is no simple answer. Indeed, they have to be issues for which the tutorial team does not have an answer if you are to avoid the students playing 'guess what's in my head' games with the staff. Yet the course team needs some kind of framework to keep the teaching/learning activities on the same track where there are over 300 on the course and many tutors working with the groups.

A solution to the problem of finding a structure that suited such an enquiry approach was partially solved for the early courses by reference to the views of two Americans looking at English primary schools. Berlak and Berlak (1975) considered what seemed to be going on in such schools and this paper was later developed into the book (Berlak and Berlak, 1981.) The latter provided a framework of dilemmas that the authors had identified in the practice of the primary schools. These formed the basis of the first-year programme in the course. This develops the skills of enquiry through the active investigation of some of the questions raised in the book as they relate to societal, curriculum and control sets of issues. The most important feature, however, is not the issues on which the course is focussed but the processes which form the experience of the students.

The work needs to be closely linked to the development of 'theory in use' or in the terms of the rationale of the degree programme 'a theory *of* the action rather than theory *into* action'. From the beginning the bases are that the student has to learn to cope with the dilemmas of teaching and that dependence on a tutor does not help him/her to face these dilemmas. 'Instruction is a provisional state that has as its object to make the learner or problem solver self-sufficient' (Bruner, 1971).

For self-sufficiency to develop both staff and students have to be inclined towards the process of learning from experience. The tutors are supported by a certain amount of myth-making that has been built up over some years, that the process-objective-based programme is the best way forward. It links with the quite extensive recruitment of primary teachers into the team with their belief that a fair measure of learning through activity is the best approach to primary education. It seems sensible, if possible, to educate prospective primary teachers on the same basis. In addition, a large scale survey of employers carried out by the Polytechnic (Lindsey *et al.*, 1964) shows that employers in general are interested in students who have problem-solving skills. The present position in classrooms reinforces the need for the teacher to be able to face dilemmas and to resolve them effectively almost day by day. In this the teacher is frequently without much support and guidance from others.

One important factor was the decision made, and supported by one of the external examiners, that the formal assessment should test as much as possible the processes that the course was supposed to be developing. It has been the assessment procedures that have pressed the students into experiences that are very real to them and that are highlighted in the exercise of assessing their own work. It is also critical to the philosophy of the course that from the first week in the first module the course engages the student in action and in that module a major part of the assessment is the group grading of a group project. Each member is awarded the same mark as the rest of his/her group and no internal marker can change the grade, although the external can and has done. It is important for the students to feel that the exercise of self-evaluation is a real one and not something that can be set aside by the tutor. The general process objectives are laid out in the description of the course which goes to every student at the start of the programme. Criteria for the assessment are given to the groups and expanded on by them through discussion at an early stage. So it is clear to the students how the group report will be assessed. The reality of the need to work as a team and to evaluate your own work is thus built into the assessment system. The emphasis on enquiry is brought about by requiring groups to focus on the issues that arise from the dilemmas of the Berlaks through examples that are locally alive.

At the time of the establishment of the course, nursery education in Oxfordshire was under attack and being considered for closure. In England, local authorities may choose to establish schools for the 3–5 age range but are not compelled to do so. When finances are reduced the question arises of whether money should be spent on education which is not required by statute. In this case the issue of closure of nursery schools and units was a live question with a very active pressure group acting for their continuation on educational grounds. At exactly the same time the Youth Training Scheme was being introduced and rapidly expanded. This is funded from another source, the Manpower Services Commission, which has direct funding from central government. There is some similarity with the Participation and Equity Programme of the federal government in Australia. Although these two sectors of the English educational system, nursery education and YTS, are funded from different routes the question is how the nation wishes to distribute the funds available and it was this which raised the first dilemma of the programme. In both cases local people were actively engaged in supporting one or other of the cases and were interested in presenting their position to the students. The clients in these cases, the under-5s and unemployed school leavers, were both outside statutory provision and hardly any of the students had previous experience of these parts of the education system.

To illustrate that problems such as these have many facets, the courses bring in 'witnesses', people from the real world who are themselves directly involved in the debate. A witness is brought in to answer questions and not to present information. If the group does not ask the question it remains unanswered so that the students are active in the process of finding out from the witnesses and quickly establish that different people have different views on the problem being considered. Incidentally, it is easier than usual to get a wide range of people to help on this basis as nothing is prepared and they are briefed that an answer — 'I don't know' — is perfectly acceptable.

Another feature of the programme is the inclusion of simulated activities that focus on the feelings of those involved in decision-making. Some of these are group activities, such as 'starpower' in which the participants are brought to feel the emotions of those who are denied equal rights in bargaining through a game in which counters are traded. Others are linked to dilemmas of decision-making as when a group has to decide who will be jettisoned from a sinking raft. Some of these activities which are viewed as most threatening involve individual students reviewing their lives and looking to the future.

Much of the time in the groups is spent collecting material for their group reports and in writing up the various sections. At these sessions tutors act as facilitators supporting the group as it works towards the consensus that will form the report (envisaged as a back-up report for a sub-committee of the Education Committee of the local education authority). Groups are encouraged to use diagrams and charts to facilitate clear and rapid communication.

There is a content element in the programme, involving visits and a core of lectures which sometimes take a traditional format. However, most of the information needed is discovered by the groups as they go about the work. The relative lack of formal input is felt to be unsettling by some students but the course team have learnt that the majority are eager to take part and find out for themselves. Some problems have arisen from interaction in the groups, as they try to write the report, particularly in relation to students who do not contribute as they are expected to by the others.

The course described is only one of five taken by the student in the first year. Two others are also based on the Berlak dilemmas and there is a second strand to the coherence of the programme provided by two more. This links the enquiry approach to the child in the school. In these two courses the student examines how children learn in the classroom in the areas of mathematics and science and, in the next term, language. In these courses the child, as an enquiring learner, is the focus and students are discouraged from teaching but rather observe as the child enquires in these curriculum areas. The course reinforces the view that learning is not about the transmission of knowledge at either the student or the child level — child and student cooperate to reveal how the child thinks and enquires about materials presented. The first time that the programme was run the committee concerned with the course asked that the first module be as fully evaluated as possible.

An evaluation model was agreed (Stake, 1967) and information was collected about the antecedents, transactions and outcomes by a range of data gathering approaches. These included a questionnaire but also an open meeting of the students with a group of tutors, none of whom had actually taught on the course.

There were wide ranging responses from the students about the programme. The questionnaire was rather a blunt instrument from which to gain a full view, but the open-ended questions produced interesting responses. For some students the programme had been traumatic and they were highly critical of the 'lack of content'. However, for most, the unit had provided a learning experience which they valued. The focus of difficulty and dissatisfaction was the group assessment of the project reports. Many groups had met difficulties in getting some of their group members to attend the meetings that they had arranged and getting them to complete their share of the work. There were cases where some students had been ill and missed some weeks of the course when the project was being written. The idea that all in the group would be awarded the same grade was accepted as an ideal, but proved difficult in reality when the workload of the students was seen by themselves to vary. They accepted that it was part of the exercise for them to deal with aberrant group members but in some cases were simply unable to do so. In other situations difficulties were resolved and in at least one case a pair of students worked all night to meet the standards of the rest of the group by rewriting their contribution. One item that many commented on in various ways was that they had got to know the other students in a way that had not happened elsewhere in their courses. The students tend to arrive in the polytechnic as rather competitive individuals with an inclination to work alone and even to conceal sources from each other. As the model of a teacher taken by the rationale was based on cooperation to solve problems and the development of interpersonal skills, this result was important. While the community of enquirers (the student group) sometimes had difficulties and lost a few members, the project reports and assessment sessions illustrated that the general focus was shared and that the skills required for cooperative problem-solving were exercised.

There were no difficulties with the external examiner and although certain improvements were suggested, the overall approach was fully supported. The criteria for the whole course were clearly laid out for the students at the start and efforts to assess their performance against the criteria were accepted as valid attempts, even by students who were upset by the results. The students who were the focus of the detailed study are now in their fourth year but the programme continues with relatively little modification. Although we cannot demonstrate it clearly, the tutor team believe that we do have a course which develops the skills and attitudes needed to become an enquiring teacher. Certainly other programmes in the degree which have since taken up the idea of group assessment report that the education students immediately take the lead in getting the group organized and adjusted to the process.

Perhaps the enquiring teacher can be effectively developed only by initial teacher education programmes where the processes necessary to an enquiring approach are an essential aspect of the course. In the belief that practical problem-solving is at the heart of helping children to learn, the team see it as the only effective way to prepare students for the future.

References

ARGYRIS, C. and SCHON, D. (1974) *Theory in Practice: Increasing Professional Effectiveness*, London, Jossey Bass.

BERLAK, H. and BERLAK, A. (1975) 'Towards a political and social-psychological theory of schooling: An analysis of English informal primary schools', *Interchange*, 6 March.

BERLAK, H. and BERLAK, A. (1981) *Dilemmas of Schooling: Teaching and Social Change*, London, Methuen.

BRUNER, J.S. (1971) *Toward a Theory of Instruction*, Cambridge, MA, Belknap Press.

GAUTHIER, D.P. (1963) *Practical Reasoning: The Structure and Foundations of Prudential and Moral Arguments and Their Exemplification in Discourse*, Oxford, Oxford University Press.

LINDSEY, R., THOMAS, S. and SHIRES, H. (1964) *The Value of a Modular Degree*, report commissioned by Dr David Watson, Oxford Polytechnic.

REID, W. (1975) *Thinking about the Curriculum: The Nature and Treatment of Curriculum Problems*, London, Routledge and Kegan Paul.

SCHON, D. (1971) *Beyond the Stable State: Public and Private Learning in a Changing Society*, London, Temple Smith.

SCHON, D. (1983) *The Reflective Practitioner*, New York, Basic Books.

SMITH, L.M. and GEOFFREY, W. (1968) *The Complexities of the Urban Classroom: An Analysis Towards a General Theory of Teaching*, New York, Holt Rinehart and Winston.

STAKE, R. (1967) 'The countenance of educational evaluation', *Teachers College Record*, 68, 7.

ZEICHNER, K. and TEITELBAUM, K. (1982) 'Personalised and inquiry-orientated teacher education: An analysis of two approaches to the development of curriculum for field-based experience', *Journal of Education for Teaching*, 8, 2, pp. 95–117.

6 The Interrogation of Case Records as a Basis for Constructing Curriculum Perspectives

Susan Groundwater-Smith

Introduction: Examining the Curriculum Terrain

The unifying theme for this discussion is 'critique', an approach to enquiry which is conducted in ways which have the potential for improved practice based upon enlightened understandings. Critique, in this instance, is evolved as a result of collaboration between enquirers, wherein they investigate in a manner which is predicated upon self-reflective and socioculturally reflexive deliberation. (The construct 'reflexive' refers to the practice of being able to perceive not only that one's personal history is influential in shaping one's world view, but also that this history is located in the midst of a larger sociocultural canvas which too must be deliberated upon.)

Curriculum work spans a great variety of perspectives and practices which may be contrasted in several ways. For some it presents itself as a series of segmented activities bounded by technical guidelines and is largely unproblematic. For others it is perceived as an intricate web of actions, apparently seamless and credible, but paradoxically subject to a plethora of opposing tensions and pressures.

I shall take the view that it is the latter representation which is the more appropriate and explore this map of curriculum work within three intersecting and overlapping categories: text, context and pretext. That is, I shall briefly examine the cultural artefacts of curriculum work as well as the media by which it is expressed; the settings within which it occurs; and the reasonings which underpin its practices. Or, to put it another way, the what, the where and the why of curriculum work will be examined. I will suggest that such a trilateral portrayal will secure and identify curriculum work in ways which will disabuse us of the notion that its endeavours are amenable to simple, allegedly neutral functional analysis, but will enable us rather to see that what is required is a demanding, ongoing interrogation, both reflective and reflexive in nature.

In the first instance, to represent curriculum work as text is to expose the embedded 'geomorphology' of the many competing and varying curriculum theories. The rises and falls of such theories have been sketched in by many including Lundgren (1983) who characterizes them variously as classical, realistic and moral curriculum codes. He reminds us that we need to locate these texts in the demands and pressures of the day. Indeed, such a sociohistorical analysis is well supported by Foucault (1972) who argues that the historical lens is vital to an understanding of contemporary, burgeoning rationalization in all fields of social endeavour. This rationalization has been expressed in curriculum work, Lundgren argues, by the hegemonic insistence upon the equation of curriculum theory with learning theory to the exclusion of social theory.

Today's curriculum texts (this term 'texts' is inclusive here of writings embracing prescriptions for practice) or discourses have grown out of reasoning following World War II and the advent of the space race marked initially by the launching of the first Russian satellite in 1957, and continued into the eighties in the US 'Star Wars' project. Curriculum, that interface between teaching and learning, has been seen as that which most efficiently realizes goals which are set in behaviouristic and mechanistic ways; as Popkewitz (1985) says:

> Knowledge is presumed neutral and fixed, or at best, unattached to any social group or cultural interest. (p. 6)

Indeed, Tyler (1969) defended his scientistic and mechanistic means of assembling curriculum knowledge, via the generation of behavioural objectives, with some impatience:

> Any of the objections given by teachers to instructional objectives seem to be predicated upon inadequate conceptions of education, curriculum and instruction. (quoted in McDonald Ross, 1975, p. 355)

Certainly there has been, in recent years, a much greater recognition of cognitive diversity, but nonetheless, the significant drive has been to find more effective means of specifying curriculum objectives rather than problematizing their whole *raison d'être*.

Although there was some flirtation during the seventies with 'open' procedures which allowed learners more actively to construct their own knowledge (this counter-ideology has been well documented by Abbs, 1982), the general regression to this rationalistic stance has been noteworthy in most English-speaking countries.

If the study of curriculum work as text is the study of the meaning of the artefacts of curriculum, then the study of curriculum work as context is the study of that total environment wherein the meaning is embedded. As Halliday and Hasan (1983) put it:

> There is text and there is other text that accompanies it: text that is 'with', namely the context. This notion of what is 'with the text', however, goes beyond what is said and written: it includes other non-verbal goings on — the total environment in which a text unfolds.

The environment itself generates a complex, interactive dynamic which affects bilaterally the selection of text (both in the commonsense meaning of published materials and in the sense of policies) and the modes of delivery. The context in which schooling occurs shapes the curriculum itself. An example which is illustrative of the context of curriculum work as a major problematic is Keddie's now classical study of teachers' perceptions of their students and how these affected their pedagogical practices. Keddie revealed how the typifications and categories used by teachers, regarding their students, influenced their curriculum choices. Moreover, these belief systems revealed themselves in an extensive study in Australian schools conducted by Connell, Ashenden, Kessler and Dowsett (1982) in which it was indicated that teachers' assessments and assumptions regarding a child's social origins distorted the curriculum itself in significant ways, so that the experiences designed for middle-class students were consonant (or organic) to their general life experiences whereas those designed for working-class students were diminished and depleted.

It is useful, therefore, to examine the interplay between text and context as an interplay between intentions and operations set against a sociohistorical backdrop. Certainly a number of curriculum researchers have explored the nexus between planning and implementation (cf. Cohen and Harrison, 1982). However, they have not concerned themselves with the grounding of the case in the articulations between the state, the economy and the schools themselves. Given our current social arrangements for schooling and the role played by government (and indirectly, business and industry) in resourcing and providing directions in policy-making it seems to me to be cavalier indeed to leave this territory uncovered.

Apple (1979) has argued both by an analysis of cases and by reasoning that the relationships between planning and practice can only be explored fruitfully if it is recognized that curriculum work is undergirded by social and economic ideologies and their institutional affiliations. It is to these underpinnings that I now turn.

Public pretexts for curriculum work are generally voiced in liberal and humanistic ways:

> The central aim of education which, with home and community groups the school pursues, is to guide individual development in the context of society through recognizable stages of development, towards perceptive understanding, mature judgement, responsible self-direction and moral autonomy. (Aims of Primary Education in New South Wales, 1977, p. 14)

The rhetoric of liberal democracies is to guarantee free, secular, universal state schooling which will confer upon its participants equality of opportunity, if not equality of outcomes. Some curriculum theorists have been at pains to point out that such rhetoric acts only to elucidate the surface features of curriculum work and that there is an additional and more insidious agenda (Bowles and Gintis, 1976). It is contended that schools are social sites wherein two forms of knowledge are transacted; the one being overt and publicly stated, the other covert and transmitted as values and beliefs via social relations, artefacts, organizational structures and routines, i.e. the 'hidden curriculum'. The school plays contradictory roles at one and the same time by teaching about democratic values but demanding, in its own environment, social control.

The difficulty with many of these analyses of curriculum work as pretext is that they lead to a significant apportioning of 'the blame' to teachers within the school without seeking to locate them in their own historical and cultural spaces. It is important to make the distinction set down by Giroux (1983a) which separates ideologies about school and ideologies in school. Giroux makes a plea for a climate of questioning which will lay bare the normative assumptions underlying our modes of representing curriculum work:

> Furthermore, if the notion of the hidden curriculum is to become meaningful it will have to be used to analyse not only the social relation of classroom and school but also the

structural 'silences' and ideological messages that shape the form and content of school knowledge. (p. 61)

What is singular about Giroux's approach is that he sees such an identification of the pretext for curriculum work as the beginnings of a move from the practical to the emancipatory. Thus the gaining of authentic insights into curriculum work, in all of its manifestations, text, context and pretext, requires a reappraisal of the ways that we come, over time, to know about and understand curriculum practices. It is to 'ways of knowing' that I would like now to turn.

Coming to Know

An important observation to make at the outset is that there is a distinction between information and knowledge. This is not just a quibble about shades of difference since the one may be seen as a significant variant of the other. Stenhouse (1979) put it most succinctly:

> Information is not knowledge until the factor of error in it is appropriately estimated. (quoted in Rudduck *et al.*, 1983, p. 141)

Essentially, what Stenhouse is saying to us is that we are the inventors of our own knowledge and the quality of the invention is dependent upon our ability to evaluate the information which is available to us, be it sensory, first hand information or vicarious, received information. This involves us in a never-ending stream of judgments, of broad and fine discriminations, so that the gaining of knowledge is a transforming process. As such it is personal, dynamic and never complete. This representation of the knowledge-gaining process applies to both knowledge about things and knowledge about ideas, it embraces the physical and the imaginative worlds.

While it is not yet entirely clear what the relationship is between language and thought, it is generally agreed that language and the construction of knowledge are closely linked. The influential Bullock Report (DES, 1975) put it in this way:

> It is a confusion of everyday thought that we tend to regard 'knowledge' as something that exists independently of someone who knows. What we know must in fact be brought to life afresh within every knower by his (sic) own efforts. In

order to appreciate what is offered when we are told something, we have to have somewhere to put it .... Something
approximating to 'finding out for ourselves' needs therefore
to take place if we are to be successfully 'told' .... The
development of this individual context for a new piece of
information, the forging of the links that gave it meaning, is
a task we continually tackle by talking to other people.

That this knowledge is personal does not mean that it is diminished in any way, that one dismisses the position as 'merely subjective'. Rather, from this perspective we can rigorously account for
the place of judgment and critical reflection. The problematic is not
one of subjectivity but of the conditions under which judgments are
arrived at. Carr and Kemmis (1986) point out that educational
practices are *always* conducted in the light of judgments made by
practitioners, but that too often these judgments are based largely
upon habit, precedent and tradition rather than by way of informed
critical reflection. Knowledge which, in a sense, is 'right knowledge'
(Kemmis, 1982, p. 3) is knowledge which is truly emancipatory in
its nature; which will enable the knower not only to know, but to
act; not only to act, but to act correctly ... wisely ... justly. This,
of course, is not to say that there is one single way of acting, but
rather that the action must be undergirded by prudence brought
about by careful deliberation.

The interplay between knowing and acting is central to the
arguments of Carr and Kemmis. Knowing is not of itself an end,
but is a propellant moving the knower forward to improved and
more productive actions. This view is taken up by Giroux (1983a)
who argues that a socially critical view provides us with the theoretical tools for reform and change. The knower, in this way, is
released from potentially oppressive and culturally reproductive
practices and is motivated towards a commitment to a struggle for a
better and more equitable world.

A strong source of influence for Carr and Kemmis (1986) and
Giroux (1983b) has been the collection of writers/philosophers related to the 'Frankfurt School' of critical theorists. Most noteworthy
of these has been Jurgen Habermas. The scope of this writing does
not allow for a full analysis of his influence and a brief gloss would
not do credit to the complexity of his position. Rather, I would
prefer to acknowledge his considerable and continuing impact upon
the evolution of critical theory, particularly as it applies to gaining
understandings of curriculum work.

This brings me to the implications of all that I have said thus far for practical work.

Providing the Means to Craft Curriculum Knowledge

I want to couch this portrayal in personal ways for it has been my own practice as a lecturer in curriculum studies in both pre-service and in-service teacher education which I have sought better to understand and improve. Three contiguous events led to the evolution of the Curriculum Issues Project. One was reading in the area of critical theory and reflecting upon its implications for my own practice. The other was working, all too briefly, with Jean Rudduck on the British Library Project. The elements of the story to be told were all there in the form of the case records collected, under the guidance of Lawrence Stenhouse, from a large number of schools in England and Wales. The challenge was to craft a portrayal from the many different and often contradictory perspectives in the case records. The experience of: challenging and defending analyses; taking account of Jean Rudduck's constant evocation to 'attend to the voices of the case records'; and sharing and shaping incomplete ideas in a collegial way was emancipatory for me in that it led me to re-examine many taken-for-granted features of my practices. And the final experience was to develop insights with Bev Labbett, then working at the Centre for Applied Research in Education (CARE) at the University of East Anglia upon aspects of the Microelectronics Education Program (MEP) regarding the means by which one could construct a curriculum wherein 'correctness' was not an overarching consideration and where the 'problem' itself remained the responsibility of the learner rather than being taken over by the teacher too precipitously.

Whereas I had planned to contextualize students' learning experiences in relation to curriculum issues by providing them with case studies as protocol materials, I now came to see that the process of constructing the studies was itself the essentially empowering feature. The role of the students would change from investigating materials which had already been transformed several times to working, where possible, with materials which were closer to the primary sources. I sought to create conditions under which learners could become active enquirers within the framework proposed by Nias (1984). This framework assumes *inter alia* that learners will know (or learn) how to undertake such enquiries; that the issues will be substantive; that educational theory can be derived from the enquiry; that the knowledge will be personal; and that, furthermore in a cumulative and formative sense, the enquiries will assist the individual's professional development.

Consequently, the project was designed to provide resources and conditions whereby participative, collaborative enquiry could be undertaken and the participants could both evolve a personal critique as well as contribute to collective understanding. Particularly, by including policy statements, accounts of teachers' planning and 'snapshots' of practice, it was hoped that the connections between intentions and operations might be perceived. The course held the following aspirations:

(a) To set up through the case records a resource which allows the learner to become a skilful researcher/interpreter of curriculum actions;

(b) To create an environment wherein it may be seen that there are alternative explanations, i.e. that there is no one correct answer, but that each explanation in itself must be judiciously defended; and

(c) To empower the students to see themselves as creators of theory.

Fundamental propositions were also set down:

(a) It will not be possible to pre-define with precision what the outcomes will be;

(b) The principal issues must emerge from the data and the learners' interactions with them;

(c) Although all learners will have the same information there will be a diversity of interpretations;

(d) The thrust is to create sufficient intellectual space for the learners to experience problems rather than invading their space by telling them what they need to know;

(e) There will be uncertainty but this should not descend into chaos;

(f) At times, learners will explore unproductive avenues and this is part of the enquiring process;

(g) The roles of listening, questioning and speculating will be more appropriate for the teacher than those of criticizing and/or explaining.

The course was prepared to cover the equivalent of one semester and was broken down in the following manner:

Week 1

(a) Meeting each other in curricular terms. The intention here was to open up talk about curricular issues by basing them upon personal experience. This would acknowledge the personal lens through which we all experience the world. Members were instructed to break into groups thus: 'each time you join a group meet and talk with each other in terms of the criterion for the group's formation and its relationship to curriculum decision making.'

Division   (i)   Most schooling in streamed classes/most schooling in mixed ability classes;

(ii)   Secondary schooling in a co-educational/single sex school;

(iii)   Being a teacher as well as/never having been a parent;

(iv)   Having a preference for arts/science subjects.

(b) Writing about personal experiences of schooling following the readings of extracts from:
Portrait of the Artist as a Young Man
David Copperfield
My Brilliant Career
Where the Whistle Blows

Weeks 2, 3, and 4
Identifying issues within one school. In small groups students select a school and collaboratively draw together a portrayal of that school's curriculum concerns and actions.

Week 5
Presenting the findings in a plenary session.

mid-semester break

Weeks 6 and 7
Identifying issues across schools. Working in small groups students again collaborate to locate issues by making comparisons and contrasts and seek further perspectives by examining the relevant literature.

Week 8
Presenting the findings in a plenary session.

Week 9
What would I do? Taking a fragment from the case records the student projects himself or herself into the situation and proposes his or her actions.

Weeks 10 and 11
Directions and strategies for change. Additional resource people were invited to these sessions.

Individual essays identifying and debating curriculum issues were to be handed in four weeks later.

The records themselves were materials collected from four different primary schools in the Sydney Metropolitan area in Australia. Each school was regarded as distinctive in that it was drawn from a particular community with all of the attendant sociological, economic and ethnic implications, but also the schools could be regarded as part of a larger whole in that they were all schools of the NSW State Department of Education and thus governed by that Department's policies and practices. Each record contains negotiated transcripts of interviews with teachers which probed their professional histories and personal philosophies, as well as lesson observations. School curriculum policy documents were included as were community profiles and census materials from the Australian Bureau of Statistics.

The records are not regarded as ever 'complete'. Recently a video tape was made at one school 'Try Seeing It Through Our Eyes' which represented an attempt to capture something of the children's views of schooling. As Walker and Wiedel (1985) have already demonstrated, photographs can be a powerful means of generating critical talk about the lived life of the classroom. In this instance a small group of children were given simple cameras, film and flash cubes. They were invited to take photographs throughout the school day of experiences and events which moved them. They were then interviewed in pairs regarding the meanings behind their photographs. The process allowed for the emergence of a multiplicity of perspectives of the same events. A videorecording crew was present throughout the sequence.

In terms of their interactions with the materials the orientation of the learners' social discourse was necessarily towards 'problem-setting' rather than 'problem-solving' (cf. Smyth, 1985, p. 2). The concerns were to raise issues, grounded in practice, in such a way that vigorous debate would follow, and through this a clarification of the position taken up by any one protagonist. Learners were required to confront and tease out both the inconsistencies in their own positions and the genesis of their own ideologies. The engagement with the project, then, was clearly a reflective one, remembering that:

> Reflection is a practice which expresses our power and reconstitutes social life by the way we participate in communication, decision making and social action. (Kemmis, 1985, p. 140)

While not generous in its time allotment, there was sufficient room in the project for reflection to occur. Ingvarson (1985) has suggested that activities and courses in teacher education, particularly in-service education, need to be planned over longer periods of time, with intervals between sessions. While he was arguing to support action-oriented courses, the same holds true for those for whom the action is the raising rather than the solving of problems. The strategy is necessarily a powerful, but preliminary one. For as Mezirow (1981) says:

> A self-directed learner has access to alternative perspectives for understanding his or her situation and for giving meaning and direction to his or her life, has acquired sensitivity and competence in social interaction and has the skills and competencies required to master the productive tasks associated with controlling and manipulating the environment. (p. 21)

By adopting, albeit on a modest scale, strategies to facilitate such a reconstructive process, it is my hope that not only will the students become more prudent and reflective in their practice, but that I too, as a teacher-learner, will continue as an enquirer who seeks to improve her practice.

References

ABBS, P. (1982) *English within the Arts*, Sevenoaks, Hodder and Stoughton.

APPLE, M.W. (1979) *Ideology and Curriculum*, London, Routledge and Kegan Paul.

APPLE, M.W. and WEIS, L. (1983) 'Ideology and practice in schooling: A political and conceptual introduction', in APPLE, M. (Ed.) *Ideology and Practice in Schooling*, Philadelphia, PA, Temple University Press, pp. 3–34.

BOWLES, S. and GINTIS, H. (1976) *Schooling in Capitalist America*, New York, Basic Books.

CARR, W. and KEMMIS, S. (1986) *Becoming Critical*, Lewes, Falmer Press.

COHEN, D. and HARRISON, N. (1982) *Curriculum Action Project*, Sydney, Macquarie University.

CONNELL, R., ASHENDEN, D., KESSLER, S. and DOWSETT, G. (1982) *Making the Difference*, Sydney, George Allen and Unwin.

DEPARTMENT OF EDUCATION AND SCIENCE (1975) *A Language for Life* (The Bullock Report), London, HMSO.

FOUCAULT, M. (1972) *The Archaelogy of Knowledge*, translated by A.M. Sheridan Smith, New York, Harper Colophon.

GIROUX, H.A. (1983a) *Theory and Resistance in Education*, London, Heinemann Educational.

GIROUX, H.A. (1983b) *Critical Theory and Educational Practice*, Geelong, Deakin University Press.

HALLIDAY, M.A.K. and HASAN, R. (1983) *Language Context and Text: Aspects of Language in a Social Semiotic Perspective*, Geelong, Deakin University Press.

INGVARSON, L. (1985) 'Policy related issues in school based professional development', paper presented at the annual conference of the Australian Association for Research in Education, Hobart, November.

KEDDIE, N. (1971) 'Classroom knowledge', in YOUNG, M.F.D. (Ed.) *Knowledge and Control*, London, Collier Macmillan.

KEMMIS, S. (1982) *Three Orientations to Curriculum*, Geelong, School of Education, Deakin University, mimeo.

KEMMIS, S. (1985) 'Action research and the politics of reflection', in BOUD, D., KEOGH, R. and WALKER, D. (Eds) *Reflection: Turning Experience into Learning*, London, Kogan Page.

LUNDGREN, U.P. (1983) *Between Hope and Happening: Text and Context in Curriculum*, Geelong, Deakin University Press.

MacDONALD, R. (1975) 'Behavioural objectives: A critical review', in GOLBY, M. GREENWALD, J. and WEST, R. (Eds) *Curriculum Design*, London, Croom Helm.

MEZIROW, J. (1981) 'A critical theory of adult learning and education', *Adult Education*, 32, 1, Fall, pp. 3–24.

NIAS, J. (1984) 'Teaching enquiry-based courses: Implications for the providing institution', opening lecture, Downing College Conference, Cambridge, 16–18 July.

POPKEWITZ, T. (1985) 'History and social science: Considering an historical sociology of schooling', Geelong, School of Education, Deakin University, mimeo.

PROSCH, H. (1971) *Cooling the Modern Mind* Skidmore College Faculty Research Lecture.

SMYTH, J.W. (1985) 'Teachers as clinical inquirers into their own practice', paper presented at annual conference of the Australian Association for Research in Education, Hobart, November.

STENHOUSE, L. (1979) quoted in RUDDUCK, J., HOPKINS, D., GROUND-WATER-SMITH, S. and LABBETT, B. (1983) *Independent Study, Books and Libraries and the Academic Sixth Form*, a report to the British Library Research and Development Department.

WALKER, R. and WIEDEL, J. (1985) 'Using photographs in a discipline of words', in BURGESS, R. (Ed.) *Field Methods in the Study of Education*, Lewes, Falmer Press, pp. 191–216.

7   A Research-based Course in Science Education

Ian Robottom

Introduction

In this chapter I wish to describe some developments in a research-based science education course at Deakin University. The terms 'research-based' and 'enquiry-based' may, of course, be variously interpreted; the Deakin course is 'research-based' in that it *requires students to be participant enquirers into their own practices as teachers of science*. The intention in this chapter is firstly to *describe* the course's structure, pedagogy, assessment, and research orientation; and secondly to *cite some issues* arising from the experience of the course.

The Course

History of the Course

The course 'Biosocial studies' is located in the third year of the three-year BA (Ed) teacher education program at Deakin University. In this mainstream teacher education program, there are separately timetabled courses in teaching studies and curriculum studies, and the practicum is separate from these again. The mainstream program has been described as a 'structured dichotomy':

> In fact, for reasons that are partly historical and partly pragmatic, the practicum has tended to be organized as separate 'school experience rounds' located *before* the course

proper has begun (in February, while lectures commence in March), in the middle of the year, and at the end of the year *after* the 'formal' part of the course has been completed. Student-teachers experience over 100 days of teaching in schools, but there is a *structured dichotomy* between the 'content' of the program on the one hand and the practicum on the other. (Robottom, 1986)

The science education course within this teacher education program aspired to promote an 'enquiry science' perspective — that is, it encouraged the teaching of *science* as a field of enquiry. However, the perspective on professional development in science teaching embedded in the structure and processes of the course was not enquiry-based — that is, it did not encourage professional development as educational enquiry. This point can be illustrated with reference to the status ascribed to the educational theories presented in the course: the course materials contained accounts of theories on children's thinking in science — theories on causality, problem-solving and child development. The work of such theorists as Laurendeau and Pinard, Kuslan and Stone, Inhelder and Piaget, and Suchman was presented in an unproblematic way, and implications for 'good science teaching' were drawn and presented to students in an equally unproblematic fashion.

> Students *are* provided with opportunities to engage in activities related to the work of these theorists — for example, students are required to analyse a prepared transcript of a clinical interview with a child attempting Piaget's 'balance problem' — but the status of implications for science teaching of such work is assumed. There is no opportunity for students to put to the test the propositions about teaching embedded in the provision of such theories and attendant 'implications'. Thus the course tends to manifest a view that development of theories about teaching is the preserve of outside theorists, and it is the role of student-teachers (and teachers) to put uncritically into classroom practice the practical implications derived from these theories. (*ibid.*)

For the last three years of offer of 'Biosocial studies', a parallel alternative pilot program of teacher education, was in operation. As the name implies, the 'School-based teacher education' program

(SBTE) required student-teachers, for substantial periods at a time, to carry out nearly all their education-related activities in a school — their teaching and curriculum studies tutorials, subject method tutorials, and of course their practicum activities. In each semester, students spent a full *ten weeks* actually working in a school (Henry and Charles, 1985). However, the differences between the SBTE form of operation and that of the mainstream are more fundamental than the *site* of these activities. Underpinning the SBTE program is the philosophy that the educational matters for consideration in the program ought to be topics and issues about teaching that arise as an outcome of the student teachers' engagement in the practical work of classroom teaching. Teaching and curriculum studies are integrated with the practicum — the substance of these studies is understandings generated as students participate in participatory enquiry into their own teaching practice. Tutorials are then based on issues — substantive issues to do with improving aspects of teaching and curriculum, and methodological issues to do with improving the research engaged in — that are progressively identified by students during the course of their educational enquiries. An attempt is made in the SBTE program to ensure that the student-teachers have a strong say in negotiating the curriculum of the program (Robottom, 1986).

Structure of the Revised Course

'Biosocial studies' was revised in 1986. In point form, these changes were:

- The practicum (school experience) was organized into a 'long and thin' pattern of two days per week for most of the academic year.
- In the practicum, student-teachers were allocated to classrooms in *pairs*, rather than singly as in the past. The reason behind the pairing of students in the practicum was that this arrangement was thought to be consistent with the collaborative, participant nature of the enquiry students were expected to engage in.
- The curriculum studies courses scheduled for third year were given the responsibility for organizing *one day per week* of practicum time — these course teams determine the activities conducted by students on this one day per week.

- This arrangement holds for the whole year, enabling an *immediate and ongoing opportunity* for student-teachers to test in the classroom the propositions encountered in the course. The practicum is seen as an essential part of the curriculum studies course — a part which provides a context for student-teachers themselves to develop further their theory of teaching through the application of a form of educational enquiry into their own teaching of a particular curriculum area. The *substance* of the course is the set of understandings that emerges from the testing (through participant research conducted during the practicum component of the course) of propositions about science teaching and science curriculum encountered during the parallel non-practicum component of the course.

- An attempt is being made to structure the interaction of theory and practice as explained above through the development of 'tasks'. Each task identifies a particular educational problem relating to science education, provides a sample of the relevant literature of the field, and requires student-teachers undertaking the task to research some of the claims made in respect of the identified issue in the literature. Student-teachers negotiate their own science education curriculum by completing some out of a range of prepared tasks, and by writing and then carrying out their 'own' tasks designed on a matter of particular interest to themselves. In brief, each task requires that the student-teachers actually try out a range of different science teaching strategies and reflect critically on their science teaching, making explicit their own theories about science teaching, and considering their own theories in relation to theories advanced in the literature of the field and to their own practical teaching experiences.

- Assessment: tutors' appraisals of students' work in tasks are the main form of assessment. The criterion invoked in this assessment is the extent to which the requirements of the tasks are complied with. As in most courses of the BA (Ed) program, assessment is competitive — students are awarded grades for their work in the course which contribute to an aggregate list at the end of third year. This aggregate influences directly the students' opportunities for employment.

The Course's View of Student-teacher Professionalism

In 'Biosocial studies' an attempt was made to reconstrue student-teacher professionalism — to try to alter the traditional relationship of 'student', 'theory', and 'teaching practice'. As pointed out elsewhere (Robottom, 1986), the differences in the revised 'Biosocial studies' course are more than structural:

> As in the SBTE, the philosophy guiding the course is that improvement in teaching requires the development of a personal theory of teaching through the interaction of theory and practice. Rather than 'importing' uncritically-accepted educational theories and searching for 'implications' for good teaching — a process which renders the professionalism of the student-teacher subordinate to that of the originators and disseminators of those educational theories — theories are treated as problematic and as the source of propositions that can be *put to the test* in the classroom by the student-teacher. This process builds up the notion of student-teacher professionalism to the status of educational researcher — theory-tester rather than theory-consumer.

This endeavour proved to be more difficult than anticipated.

Some Issues

The revisions described briefly in the preceding discussion are not yet fully tested. Difficulties were anticipated in the form of concerns from various quarters about the lack of systematic 'coverage' of tried and true science education topics — both teaching strategies and teaching theories about 'how to teach science'. What this revised approach sought to do was to diminish what was seen as an artificial dichotomy between theories and practices as expressed in a structured separation of science education 'content' and the practicum. By providing student-teachers with the opportunity to exercise a form of enquiry into their own science teaching, it was hoped that an improved professional capacity in educational research would enable them to become more independent in organizing their own professional growth. In the event, issues that did emerge were as follows.

Award-bearing Course: Effect on Participant Research

The course as a whole recognizes recent developments in curriculum studies in Australia that seek to explore issues associated with a *democratic curriculum*. Accordingly, the prepared 'tasks' adopt a politicized view of science education. Their concern is with such issues as sexism in science and science teaching, participatory learning/negotiated curriculum, activity-based learning, and the professional status of teachers. The two minimal requirements of the tasks are that students actually teach some science lessons, and that they adopt a politicized perspective as they enquire into some democratic curriculum issues in science teaching.

The tasks are written in a structured way. They set out fairly detailed requirements of students — as evident in the comments relating to the written report to be submitted for assessment:

Summary of requirements
To summarize, your requirements for science in this block are:

(i)   read the task library;
(ii) prepare a position paper on sexism in science teaching;
(iii) teach six science lessons in which your beliefs or some of the claims of authors in the field about sexism in science teaching can be tested through your own action research;
(iv) table and speak to some evidence of your work in weekly tutorials;
(v)   prepare a written report of at least fifteen pages describing your action research. This report should include:

- a bibliography of readings actually read;
- your position paper, reworked in the light of your research;
- an account of what you learned about sexism in your teaching or in your school through these six lessons;
- an account of any shifts in your personal position on science teaching resulting from your action research;
- an account of what you learned about the limits

> imposed and opportunities offered for girls in sci-
> ence teaching by your own teaching or by your
> classroom setting;
>
> - an account of your monitoring and analysis pro-
>   cesses;
> - a diagrammatic summary of each action research
>   cycle;
> - a critique of the claims made in reading 6 about the
>   appropriateness of action research to explorations
>   of sexism in science teaching.

There is evidence that the detailed character of these written tasks
acted against their intent to foster a critical or politicized perspective
by students in relation to the personal and institutional factors that
shape their practical action. The requirements of the tasks, while
justified by an interest in directing attention to the relationship of
understanding, situation and practice, in the event were seen as
suggestive of an impositional directive that is contrary to the alleged
responsiveness of participatory research. While espousing a paradigm of professional independence in the form of participant
research, the detail of the tasks' requirements coupled with the
competitive assessment of the course, suggested the conventional
paradigm of technical competence. Further, owing to the pre-
specification of certain topics (again justified by an interest in
democratic curriculum), the tasks become an unnatural driving
organizational principle:

> It would be better if we had the chance of going into the
> school, looking at the children, taking a few lessons in pairs,
> and then making a choice for ourselves about what really
> needs research, we should do it that way, rather than choos-
> ing a task in advance and going out and sticking to that task
> ... otherwise you're forced to change your teaching style to
> suit that task, to get the results, like including lots of activi-
> ties when that isn't really what you want to do. That's not
> the idea of classroom research by teachers. You're supposed
> to be teaching naturally ....

In response to comments like this, we altered the course requirements to encourage a more narrative form of reporting; this change
seemed to result in more readable, 'natural' accounts of enquiries.

Experience in working through the tasks did appear to create
for students an enquiry perspective in the practicum, with students
seeing an ostensibly 'method' course as a research course:

Besides the fact that we have to take six science lessons a
week, all this research (which is good, I think) could apply
to anything. It's not as if we were learning about Biosocial
studies, it's just learning about classroom research and it can
be applied to anything. I'm not saying this is a bad thing,
but they're telling us that Biosocial studies is going to teach
us about those things specifically . . . .

We're not getting any workshops, resource materials or anything to help with our lessons, but we are learning from our
own mistakes and experiments. We're learning because we're
forced to go out and take science lessons that we have never
taken before. We're forced to find our own resources and
things like that . . . which is good in a way because that is
what is going to happen next year.

And at times there were signs of the adoption of a critical perspective in the students' reflections on the educational settings of which
they were a part during their practicum, as shown in the comments
of three different students:

However, after taking my lessons I did in fact find that the
skills that have been prescribed [in the state science curriculum guides] for a particular year level were far too narrow.
Because what I found from testing the claims of the two
skills I researched from *Implementing Science* [the state science curriculum guides] was that these children had a lot of
difficulties with these skills . . . I found that prior experience
is a large contributing factor to whether the children can or
cannot display these prescribed skills. It was obvious that
these children had never studied graphs before and they
were not given much time to do any creative writing let
alone having to give reasons for findings or draw conclusions to anything they have discovered. Science is not a very
large part of the curriculum at Barwon Heads and by not
allowing the children to get involved with science or related
activities they are not developing such related concepts and
skills to their fullest potential.

I would highlight a point that the process of this task has
raised for me. Although the knowledge and expertise of the
authors of these (science curriculum) materials may be high,
they are writing for the 'general' school grade in Victoria.

One must wonder whether such a grade exists. The components of any one 'classroom' vary so greatly that it is impossible for two identical classes to ever occur, so that it would be impossible to even write a specific list of skills that would suit all science classes at all levels.

Although I have looked at only *one* class of children, at *one* particular time over a *brief* six week period and concentrated on only *four* of the several claims made in *one* article of curriculum material, I now believe that it should ultimately be the teacher who devises the prescriptive details of the science objectives for his/her class, renewing these each year.

After analyzing all of this data from my first lesson it was very obvious that my periods of wait time did not fit into Tobin and De Ture's scenario for the average teacher. In fact my wait time varies dramatically throughout the lesson, due to the style of question I was posing. I had forecasted in my position paper that the fact of constant pacing of the lesson might restrict my wait time to the minimal. I felt that I might have been scared of leaving periods of silence. In practice this was not the case.

I also discovered that I was unhappy with the definition of wait time. It seemed to involve a great deal more than periods of silence. In fact it seemed to involve passages of interaction as well. Therefore it would be difficult to classify wait time, as one would need to decide where the actual question ended and additional comments took over.

I also discovered that the length of the children's answers varied greatly throughout the session. They did not seem to correlate directly with the amount of wait time, however I was unsure of the reason for the variation at this time.

A second premise of (De Ture and Tobin's) research is that a long answer is necessarily a better answer. This, I am sure, is not so. The issue of 'better' answers is one which requires much more investigation. I can see the value in allowing children time to think about interpretive type questions, however I also believe that periods of silence are not the only way in which a teacher can provide this time. Deeper thinking is a skill to be developed within children. This development requires much more than leaving extra periods of silence in the classroom.

These quotes from students' assignments reveal some of the strengths of participatory research by students in a teacher education course. Some of the strengths are that the students are gaining confidence and ability at making their own judgments based on direct teaching experience; they are adopting a healthy scepticism about the educational claims of others; and they realize the locatedness of educational 'findings'.

Institutional Resistance

There appears to be a resistance to the adoption of an enquiry perspective in the practicum of primary teacher science education courses. This resistance was encountered from a number of quarters. Perhaps as a result of their own life histories, students themselves harboured strong expectations about the character of a proper science education course: in tutorials, there were demands for 'tips for teachers', with pressure applied to staff to provide the 'solutions' to practical problems concerning content and activities.

Reactions in the schools were mixed. In some cases, students and teachers worked collaboratively on problems:

> In my case the relationship with the classroom teacher worked well. The teacher had been wanting to promote an enquiry thing in kids. Both of us found the problem — I tried one day, trying to get the kids to think up an idea and they just — 'we don't know what you're talking about' — I tried everything and I couldn't see the point of continuing at that point in time and he thought that was the best thing to do in those circumstances. So the next day he tried it and he had the same problem. It was good that he was experiencing what I was experiencing. Gradually we overcame it.

However, resistance was encountered in some of the schools involved in the practicum:

> The idea of devoting half a day to science and half a day to the arts was out of the question. There were expectations by the Principal (school coordinator) that we remain in our classroom when not involved in teaching, and study the classroom teacher. All reflection for us was done outside school hours.

> During the time spent at Deakin we have been encouraged to question teaching strategies, yet on teaching rounds, our role model (the teacher) often prefers to teach in an unquestioned, directed way.

> My teacher seemed to want a nice finished product that would be the result rather than seeing the process that we were going through.

There was also resistance from within Deakin's BA (Ed) program, surprisingly from some staff who actually teach in courses concerned with curriculum design and development. From our point of view, educational changes of this scale (integrating the practicum and the 'method' course; the substance of the course more concerned with the notion of 'science teacher as researcher' than with 'tips for teachers' or 'the good oil'; a two-day-per-week practicum for the whole year; paired allocations of students in the practicum) are *practical activities*. It is to be expected that the extent and character of problems and issues can only be appreciated by working through the proposed change; they cannot be prefigured in any comprehensive way. And in this case, students, teachers and supervisors alike spoke of a number of issues concerning the organizational changes associated with Biosocial studies. Many of these concerned the paired allocation of students in the practicum, something the course team felt was justified by the need for collaborative, participatory enquiry in science education.

We came to see the rise of problems and issues such as those concerning the paired allocation of students as an inevitable outcome of a change effort, not a pathological condition to be recoiled from. In fact the now much greater appreciation of the existence and complexity of educational *problems* by all participants in the change effort is, we believe, evidence of professional growth — to be able to explicate an educational change effort in terms of its tensions and contradictions is to demonstrate an (at least partial) understanding of its meaning and significance. Some staff, however, did not see things this way, and exerted a negative influence through efforts to resist the sustained two-day-per-week practicum.

This experience confirmed the view that one of the main problems of trying to bring about change from within a mainstream context arises when that context is seen as unproblematic by others. In this case, teaching, curriculum and educational change were not widely seen as problematic by students, teachers or colleagues. The 'participatory enquiry' perspective of Biosocial studies came to be seen as idiosyncratic — as an uncertain anomaly among the other, secure, courses in the program. There now appears to be the need to address the issue of changing the context within which the course is located, to make participant research more 'mainstream'.

On the basis of the Biosocial studies experience, it is clear that strong support needs to be given to changing the context of the overall program. A seemingly appropriate set of guiding principles actually exists: these were generated in a formal review of the School's BA (Ed) program and approved by the School's Board of Studies over three years ago but have since largely lain dormant. These principles are:

- Courses should be *research-based*. They should relate to staff research work and engage students in research, to encourage students to adopt a research stance to their own teaching. Consequently students should be engaged in problem-solving tasks which press them to adopt a critical attitude to the issues of the course.

- Courses should be *practice-based*. Students should use courses as explicit mechanisms for exploring and extending their potential as teachers.

- Courses should provide a series of tasks and experiences from which students can construct their own model or view of teaching and education. Therefore the program should develop increasing autonomy and responsibility in the student as a learner-teacher and teacher-learner; while earlier courses may be more tightly structured, later courses should allow greater opportunities for self-initiated and self-directed enquiries by students.

- The course should emphasize *the fundamental interrelationship of theory and practice*: it should encourage students to reflect critically on theories by reference to actual teaching practices (their own and others'), and to reflect on actual practices by reference to available theories (their own and others').

- The value of critical reflection will also be emphasized in relation to the pedagogy of each course. *The arrangement of pedagogy of each course should be explicit and self-disclosing so that students can reflect critically on how the activities of the course have related students, teachers, knowledge and the learning context.* Research tasks, the nature of teaching and the character of assessment should be open to negotiation and valuation by students and staff.

The 'Science'–'Education' Tension . . .

One of the tensions that emerged in the Biosocial experience was the tendency for students to adopt an exclusively applied-science approach in studies of their teaching — in short to apply a science paradigm in the study of education issues in science education. This tendency was expressed at the level of design and the level of reporting.

A number of students designed a study of their science teaching around a 'controlled experiment' model. For example, students investigating 'constraints to activity-based teaching in science' wanted an initial lesson that was intentionally didactic in character in order to provide a baseline against which to compare any advantages of teaching in a more enquiry-based way. It was almost as if students were setting up their own straw man of teaching which they could knock down with changed practice, thereby claiming improved teaching. The issue here is that 'improvements' within two different paradigms of teaching may be incommensurable — whether it makes sense to compare the relative success of two teaching approaches when those different approaches themselves make different assumptions about what counts as 'good teaching'. The 'success' of different approaches to teaching may be intelligible only in terms of their respective assumptions.

At the level of reporting, some students seemed to expect to be able to ascribe classically scientific status to the outcomes of their educational enquiries:

> However in the issues we investigated we could not find any conclusive proof about any one issue which may have led to girls disliking science . . . we could not conclusively say why boys dominate and why they have better manipulation skills.

There is evidence that the science inheritance (notions of 'objective'; 'conclusive'; 'measurement'; 'progressive'; 'linear'; 'positive' . . .) associated with the area of substantive interest (it is, after all, *science* method we are dealing with) is confounding the view of the character of educational enquiry, which is seen as properly needing to share those same characteristics. Educational enquiry is intended to be empirical and open, but is probably rarely conclusive or positive. Put another way, tension exists between the 'science' paradigm and the 'educational enquiry' paradigm in this science education course for teachers.

Theory and Practice in Professional Development

There seems to be a definite distinction in many students' minds between 'the tasks' and 'real teaching'. The tasks, of course, were written to encourage exploration of teaching issues through actual science teaching practice. The minimal requirement of all tasks was the teaching of five or six science lessons over the period of the teaching round — and in several cases the requirements of the tasks caused students to teach science lessons for the first time. However, for several students, the work they conducted on tasks was in some sense different to 'real, worthwhile teaching'. 'Task time' was seen as competing with 'teaching time' during the practicum. To be researching one's own teaching as one taught was seen as different to the real thing of simply teaching — and not only different, but in some sense of lesser value.

> Unlike other lessons whereby you are 'teaching' the children something, these ... research lessons provided a set-up situation, purely so we can collect data that we require. It makes me question whether the children got anything out of the five lessons or not, except the experience that I offered them and the skills they were made aware of.

> When are we going to learn from you how to teach science?

> All this task stuff is a waste of time compared to real teaching.

> Just what *is* science teaching?

There is a clash of two views of teaching education here: on the one hand, there is an interest in tried and true 'tips for science teachers' and a desire for teaching opportunities to put these tips ('the good oil') into practice in a way that is unencumbered by the 'additional' demand of having to engage in a research project; and there is an interest in professional development as participant educational enquiries within a context of science teaching. In our experience, students reaching the third year of their teacher education course tend to have already been socialized into the former view of teacher education, and perhaps the ethos of teacher enquiry will need to be revealed with greater across-course coherence if substantial change is to occur.

Acknowledgement

The course referred to in this discussion is called 'Biosocial studies'; its course team comprises Rod Charles, Giovanna Di Chiro, Ian Robottom and Richard Tinning. The author acknowledges the contributions of the other members of the course team to the development of this chapter.

References

HENRY, J. and CHARLES, R.C. (1985) 'Collaborative relationships within school-based experiences', *South Pacific Journal of Teacher Education*, 13, 1, pp. 53–62.

ROBOTTOM, I. (1986) 'From pilot to mainstream: Learnings from the SBTE program', *Journal of Teaching Practice*, 6, 2, pp. 32–9.

8 Enquiry-based Learning in Initial Teacher Education

Herbert Altrichter

Introduction: Identifying a New Approach and Its Associated Difficulties

For the last four years action research as a means of in-service education of teachers has been explored by various members of the Department of Education of Klagenfurt University, Austria.[1] As results were favourable, we have been encouraged to search for ways of implementing relevant elements of action research into the University's initial teacher education programme which is the prime responsibility of the Department (the University trains teachers for secondary grammar-type schools[2]).

As always, the planning of a substantial innovation raised a number of problems. *Inter alia* these were:

(i) that although we had considerable experience with in-service training based on action research and although we had read papers about efforts towards developing enquiry-based initial education programmes,[3] we had *no direct experiences ourselves with action research within initial teacher education.* It was clear that there was no ready-made solution which could be easily implemented to start with, so the development of the programme had to be done during the project itself. This fits the philosophy of action research, which claims that curriculum development should be negotiated with those for whom the curriculum is intended. Nonetheless, this process generates its own insecurities;

(ii) that to *find partners* for this kind of developmental work may be problematic. This proved to be not too difficult at the institutional level. Due to the long-established cooperation with the University, the local education authority (responsible for the province Klagenfurt University is situated in) and the regional institution for in-service education of teachers were quite willing to embark on a project whose outcome was not very clear in advance. Funds for realization and evaluation of the project were obtained from the Ministries of Education and Science.

Partners had to be found also on an individual level. University tutors from different departments, willing to cooperate in this innovative programme, were recruited through personal contacts; the local education authority advertised to recruit teachers to be responsible for the teaching practice elements of the teacher training programme;

(iii) that since the majority of the project-team members could not be expected to have done action research in their own classrooms, the project was to *provide opportunities for them to become acquainted with action research* and to gain personal experience of it by conducting an investigation concerning issues in their classrooms;

(iv) that it became impossible to *involve student-teachers in the planning stage,* since in the Austrian university system you cannot get hold of a group of students which will attend your course a year in advance. During the preparation of the project and during the first steps of its realization two students, who had already finished the teacher education programme in its old version, were called in to represent the students' point of view. Although their participation was very helpful, they decided not to continue because they felt they could not act as representatives for their younger colleagues. As a result the following stance was adopted by the project to compensate — at least to some degree — for the lack of student advice. Since teachers and university tutors will encounter a new group of students every year, the concrete realization of the programme will have to be negotiated with this specific group and adapted to the specific circumstances. Thus, the development work of the project should yield a framework and some guidelines for the teacher education programme, but the detailed development work for each specific course will have to be done by the participants during the course itself;

(v)   that we realized that *action research by student-teachers would be a problematic thing in itself.* On one hand we hypothesized

- that a research stance (which is deemed to be favourable for the professional development of both the individual teacher him/herself and the teaching profession) is more profound and more suitable to build on during subsequent in-service phases if its foundation has been laid as early as during the student-teachers' first experiences in practice;
- but on the other hand we thought that action research during initial teacher education is particularly difficult because student-teachers cannot draw on a body of professional experience in the same way as experienced teachers can and because student-teachers are sometimes confronted with more problems than they can investigate; and finally

(vi)   that the project involved a great deal of bureaucratic *complexity*: i.e., two ministries, three local agencies and three university departments were participating. The project comprises in-service experiences, programme development, implementation and evaluation in the course of one and a half years. Teachers, University tutors, student-teachers, and administrators are involved to a high degree. We decided to reduce some complexity by concentrating on the core elements of the University's initial teacher education programme, such as:

- an educational course of three hours per week for one semester, concentrating on the teaching-learning process, lesson preparation and evaluation;
- a subject-matter teaching methodology course of two hours per week for one semester;
- and the whole teaching practice section of the teacher education programme consisting of an introductory teaching practice unit (two hours per week/semester) and the main teaching practice unit (three hours per week/semester).

Also, it was decided for the present to launch the innovative project for two of the University's subjects only, that is English and German.

Strategies for Implementation

The following strategies evolved as a means of coping with the variety of problems mentioned before. The project itself aimed at an innovation in the initial teacher education programme at Klagenfurt University by integrating elements of enquiry-based learning into its core courses. This innovation was to be conducted in a specific way: the development, implementation and evaluation were to be performed by all those persons who have teaching responsibilities within this programme — both University tutors and school teachers responsible for the students' teaching practice. During the phases of implementation and evaluation students would be involved as well.

The members of the project were organized into three different kinds of teams (see figure 1).

Figure 1: Members of the project

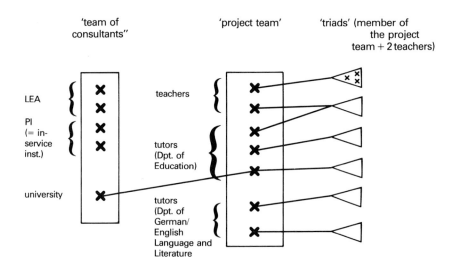

The *'project team'* consisted of two teachers working in the teaching practice section of the programme, two tutors who are subject-matter teaching methodologists from the respective university departments (English and German) and three University tutors from the Department of Education.

The project team's task was:

- to prepare seminars, project meetings, working papers and other organizational measures in a way that gives all the project members the opportunity to participate in developing, implementing and evaluating the programme;
- to provide channels for the exchange of ideas, information, problems and possible solutions between all members of the project.

The main working units of the project where the so-called *'triads'*. Each of the eighteen teachers involved in the teacher education programme was a member of one triad but care was taken to make sure that each triad 'hosted' at least one member of the project team. The triads were to meet every three to four weeks, giving their members the opportunity to discuss their work, report on their problems and develop further action strategies. If a triad wanted to communicate an idea, a question, a suggestion, etc. to the other triads, this was to be done via the participant also working within the project team. During the next meeting of the project team the 'message' would be passed on to the other members of the project team and consequently by them to the other triads.

Finally, there was a *'team of consultants'* consisting of two representatives of the LEA (both of them inspectors), two representatives of the regional in-service institution and one representative of the University who also participates in the project team. This team was meant to advise the project's work at some pre-specified dates, to give critical feed-back and suggestions for the transfer of project findings into normal school life, and to back the project's work within the regional administration.

Phases and Events

The Preparatory Phase (September 1985–March 1986)

During the months before the actual start of the project some preparatory steps had to be taken. After the first informal negotiations between representatives of the University and the LEA, the 'team of consultants' and the 'project team' were constituted. The latter had to discuss the preliminary project rationale and develop it into the first organizational steps. Teachers were recruited through an advertisement; an information meeting was held for those answering the advertisement. Participants at this three-hour meeting were informed about the current state of the project team's thinking and were given the opportunity to discuss the pros and cons of the proposed approach in small groups. After this meeting one teacher cancelled her participation because of fear of work overload, one because of an accident; thus, two other teachers were nominated.

Phase 1: 'In-service Training' (April 1986–July 1986)

This initial procedure had two aims:

- to give all participating teachers (both from school and University) the opportunity to gain first-hand experience of 'action research';
- based on these experiences all participants were to develop the curriculum for the core elements of the teacher education programme.

We started with a *one-and-a-half-day seminar* which introduced the participants to 'action research' by simulating an entire (but condensed) research process (see figure 2). During this weekend the triads were constituted, too. There was also some time to think about aspects of each member's own classroom practice which would be worth researching. During the following three months every participating teacher (both from schools and University) was to do some research on one aspect of his/her classroom and to prepare a case study on his or her research process and findings. Support and advice for the teacher-researchers were provided by the colleague-consultations of the *triads* which met every three to four weeks, and by working papers concerning 'typical research problems' (for example, 'clarification of research starting points') which were issued by the project team.

Phase 1 was completed by a one-week *summer seminar* consisting of two parts. During the first two days the participants' case studies, their substantive findings and their experiences as researchers were discussed and scrutinized for their relevance concerning initial teacher education. During the last three days groups of teachers developed and prepared improvements for the core courses of initial teacher education at Klagenfurt University which were to make use of their own enquiry-based learning as teacher-researchers during phase 1.

Figure 2: Project: 'Enquiry-based learning in initial teacher education'

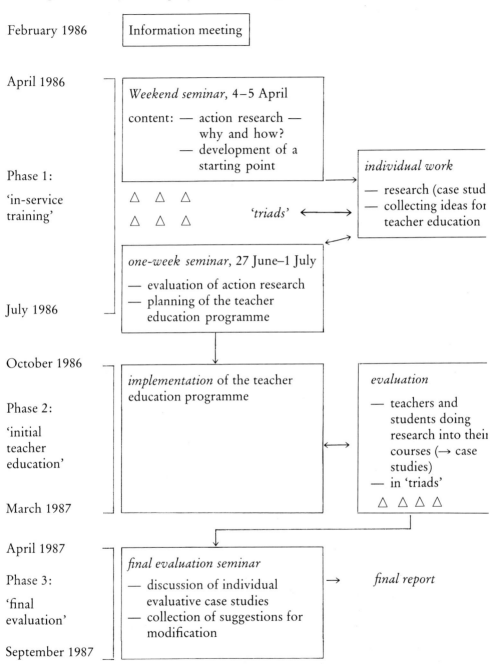

Phase 2: 'Initial Teacher Education' (October 1986–March 1987)

During phase 2 the project members implemented — in their function as tutors and teachers for the students' teaching practice — their innovative curriculum. They were to evaluate the implementation by monitoring their own performance as tutors and teachers of teaching practice. Each triad (which acted also as a basic unit of evaluation) provided at least one case study reporting on the triad's members' action research into their innovatory efforts.

Phase 3: 'Final Evaluation' (April 1987–September 1987)

During a *'final evaluation seminar'*, in which all the project's members plus some students participated, the first version of a joint evaluation report was to be prepared using the following procedure.[4] The participants were asked to formulate before the seminar about 'five evaluative statements' which should appear in the final report. During the seminar, small groups of participants read all the triads' case studies scrutinizing them for data which could substantiate, invalidate, or differentiate their 'evaluative statements'. They were also to discuss and formulate consequences for the modification of the original innovation and for its implementation into the regular initial education programme. To give an idea of the format and content of the small groups' evaluation reports an excerpt is printed below:[5]

16. For student-teachers, who are facing a situation they are not familiar with, a semester is too short to prepare a case study.

Data
The sentence is corroborated by student's statements as documented in Case Study 20, p. 4 and Case Study 27, pp. 5. 'Everything is new to me. I have hundreds of questions, not one' (Case Study 20, p. 4).

Commentary
The sentence does not complain of the time consuming character of 'enquiry-based learning' in a general way, but refers to the specific features of the student-

teacher's role. This role is (inter alia) characterized by the fact that facing a multitude of new impressions and experiences in practice makes it difficult to concentrate on a more thorough reflection on specific aspects of one's own teaching (see 'Sentence 20' for an analysis of main features of student-teacher's role).

Suggestions

S 1: The study regulations of the teacher education programme should be altered. School practice of students should be extended to one year (with varying presence of students in schools). Better opportunities for cooperation and coordination of supervising teachers and university lecturers should be provided (cooperation in seminars should be secured by the study regulations).

S 2: Prolonged school practice would make it possible to start with an 'orientation unit'. Within this unit students could reflect on their prior experiences as pupils in relation to their future role as teachers and orientate themselves with regard to the variety of new tasks they are facing (see Case Study 27, pp. 15 for more elaborated suggestions).

S 3: Forms of 'enquiry-based learning' which take account of the specific situation of student-teachers should be devised and tested. E.g., Case Study 20, p. 7 suggests that students' research stance should be developed in smaller steps. A diary could serve as a medium to reflect the multitude of new experiences; the assignment could consist of some excerpts from the diary plus reflective commentaries. . . .

Some Experiences

The final evaluation report will most probably consist of a collection of the small groups' evaluation reports and a summary of their main statements which have to be prepared by the project team. Since this final report has not been finished and negotiated at the moment I shall concentrate on some experiences of the first phase of the project based on data from my research diary and two case studies.

Phase 1 was a real venture; a lot had to be achieved during a short time which was also meant to serve as a foundation for subsequent work:

- During phase 1 the *action research* of the teachers had to be *initiated and sustained*. There was only very little guidance and support from 'central experts'. Instead support was meant to be given via 'colleague consultation' within the triads. However, three of the triads did not include a single member who had completed an action research case study before embarking on the project. Poor action research — since it was thought of as a foundation for developmental work — could also impair the quality of the innovation which was to be designed. Although all the participants were fairly experienced teachers who had previously participated in developmental projects or given in-service courses, three months is a limited time within which to complete a case study and reflect on what you have done.
- During Phase 1 the *developmental work* had to be *initiated and sustained* as well. Three days during a residential seminar is not very much time for such a large group to collaborate in planning and preparing the core of a teacher education programme, though it was more time than used so far for collaborative preparation. It was a great advantage that all the project members had taught in the teacher education programme before, thus being able to contribute valuable experience they could draw upon during developmental work.

The *one-and-a-half-day seminar* consisted of 'a simulation of an entire but condensed action research process' plus some amount of time for constituting the triads and formulating starting points for each participant's own research project. This seminar has proved a useful initiation to action research within the heavy support structure of a University course, but it was rather doubtful if it could fulfil its task within the more loosely organized network of triads.

The experiences and observations of the 'research simulation' were discussed and evaluated during one of the final sessions of the seminar. This — for us impressively profound — discussion was summarized as a set of twenty-three hypotheses formulating important conditions of teacher-research. An excerpt of a working paper collecting these hypotheses is printed below:[6]

Experiences:	• There was too much research.
	• Data were selectively analyzed, some were absolutely neglected.
	• The camera was too loud and disruptive.
Hypothesis 21:	It is useful to design data collection with regard to one's own working capacity in order to gather not too many data which cannot be used afterwards. However, one has to be aware that all data cannot be used to the same extent.
Hypothesis 22:	It is a quality standard of teacher-research to minimize disruption of learning.
Hypothesis 23:	Some research instruments can be used as teaching methods which are relevant with regard to the educational aims (for example writing diaries; group discussions).

There was the idea that this working paper could serve as a basic document for both monitoring the research and developing the project members' conception of action research. Since this document included what the participants thought to be important for action researchers at the end of the first seminar, their further experiences could be used to test, modify and augment this stock of practical knowledge concerning research. In spite of the tight deadline, seventeen out of eighteen project members succeeded in completing their *case studies* before the summer seminar. The size of the case studies ranges from six to seventy-six pages; similarly, their quality varies — some worth being published on the spot, some only very rough drafts for internal circulation. On the whole, however, they are far above expectation, considering the circumstances under which they were researched and written.

Feedback about the *summer seminar* revealed that participants highly valued discussing their case studies in small groups composed of people who had done research into similar problems. However, there was considerable reluctance to participate in two plenary sessions attempting to systematize the discussions of the small groups and to produce a set of common findings, hypotheses and open problems of the project teachers. Concerning the developmental part of the seminar, most of the teachers valued the opportunity to collaborate in preparing the teacher education programme together with the University tutors (and vice versa). The results of the development work are guidelines and ideas for learning situations for the four core units of the teacher education programme. The main features of these guidelines (among a whole variety of innovative suggestions) are:

- *Enquiry-based elements were introduced into the teacher education programme.* The student-'teachers' first steps in practice were conceived as an alternation of reflection (on their actions) and action (on the basis of their reflections). Students were to be asked to write a 'research diary' about their experiences in school practice and to prepare a case study on an aspect of their teaching they wished to concentrate on.

- *Coordination of the university lecturers' and the supervising teachers' work was improved.* Based on their experiences from previous years teachers suggested amendments in content and format of the university seminars. Participation of school teachers in university seminars was increased.

- *Importance of supervision in practice was emphasized.* The sessions during which supervising teachers and student-teachers reflected on their experiences in practice and prepared plans for further activities were seen as central elements of the programme. A variety of ideas was collaboratively developed to make supervision sessions more worthwhile and varied.

- *Organizational changes were devised to adapt the existing framework to the altered intentions and learning situations.*

This developmental work may not have led to a restructuring of the teacher education programme as radical as some dedicated followers of action research may wish. Rather it may be conceived as a further development of the existing structure into which — among other things — enquiry-based elements have been introduced. It will depend in the next months whether we succeed in keeping this emerging spirit of cooperation and development going — even into the direction of more profound changes in the organizational framework of the programme. That such changes could be worthwhile is indicated by some statements in the small groups' evaluation reports. But this is another story I have promised not to tell.

Acknowledgement

I am very grateful to Bridget Somekh and Heinz Tschachler who gave critical feedback and advice concerning language and content of this chapter.

Notes

1   Our understanding of action research was influenced and stimulated by the work of John Elliott (1981 and 1984) and Donald Schön (1983). For publications (in English) originating from our department see Posch (1986); Altrichter (1986a and 1986b).

2   In Austria the secondary school system is divided into two parts (see figure 3). Teachers attending the project came from the grammar-school-type stream of secondary education (called 'top-level secondary general schools' in the figure) because universities are exclusively responsible for the education of these teachers. Teachers from 'Hauptschulen' (called 'compulsory secondary general school' in the figure) are trained at post-secondary 'Paedagogische Akademien' ('teacher-training academies').

Figure 3: The Austrian school system

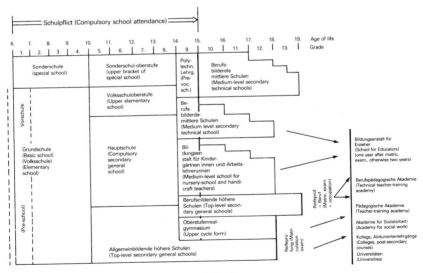

Source: Federal Ministry for Education and the Arts

3   For example, Tickle (1984); White (1986).
4   This procedure was inspired by Miles and Huberman's (1984, pp. 71) 'Developing propositions'.
5   The excerpt shows the main features of the small groups' evaluation report. They contain:

- *'Sentences'* which are meant to provide a short formulation of the evaluative statements;
- *'Data'* which substantiate or delimit the 'sentence'. 'Data' are sometimes quoted verbatim, more often there is a reference to the respective case study;
- *'Commentaries'* which interpret and differentiate the 'sentences'; and
- *'Suggestions'* which contain ideas and recommendations for the improvement of the programme as found in the case studies or developed by the respective evaluation group.

References

ALTRICHTER, H. (1986a) 'Visiting two worlds: An excursion into the methodological jungle including an optional evening's entertainment at the Rigour Club', *Cambridge Journal of Education*, 16, pp. 131–43.

ALTRICHTER, H. (1986b) 'Professional development in higher education by means of action-research into one's own teaching — A case study', in HOLLY, P. and WHITEHEAD, D. (Eds) *Collaborative Action-Research*, CARN-Bulletin No. 7, Cambridge Institute of Education, pp. 73–85.

ELLIOTT, J. (1981) *Action-Research: A Framework For Self-evaluation in Schools*, Schools Council Programme 2, Teacher-Pupil Interaction and the Quality of Learning Project, working paper no. 1. Cambridge.

ELLIOTT, J. (1984) 'Improving the quality of teaching through action-research', *Forum*, pp. 74–7.

MILES, M.B. and HUBERMAN, A.M. (1984) *Qualitative Data Analysis*, Beverly Hills, CA, Sage.

POSCH, P. (1986) 'University support for independent learning: A new development in the in-service education of teachers', *Cambridge Journal of Education*, 16, pp. 46–57.

SCHÖN, D.A. (1983) *The Reflective Practitioner*, London, Temple Smith.

TICKLE, L. (1984) 'Towards a process of professional development', paper presented at the 9th Conference of the Association for Teacher Education in Europe, Linz.

WHITE, W.G. (1986) 'Action research: A paradigm for pre-service teaching internships', in HOLLY, P. and WHITEHEAD, D. (Eds) *Collaborative Action Research*, CARN-Bulletin No. 7, Cambridge Institute of Education, pp. 2–15.

Part 3

In-service Teacher Education

While the significant difficulties of developing and implementing pre-service enquiry-based courses revolve around questions to do with the status of young students, and the tenuous nature of their contact with schools, the converse applies with inservice teacher education. Typically, teachers concerned with pursuing long-term award-bearing courses such as an MA in Applied Educational Studies, or a BEd (Hons) In-service programme, are those who are steeped in practice. They are senior teachers who are immersed in their teaching, administering and consulting roles in individualistic ways which make it difficult for them to detach themselves and question the nature and foundation of their practical knowledge.

White (1986) has observed:

> Lay people may not realize how rarely teachers speak to one another about the professional aspects of their work. They do not as a rule talk about teaching methods. Each is sealed in a classroom and guards the privacy of life in it. Students know much more about a teacher than colleagues of many years standing ... (p. 282)

The Outstation MA Programme, conducted by the University of York, which Lewis describes in the chapter which follows, is an attempt to create an experiential learning environment within which teachers may work and speak with one another. They are required to work collaboratively together to re-examine taken-for-granted features of their practice, not only in the interests of producing more enlightened practice but also to improve overall school policies and practices.

Power (1981), in commenting upon teacher education in Australia, lamented those professional development programmes which hold closely to the 'teacher defective model'. Such programmes seek to identify the deficits and weaknesses of a teacher's work in ways which are often humiliating and deskilling. The York approach constitutes a positive commitment to reflective critique which may allow for growth rather than defence.

Nevertheless, Lewis is clear that the innovation is by no means without its problems. The concept of teams is examined and while it is recognized that it is politically ineffectual to have only one teacher from one school on a course there is the problem of the team itself being an artificial creation. By this he means that the team is not one which may have arisen naturally, but is created to meet the requirements of the course. As well his chapter discusses the mismatch between the University's aspiration to improve practice in a given school and the individual candidate's quite reasonable pursuit of personal qualifications. A teacher, having completed his or her course of study, may seek for promotion. In most instances this means moving on to another school, thus leaving the original school bereft of that person's experience and his or her partner without a collaborative associate. The programme for school improvement is consequently threatened.

Lewis' very full account of the York Outstation Programme is complemented in this section by briefer notes which describe two additional in-service teacher education strategies each one with its concomitant problems and possibilities. Dennis and Burrell outline a BEd (Hons) In-service degree offered at Worcester College of Higher Education. The central place of the summer school in the programme is seen to deal particularly with the perceived needs of in-service students for a context in which genuine collegiality may be nurtured.

Stevens is also concerned with contexts, albeit in a different fashion and with a different purpose in mind. Candidates undertaking the Diploma in Education of the 14-19 age group at the North East Wales Institute of Higher Education are placed in a number of unfamiliar contexts including industrial and professional settings. The course focusses upon the students' management of these places in which they are the strangers and towards which, on occasions, they may even have a considerable aversion. Stevens not only describes the variety of placements but also outlines ways in which students are assisted in orienting themselves to this novel form of 'work experience'. There is a nice irony in the provision of such placements for teachers in an era when it has long been an accepted practice for pupils.

Finally, in this section, the presentation by Somekh examines the strategies used in facilitating the introduction of a major innovation into schools, that is the application of the micro-computer as a learning tool in the classroom.

Somekh recognizes that an innovation of this magnitude, associated as it is with complex technology, is particularly stressful.

As a means of reducing feelings of uncertainty, but not burying them, she argues for the establishment of a mutually supportive enquiry-learning network which will allow for the systematic investigation of the effects of introducing micro-computers into schools.

In outlining her approach to assisting teachers with their computing skills while facilitating an enquiry oriented approach, Somekh employs a number of strategies. She argues for a didactic beginning as a 'safe context' building exercise, particularly in this instance where the course is of a highly condensed kind; the group was told at the start what it needed to know in order to begin. Once confidence was established investigation of effects became paramount. Somekh argues for an *ad hoc* approach to the gathering of the first round of information, with a progressive and more refined focusing from thereon. The strength of this approach is that it simultaneously tackles the problems of the neophyte user of the technology and of the research procedures.

Her chapter demonstrates the beginnings of a resolution of a considerable problem in educational computing, that is how to judge its effects without becoming harnessed to the technocratic bandwagon. Papert (1985) pointed out that computers are a part of the culture of the classroom and the school, they are not apart from these sites and should not be treated in 'technocentric' ways. He says:

> We are not looking at the effect of a technological object on an individual child, we are looking at the working of a cultural process. (Papert, 1985, p. 65)

Somekh has done just this. Her portrayal also reminds us that enquiry can be embedded in short courses as well as in the substantial award bearing courses that are discussed earlier in the section.

References

PAPERT, S. (1985) 'Computer Criticism versus Technocratic Thinking.' in *LOGO 85: Theoretical Papers*. Cambridge, Ma.: MIT, pp. 53–68.

POWER, C. (1981) 'Promoting the professional development of experienced teachers', *Unicorn. 7*, 2.

WHITE, R.T. (1986) 'Observations by a minor participant' in BAIRD, J.R. and MITCHELL, I.J. (Eds), *Improving the Quality of Teaching and Learning: An Australian Case Study — The Peel Project*, Melbourne, Monash University Printery.

9 Learning Together: Issues Arising from Outstation MA Course Experience

Ian Lewis

Introduction

Terms like 'school-focussed' and 'school-based' have increasingly begun to feature in discussion of in-service training for teachers (INSET) in recent years. Their emergence can be taken to indicate one of two things: a concern to ensure that INSET makes direct connections with the real world of schools; an implicit criticism that perhaps many formal courses offered to teachers were more concerned with academic theorizing than they were with teachers' professional problems.

As an indication of its own commitment to support the professional development of teachers in the region, my own department in 1976 extended the range of its higher degree INSET programme by initiating a wholly part-time MA course in Applied Educational Studies. This was designed to provide a framework of support for individual teachers who wished to enhance their professional development through a formal investigation of some aspect of their own professional practice. The course was successful in attracting teachers from a wide range of institutions drawn from a region within about seventy miles of York. A great deal of valuable learning took place within the department as we gradually became accustomed to working more cooperatively with these teachers on issues and problems of immediate and direct professional relevance to them.

However, at the same time that this experience was growing we were also becoming aware of some important limitations of the programme. A fuller account of these is contained in Lewis (1985) and Lewis (1987b). It will suffice here to draw attention to key problems from which a radically new approach to offering formal support to teachers has emerged. They include:

- the isolation of the individual teacher, so that there was little group cohesion as they went their separate ways at the end of each taught session;
- the lack of relationship between the individual teacher concerns and developments within their own schools and local education authorities (LEAs); and
- the recognition that even if an individual teacher was successful in initiating developments or change, it did not necessarily follow that there was any impact in the school.

Essentially, therefore, we came to recognize that while the programme might have been effective in helping the individual teacher to a greater degree of professional understanding, the course was scarcely touching the problem of assisting schools to cope with the increasing pressures to which they have been subject in the 1980s. Discussion with teachers on this course, and increasing contacts with LEA advisers provided a basis from which, in 1983, the Education Department initiated what we have come to term our Outstation part-time MA course.

The remainder of this chapter will be devoted to an examination of issues which have emerged as this programme has developed and which we see as having relevance to other institutions which might also be looking for ways to develop programmes under the newly instituted Grant Related In-service Training (GRIST) arrangements. Before identifying these issues it will be necessary to give the reader some indication of the significant features of this Outstation course.

The Outstation Course

There are, in fact, four key features which differentiate the new Outstation part-time MA course from its predecessor:

(a) it is planned in conjunction with LEA advisers, who might indicate particular priorities of focus they would like the course to address;

(b) the teaching on the course takes place away from York at teachers' centres convenient for each intake, so that each new intake is, effectively, drawn from a limited number of neighbouring LEAs;

(c)   only teams of teachers, rather than isolated individuals, will be accepted onto the course;

(d)   these teams should share a common, general concern and, within this, each team member should have an individual interest of direct and demonstrable professional relevance.

To illustrate this last point, an example can be given of a team of four teachers on one of the current courses. These all share a concern for greater continuity of curriculum and pedagogy between the first year programme in their own 11–16 comprehensive school and the large number of feeder primary schools from which they draw their annual intake. The team consists of the teacher with responsibility for primary school liaison, the teacher with pastoral responsibility for the first year, a first year form tutor interested in relationships with one class, and the head of a subject department concerned at the diversity of background which children brought from their different feeder schools.

Amongst the reasons for these changes in the course were the intention that school-based teams would help to encourage more enquiry and development within a school; that they would also provide a basis of mutual support for each other throughout the programme; and that, by making the intake relatively local, the whole course group would share a number of general concerns and make for more effective cohesion.

The first of these programmes operated in Middlesbrough and resulted from an initiative from the Senior Adviser to Cleveland. It opened in October 1983 with twenty-four teachers in seven teams ranging in size between two and six members. Two of the teams were from primary schools, four from 11–16 comprehensive schools and one team came from a sixth-form college. At the time of writing we are currently in the process of selecting from applications for two new intakes for courses beginning in 1987. One of these will operate from a teachers' centre in Wakefield and the other will be the third Outstation course to be located in Middlesbrough. These will be the sixth and seventh Outstation courses to run since 1983 and plans are already in hand for courses running up to the 1990s. There does not yet seem to be a surfeit of these courses within the region, and the early indications of the new GRIST arrangements, which appear to place a premium on locally-based INSET programmes, suggest a potential increase in demand.

Our own experience of these courses indicates that once the

initial phase of discussion with LEA advisers about the course's relevance to their INSET plans has taken place, the experience of the teachers on the programme is more than sufficient to maintain a succession of such courses in a given locality. This is not to say that teachers are uncritical of these programmes — as later aspects of this chapter will demonstrate. Nor should this be taken to indicate that we feel that we are satisfied with every aspect of these courses. We do, however, take this evidence to indicate the courses do offer a high degree of satisfaction to a number of teachers and that each cohort of course members acts as the best advertisement we can arrange.

A brief aside is relevant at this stage, to provide the reader with an account of the process of initiating an Outstation course. This will be followed by an equally brief description of the overall structure of an Outstation course. It is hoped that these will provide sufficient contextual detail against which the later critical issues can be highlighted and given meaning.

Since LEAs within the region are now well aware of the existence and outline structure of our Outstation courses, we now rely on invitations from individual LEAs to consider offering the course in their area. This takes place just over a year in advance of the course taking place, i.e. around July of one year for a course to start in October of the following year. These preliminary discussions also centre upon aspects of the LEA's priorities for INSET, for example, an emphasis on encouraging curriculum initiatives. On the basis of this information we undertake to provide the LEA with an information sheet outlining the course structure, and indication of local priorities, and they are then responsible for circulating the information to their schools during the autumn term. The information sheet also identifies a date for an initial meeting for interested teachers, and this is held in the teachers' centre where the course will run.

Further details of the course and its demands and expectations are given at these meetings and questions from teachers are also answered. The application process also starts at these meetings. Forms are distributed and instructions given about key factors which we expect each application to contain. These include an outline statement of overall team interest, an indication of the individual interest and its relationship to the team interest, the nomination of referees, at least one of whom must be from within the teacher's own school.

While, as a University department, we have to retain control over selection for a course, once applications are received during the spring term, steps are taken to get information from the LEA advisers about each team. We are also concerned that applications show that teams have a real and continuing existence, and that the department has the capacity to offer supervision for nominated projects. Interviewing then takes place as early in the summer term as possible so that individuals, teams and schools can make any necessary preparations for their commitment to the course over the following two years. Teams are interviewed together and decisions are always made to accept or reject a whole team and not any part of one.

As a result of this process we expect to take on each Outstation a total of between twenty-five and thirty teachers, and find that this number will usually produce between eight and ten teams. At present, with the limitations on our staffing resources, we find that we can cope with three Outstation courses at any one time, starting one or two new courses in alternate years.

Each course lasts for two years, and the overall pattern is divided into two separate parts. In order to be able to devote the whole of the second year to the school-based investigation of the individual and team projects, with extensive supervisory support taking place within the team's school, we have incorporated the whole of the taught element of the programme into the first year. The first year, then, comprises a series of seminars and workshops occupying four hours per week throughout the year, taking place after school in the local teachers' centre. There are, in addition, regular workshops held each term at the York campus, in order to give substance to the fact that the course leads to a degree of the University, and also to provide a natural opportunity to work in the University library to all teachers.

Half of each evening, throughout the first year, is devoted to a course designed to enable the teachers to move from their initial specification of an area of professional interest to the design of a feasible investigation intended to enhance their professional understanding of that area of concern. The summer term of this element of the course is organized around workshops at which teachers report on issues and problems arising from the conduct of a pilot project designed to finalize their plans for their major enquiry in year 2.

The other half of each evening in year 1 is devoted to a series of term-long courses each of which is intended to provide fresh insights into contextual factors which might influence the individual projects. Current titles of such courses are *The Management of*

Change — which focusses attention on the fact that many projects are concerned with change in schools and that the consequences of any change are likely to go far beyond the immediate contexts of individual team members — and *The Purpose of Education* — which is designed to provide a basis for the examination of underlying assumptions behind both present aspects of the organization of schooling and also the pressures for change to which schools are increasingly subject.

The teachers' progress in year 1 is assessed and entry to year 2 is conditional on a satisfactory performance during the intensive year 1 programme. Assessment has three aspects: it is designed to satisfy University requirements; it is designed to provide us with evidence of each teacher's capacity to organize and articulate arguments on paper; it is designed to monitor progress towards meeting the demands of the year 2 concentration on the major project and its eventual reporting in a 30,000 word dissertation. The degree is awarded on the results of an examination of the dissertation. These have to be submitted by 30 September of the second year after entry to the course.

Even the above brief outline will have indicated a number of problematic areas which anyone contemplating this kind of development will need to explore. It will also have implied, perhaps, an uncritical series of assumptions which we are making, or do not appear to recognize. To show that this is not the case, even though a number of these questions will not be dealt with in this chapter, reference can immediately be made to the fact that from the very first Outstation course onwards, we have made a point of formally monitoring the reactions of the teachers on each course. These reports — Webb (1984), Munn (1986) and Webb (1987) — on the first three Outstation courses have played a significant part in the process of course development and improvement. More will be said later in this chapter on other aspects of this monitoring process.

Issues like the increasingly close relationships between the Department and LEA advisory staff, and the implications of this for teacher autonomy; or the practical problems of interviewing teams of teachers; or how we have resolved the dilemmas of course design to which Walker (1985) alludes; issues like these will not form the substance of the remainder of this chapter. They are not, however, unimportant, as anyone experiencing the development of courses designed to enhance the professional development of teachers will readily appreciate. They are for us, though, problems we feel we have addressed and over which we feel we have a degree of control.

Of more importance, as our experience of this approach has grown, is a sequence of relatively unforeseen issues which we are increasingly concerned to examine, and for which we have, as yet, no ready answers. It is because these issues were unforeseen that a decision has been made to focus attention on them for the remainder of this chapter. There is a two-fold purpose behind this decision: to alert the reader to the fact that any novel venture will contain foreseeable problems as well as throwing up new problems which will not have been anticipated; to share with the reader our current concerns in order to draw these to the attention of a wider audience and because we feel that they have a wider significance than the immediate Outstation context in which they have emerged.

The five issues to be addressed below are:-

   (i)   the idea of the team and team-work;
  (ii)   the mobility of teachers;
 (iii)   the significance of women teachers;
 (iv)   the questions teachers want to explore; and
  (v)   the implications of the degree context.

The chapter will conclude by emphasizing the need for research into such courses as a *sine qua non* of developing programmes designed to encourage teacher research, especially where these courses are based on a principle of working together.

Teams

The rationale for using teams in this new Outstation MA course grew from a recognition that the isolated teacher was likely to be politically ineffective in implementing change. A further justification lay in an attempt to counter 'the loneliness of the long distance researcher' syndrome which, in our experience, was a major motivational problem when teachers came from long distances, on an individual basis, to follow part-time courses based at the University.

The use of teams, though, has introduced us to a number of problems which we did not anticipate, and which are seen to have some relevance to our overall intentions.

First, there is the question of the pre-existence of teams either within or across schools. It is our experience that other than perhaps in some curriculum areas in secondary schools, teachers are unaccustomed to and inexperienced in working cooperatively with colleagues. Teams, therefore, have little working knowledge of each other — sometimes even little personal knowledge — and sometimes it is also clear that teams which apply for these Outstation courses are artificial creations, arising solely for the purpose of allowing each individual to register for the programme.

A second major problem for us has thus become that of trying to blend teams into cooperative working units, and to sustain these working units throughout the two-year programme. This has meant, for example, paying greater attention than we did initially to any evidence of cooperation between team members at interview, as well as making greater efforts to recognize the existence of teams within the pedagogical arrangements of the course. This last point relates to one of the dilemmas which Walker (1985) has identified: 'Should research projects be set or encouraged which focus on the particularities of specific situations? Or should projects be seen in relation to generalised, propositional knowledge?' (p. 8).

Given that access to our courses is not restricted to levels of education or to a single project area, we always have teams representing a range of schools which also reflect a diverse range of project areas. To ensure that courses reflect and react to emerging needs would, in our view, be a recipe for chaos — or, at least, an indication of risks which we are not yet prepared to take. However, it also has to be recognized that by imposing the kind of course structure already described, there are bound to be many occasions when our course is in advance of some teachers' needs, and other occasions when teachers can feel held back by overall course demands.

A third problem has been to do with maintaining group cohesion over two years, when the pace of progress and understanding can also vary from teacher to teacher. This can be further exacerbated when teachers hold different positions within a school and can sometimes be felt to have differential opportunities for their research. There are a number of dimensions to this issue of differential teacher status, and one unexpected insight relates to generational differences. Older teachers, for example, tend to be in more senior positions, but are also less likely to have recent educational experience. The tensions which can arise within teams which seem to be connected with these differences can make the task of maintaining, let alone making effective, team cohesion quite substantial. However, there do appear to be significant advantages to using teams and in spite of the difficulties indicated above we will continue to make this a central feature of our Outstation courses.

Teams do, for example, provide emotional and motivational support for each other when times are hard. Not everyone is depressed or having problems at the same time. Teams can also provide a salutory set of alternative perspectives on each member's work and help to guard against the dangers of one-sided interpretations and too much taken-for-grantedness in analyzing data. They are also a source of alternative suggestions and solutions to problems which might, in isolation, seem and prove to be intractable.

Teams can also help to spread the total work-load. They can share aspects of data collection; they can combine in wider reading than might be possible for each individual. They can, obviously, provide enormous assistance in helping each other to meet the various demands which the course makes, in research tasks and in preparing work for assessment.

Teams, though, in our experience, have rarely had a significant and long-standing existence in advance of working on our courses. If this experience is typical of schools and teachers more generally, then a great deal of thought needs to be put into creating teams before they can be helped to become effective agents for each other and for eventual change within their schools. Further insights into the issues which our use of teams has raised can be found in Webb (1987).

Teacher Mobility

One of our specific initial intentions was to see this Outstation approach as a framework for supporting groups of teachers wishing to improve aspects of their own practice through enquiry. One thing we have found is that this can clash with at least some of the constellation of motives which many teachers have for registering on the course.

Given that we are a qualification-oriented society, it is not at all surprising to find that many teachers want to enhance their qualifications. Nor is it surprising that some, at least, of these teachers see enhanced qualifications as one way through the log-jam of career development. These attitudes amongst teachers are given a further and unintentional boost because of the strong local relationships which these Outstation courses are developing with LEAs and, in particular, their advisory staff. This is a situation which is likely to affect all course-providing agencies under the new GRIST regulations.

It is our experience that while we encourage open applications from any group of teachers interested in the course, LEA advisers certainly appear to play a part in encouraging at least some team applications. These seem to come from schools which they wish to encourage in a particular development, or else they come from groups of teachers who are developing approaches which are looked on with favour.

It is, therefore, conceivable that one reason why LEAs have seen a major advantage in having one of our Outstation courses in their area is because it provides an opportunity, in financially straitened times, of showing a commitment to valued projects/ individuals/schools, when other avenues traditionally used for such purposes are rapidly closing.

Whatever the complex array of factors which influence such situations, there is certainly evidence that advanced qualifications are playing a significant part in giving teachers potential access to pro-motional opportunities. We have found, in consequence, that where appropriate jobs crop up, either shortly after a course has finished, or even while one is in progress, a number of teachers try, and frequently succeed in getting a 'better job'. This is not a new feature of any qualification-giving in-service course in Britain. Within the Outstation design, though, it has become a source of concern. With teachers' salaries a major bone of contention, and with falling school enrolments producing a major problem of limiting career opportuni-ties, it is clear that many teachers face a divided loyalty between themselves and their schools.

When the focus of the research in which they are engaged lies within their own institutions, this can produce a situation similar to that which Nicoll (1982) uncovered in her study of the impact and take-up of Schools Council Projects: that innovation and develop-ment are frequently tied to the individuals who initiated them. When these move elsewhere there might be little evidence, after-wards, of any effects which their work has had. This clearly has implications for the nature of the research in which teachers are engaged and this will be discussed in relation to teachers' questions in a later section of this chapter.

Providing an effective course which can attract, sustain and support groups of teachers in developing their understanding through enquiry is not, of itself, sufficient unless steps are taken to ensure that the parent institution is also affected. Consideration therefore needs to be given to the institutionalization of such changes which teams' researches indicate as worthwhile. Osmosis is not a suitable principle to adopt in hoping for growth and development out of team projects. The course as catalyst is not a useful model either. Unless formal steps are taken to ensure that a school is acting on the outcomes of its teachers' enquiries, the fact of these teachers moving elsewhere to further their own careers can easily lead to a significant lack of impact, in spite of all the work which might have been put in.

To draw attention to these points is not to imply that we have found solutions. Any answers must also address questions of where the onus lies for ensuring some degree of institutional response. Is it the responsibility of the course providers? Is it the responsibility of the LEAs and their advisers who encourage us to bring our courses to their teachers? Should it be the responsibility of the teachers themselves? Or do their schools, through committing themselves to support for teams, need to make a contractual obligation to ensure the furtherance of the work the teams have begun?

There are no easy answers to these questions. By recognizing them, though, we also recognize the need to develop even closer working relationships between course providers, teams, schools and LEAs, in order that the maximum benefit can be derived.

Women Teachers

A slight hesitation marks the broaching of this issue, not because it is unimportant; it is not! But the writer is aware that his own gender and socialization might conspire to prevent him from doing justice to a major structural and personal issue which affects many of the teachers who are following our Outstation courses.

One simple fact which we noticed from the first of these courses in 1983 was that they attracted a larger number of women teachers than we have experienced on any of our York-based programmes. This is a situation which still continues. On the five courses we have run so far we have registered sixty-three women teachers out of a total of 131. An informal check with colleagues in other in-service institutions reinforces the view that taking advanced courses out to teachers does produce a higher proportion of women teachers on them.

The only explanation we can offer for this phenomenon is that the local availability of courses helps to remove a major barrier to involvement for women teachers to a far greater extent than for their men counterparts. We take this as being indicative of the fact that, by and large, married women teachers in particular are victims of social expectations which require them to be full-time housewives as well as being full-time professionals. A consequence of these expectations for married women teachers is that many of them will find it very difficult, if not impossible, to cope with the demands of their jobs, as well as the demands which their families make of them, in addition to adding a substantial regular journey in order to follow a demanding course at some distance from their homes. Such restraints do not appear to operate in relation to men teachers.

It is also noticeable that a good proportion of women teachers on our Outstation courses are employed in sectors of the education system which are generally unrepresented on advanced courses. For us these include infant and junior schools, special schools and at least some of the growing variety of LEA support service units, for example, a language support unit which provides materials and peripatetic teaching support for early language learning in schools.

Comments are often made by those responsible for coordinating advanced courses for teachers that LEAs sometimes seem to operate with naive and stratified views about matching levels of course qualification with the age-range in which teachers work. Our own experience of teacher secondments suggests that secondary and further education teachers seem to be allowed, more readily, to follow long and Masters' courses, whilst infant and junior teachers are, more often, to be found on the short, practice-oriented programmes.

Personal and structural features of British society would thus appear to combine to make it that much more difficult for women teachers to enhance their qualifications and, thereby, their career prospects within traditional arrangements. We have, therefore, been gratified and encouraged by our Outstation experience, both by the numbers of women teachers and the numbers of teachers from these underrepresented levels of schools, who are attracted to these programmes. All the evidence points to the local accessibility of these courses as being a critical factor in achieving these high levels of representation.

One last point, in this section, of which we are only just becoming aware as we become more sensitive to our teachers' experiences on our courses: married women teachers report more instances of family pressure on them as they try to divide their time between teaching, research and their families. It looks as if families are not always ready to be as supportive of professional development for married women as they might be, especially when this is seen to reduce home commitments. This can be seen as yet another source of pressure which might lead to further discrimination against the enhancement of professional development for women when their situation is compared with that of their men colleagues.

Teachers' Questions

It should already be clear that our experience with Outstation courses has alerted us to many issues which we had not anticipated. Our responses to these are already beginning to influence our planning and the organization of relationships with teachers within the courses. Nowhere is this more in evidence than in the major changes in our thinking in relation to expectations of the kinds of research which these courses are designed to support.

Initially the expectation was that all the teams on our Outstations would be engaged in 'action research'; the course introducing teachers to ways of researching their own practice was predicated on this assumption. It is worth clarifying at this point what this initial view entailed. Kemmis (1983) has indicated one strand in stating that: 'Action research is trying out an idea in practice with a view to improving or changing something, trying to have a real effect on the situation.' This quite clearly indicates that action research involves enquiry into action which is taking place, and is not merely intended.

The Open University course, *Curriculum in Action* (1981), adds another two key aspects, as indicated in the six questions around which the course is developed. These require a teacher engaged in enquiry to ask:

> What did the pupils actually do?
> What were they learning?
> How worthwhile do they think it is?
> What did I do?
> What did I learn?
> What do I intend to do now?

This approach is chosen to emphasize the additional features associated with action research: that it is self-reflective and that it is conducted on the basis of a continuous process of action, monitoring, analysis, development.

Our initial expectation was that the teams of teachers who embarked on an Outstation course would be enthusiastic for and already committed to programmes of change. Their commitment to action would thus provide the impetus for us to encourage them in research associated with it. We did not expect fully fledged, clearly defined research questions, but we did expect to focus rapidly on ways of helping teachers to translate their professional activities into action research projects. The taught element of the first year programme was deliberately geared to providing the kind of introduction which an action research approach would require.

This situation, for current and planned courses, has changed quite drastically, and this has emerged as we have become aware of the diversity of teachers' concerns and interests. Only a minority of teachers want to embark on action research enquiries. This is not to say that the rest are unconcerned with action and change; it is, however, to recognize that as they conceptualize their enquiries it looks as if they are at stages prior to embarking on action projects. The majority of our teachers are developing projects which put a premium on gaining knowledge about practices within the schools, or else on gaining understanding about why current practices are sustained. While all these approaches will readily fall within a research tradition which emphasizes a qualitative and interpretive dimension to data collection and analysis, teachers' professional concerns do seem to embrace a broader spectrum than an action research framework would allow.

Two major factors seem to be at work here: first, there is the major constraint of the time-scale of the course, which requires an enquiry to be designed, implemented and reported upon within two years; second, there is the recognition that many teachers wish to expand their information base before they feel happy about engaging directly in school-based action. These points can best be illustrated by two examples from current Outstation courses.

A head of first year, responsible for transition from twenty feeder primary schools, and wishing to improve present arrangements, is faced with a practical time-scale which makes it difficult to undertake an action research project within the time-scale of the course. Similarly, a teacher interested in how probationer teachers accommodate themselves to their new professional jobs can justifiably argue the need to monitor a whole year's experiences in order to identify areas of weakness in a school's or an LEA's induction programmes. In both these cases there is a clear limitation on what can be investigated within a two-year time-scale. There is also, in both cases, a need to acquire information and understanding of the present situation in great detail before identifying possible areas for change.

The overall effect of situations like these is that, as stated above, only a minority of teachers on our courses are either in a position to or are desirous of adopting an action research stance; the majority operate within case study, evaluation or ethnographic traditions. While these latter cases may be the first stages of moves towards action enquiries, such enquiries will take place after the completion of the course and are therefore further influenced by points made earlier in the section on teacher mobility.

Two final points can be made in this section. The first relates to our identification of the kinds of benefit which we see teachers seeking to acquire through their involvement with research — extended knowledge, enhanced understanding, evaluation of the effectiveness of some long-term process — and using these to influence our course design. Our experience indicates that this is more productive than the initial concern with particular styles of research. The nature of teachers' own identification of benefits seems also to indicate diversity in how they see their own professional development being enhanced through enquiry. This diversity of teachers' perspectives, arising out of recognition of the variety of their research needs, is one of the important lessons for us in our Outstation experience.

This leads to the second point, which is concerned with the nature of effective cooperation between the academic community responsible for such courses, and the teachers who undertake research within them. Our experience so far indicates that there is still a long way to go before we can break down completely the traditional hierarchy of relationships which content-oriented in-service courses used to enshrine. There is more to cooperation than intention, and part of this additional requirement is identified in recognizing that a variety of approaches to research is necessary if courses are to be of value to more than a small group of teachers. To maintain, as for example Carr and Kemmis (1986) have recently done, that only through action research can teachers' professional development be enhanced is to maintain traditional academic arrogance; and also to demonstrate ignorance of the real world of teachers. In their different ways, both Gibson (1985) and Lewis (1987a) have elaborated this argument.

Ian Lewis

The Degree Context

Mention has just been made of the constraints which arise from encouraging teacher research within the rigid framework of an award-bearing course. In this section mention will briefly be made of the influence of the award itself, and the major problem we have faced with our teachers here lies in the requirement, for the award of the Outstation MA, of the presentation of a 30,000 word dissertation reporting the research undertaken. The detail of this requirement is less significant than the fact that it represents a typical requirement that the award of an MA degree will be based on examination of substantial written material of some kind.

The question which needs to be resolved is whether a reliance on a written form is the most appropriate vehicle for legitimating the results of a teacher's investigation of a professionally relevant concern. What must be the case is that teachers are, in consequence, faced with meeting three demands: they have to conduct an effective enquiry, they have to feel that the outcome is of professional benefit, and they have to meet some set of academic criteria. The problem faced by course designers is that of trying to ensure that at least these demands do not compete with each other, and at best that they might even complement each other. Hopkins (1985) gives a good account of the competing arguments about the compatability of these requirements (pp. 118–21).

There remain two final points to be addressed in this section. One of these lies in the recognition that written requirements, whatever their form, take time to produce. This means, especially in the context of a school where an enquiry has been undertaken, that much associated activity will still be taking place but cannot find a place within a written account being produced to meet an institutional deadline. The other point reflects the potential conflict, for the supervisor, between encouraging, supporting and cooperating with the teacher and the role as assessor of the eventual report produced for the award. Aspects of this dilemma have been discussed in Lewis (1984).

These points, though, are addressed to the problems of the relationship between the institution awarding the degree and the enquiry which that institution has also been encouraging. They do not address the problem, conceivably of greater importance in the context of working towards professional development, of communication of the outcomes of such enquiries within the school. Reports which satisfy academic requirements will not, readily, be suitable for a professional audience, and this creates yet another demand on teachers' time. It is also another aspect of the issues which need to be explored of linking individual and team enquiries into a whole school policy of development.

Conclusion

In identifying and exploring the above set of issues arising from our experience in developing this team-based, school-focussed, Outstation MA course, it is not implied that we have resolved all of them. This would be far from the truth. This chapter has been intended to alert colleagues elsewhere to the kinds of issues which they will also begin to face as the new in-service arrangements force them into closer working cooperation with teachers. Two important factors seem to us to emerge from our experience, and these, we believe, should become the hallmarks of any courses designed to encourage a process of learning together between teachers and members of the academic community.

The first of these follows from the experience we have had of issues outlined in this chapter, and which were not foreseen. Only experience, grounded in a commitment to working with teachers, can provide the insights required to make for effective planning and development of courses appropriate to meeting teachers' needs. Obviously some initial decisions have to be made before experience can be acquired, but since the bulk of this, for most of us, will be grounded in a traditional hierarchical relationship with teachers we cannot expect it to be an ideal base from which extensive cooperation will grow.

The second point follows from this, and is based on recognizing that attempting to help teachers to explore and understand more of their professional context demands a commitment to getting to know the precise nature of that context and the perceptions which teachers have of it. This will only develop as we move from our academic isolation and demonstrate a physical commitment to working with teachers in their surroundings to a greater extent than in-service courses have usually done.

This, though, is only part of the set of conditions which our Outstation experience has indicated are necessary for effective cooperation. The other element, through which we have come to recognize many of the features of our experience which have been described here, is a commitment to continuous evaluation of the experiences of teachers following our programmes. Mention has been made earlier of the three evaluation reports so far published on the first three Outstation courses — Webb (1984), Munn (1986) and Webb (1987) — and this has now become a regular feature of these courses. We now firmly believe that unless we are prepared to undertake the same kinds of enquiry into our own professional practices which we encourage in the teachers on our courses, we will be unable to understand and try to meet the situations in which we expect these teachers to work.

Learning together has become a kind of motto for our Outstation courses. It is hoped that this chapter has indicated that this is more than a rhetorical statement; that it is, in fact, a statement of a commitment to working cooperatively and supportively with teachers and, through a commitment to critical reflection on our own practices and the teachers' experiences of our courses, to try to improve our capacity to enhance the professional development of the teachers.

It is only through continued evaluation and reflection on our experiences that we can begin to identify the ways in which such courses can be designed to maximize the different skills and experience reflected in the different academic and teaching communities.

References

CARR, W. and KEMMIS, S. (1986) *Becoming Critical*, Lewes, Falmer Press.

GIBSON, R. (1985) 'Critical time for action research', *Cambridge Journal of Education*, 15, 1, pp. 59–64.

HOPKINS, D. (1985), *A Teacher's Guide to Classroom Research*, Milton Keynes, Open University Press.

KEMMIS, S. (1983) 'Action research', in HUSEN, T. and POSTLETHWAITE, T. (Eds) *International Encyclopedia of Education: Research and Studies*, Oxford, Pergamon.

LEWIS, I. (1984), 'The external examiner's perspective: Criteria for judging enquiry-based assignments', in NIAS, J. (Ed.) *Teaching Enquiry-Based Courses*, Cambridge, Cambridge Institute of Education.

LEWIS, I. (1985) 'Teacher action research and award bearing courses: A course organizer's view', paper presented at the annual conference of the British Educational Research Association, Sheffield, September.

LEWIS, I. (1987a) 'Encouraging reflexive teacher research', *British Journal of Sociology of Education*, 8, 1, pp. 95–105.

LEWIS, I. (1987b) 'Teachers' school-focussed action research', in TODD, F. (Ed.) *Planning Continuing Professional Development*, London, Croom Helm.

MUNN, P. (1986) *Teachers' Perceptions of Year One of the Outstation*

Programme: Bramley Grange Cohort 1984–85, York, Department of Education, University of York.

NICOLL, J. (1982) *Patterns of Project Dissemination*, London, Schools Council.

OPEN UNIVERSITY (1981) *Curriculum in Action: An Approach to Evaluation*, Milton Keynes, Open University Press.

WALKER, R. (1985) *Doing Research*, London, Methuen.

WEBB, K. (1987), *Teachers' Perceptions of Year One of the Outstation Programme: Banney Royd 1985–86*, York, Department of Education, University of York.

WEBB, R. (1984) *An Evaluation of the Cleveland Outstation Programme*, York, Department of Education, University of York.

10 Planning and Implementing a BEd In-service Degree: Not Rethinking, But Starting to Think

Doug Dennis and David Burrell

This summary account is of two degree programmes for serving teachers, the part-time and full-time modes of the BEd (Hons) In-service degree offered at Worcester College of Higher Education. Despite the necessary differences associated with part-time and full-time attendance, and also some distinctions in professional focus, both programmes are based upon the same principles, general objectives and assessment styles. The evaluation exercise referred to was undertaken as part of the quinquennial course review required by the Council for National Academic Awards (CNAA), during the academic year 1984–85, the review document being submitted in October 1985.

The programmes are regarded as 'enquiry-based' since each culminates in a professional project undertaken in the student's own school. This requires the student to identify a professional problem and then seek to resolve it by appropriate practical activities chosen in the light of theoretical considerations. The report of this work (12–15,000 words) is examined viva voce by internal and external examiners.

A proper perspective of the professional project can only be gained, however, from a consideration of the whole programmes and the ways in which they seek to prepare students for this final exercise.

The original planning (in 1974–75) began with a careful consideration of what was known of the problems associated with in-service programmes (part-time in particular), and produced a list of items such as: pressures of studying alongside a full-time job, difficulties of establishing a group identity, anxiety about returning to 'serious' study. The planning team designed a two-week 'summer school' in an attempt to meet and combat these and other problems. Two other considerations were that in-service teaching should be clearly different from initial teacher training, and that there should be clear recognition of the experience and expertise which in-service students brought with them to the programme.

A team teaching approach is adopted towards the summer school which is very intensive, involving lectures, workshops, discussion groups, group presentations, study skills and essay writing. Through these activities the course team seeks to establish students' confidence in their personal study skills and ability to present work at an appropriate level; to establish a knowledge base and introduce key vocabulary; to establish the ethos of the programme and develop the notions of acting as a mutually supportive self-help group, and also as a critical community. Student groups consist of a random mixture of age range and subject backgrounds, with the part-time programme also recruiting nurse tutors and FE lecturers. The course team views this as a positive factor in developing the critical community aspect of group interaction. Student response to the summer school has been very positive since the programme was first offered in 1977.

The programme documents identify explicitly the principal aim of 'influencing and improving professional practice by focussing throughout on the professional behaviour of the teacher'. This is discussed at some length with each candidate at interview to ensure that students are fully aware of the demands which will be made of them, as it is recognized that this approach offers potentially more threat to students than would a traditional content-based style. Early in the summer school students are offered a definition of a 'professional' as: a self-critical problem-solver whose practitioner skills are rooted in and validated by an extensive body of knowledge. It is suggested that, in terms of their own behaviour, this implies that students must be able to identify and explain the basis and nature of their classroom practice. Students are required to identify and examine the assumptions they make about: the nature of children, the nature of knowledge, how learning takes place, and then to consider the logical relationship between these assumptions and the methods and materials which they adopt in the classroom. A basic premise of this approach is that practical decisions must be informed by the best theoretical insights available and their outcomes must be objectively evaluated against recognized criteria; thus students are led to identify and examine their 'personal theory' of teaching and learning.

The teaching style adopted in both full- and part-time programmes is tutor-led discussion based on prepared reading and class-based activities. This enables students to make regular informal presentations of aspects of their teaching activities to the group and submit their own evaluations of that activity for critical comment. A wide range of approaches and activities is covered and students are expected to sample all to establish at an 'awareness level' the techniques available to them, subsequently they make a selection of those which they see as having greatest personal relevance for further investigation to a 'thoroughness level'. It is emphasized that this choice is the student's own professional decision based on their background, experience and current professional activity — a decision which a student should be able to explain and defend to tutors and colleagues. This process leads students to develop a course file which is a personally developed selection of techniques and materials for examining and evaluating professional practice in the classroom, and which has also been tested against the critical comment of fellow students.

In the part-time programme the focus of these activities is upon classroom interaction, and learning theories in the first year. The assessment item is: an evaluation of a lesson series (three-six lessons) from the points of view of interaction and appropriateness of learning theory for the lessons studied. This case study is presented and examined viva voce by both internal and external examiners. In the second year the focus moves to language (in the classroom and of subjects) and the basis of lesson planning (content, concept, interest) with a similar assessment item, again examined viva voce. Thus, by the end of the second year of part-time study students have sampled a wide range of ways of examining their own classroom practice, have discussed their relative value and appropriateness with colleagues from a range of backgrounds, made a personal selection in the light of their own professional situation and tested this in some depth through the two case studies, which have also afforded the opportunity to discuss and defend their decisions and conclusions with professional examiners. This work is seen as essential preparation for the third year which involves the student undertaking a professional project.

In the full-time programme the underlying principles are unchanged although clearly the work is more intensive. It also has a more specific focus. The autumn term equates approximately with year 1, and the focus is on 'learning difficulty and reading'. Students are 'placed' in schools for a day a week so that classroom activities can continue to form a major part of college discussions. Students are again encouraged to develop their course file on the basis of personal choices as between awareness and thoroughness levels of treatment. The school work is focussed on identifying the problems of learners and suggesting appropriate methods and materials. The work is related to the whole ability range and the 5–16 age band, teachers from whatever background are included in one group. The spring term offers a choice of focus: reading and language across the curriculum, or curriculum development to meet special educational needs. Teachers undertake a placement relevant to their focus and meet in focus groups for two-thirds of their time. The structure and approach remain the same, however, and the outcome is the production of a course file which represents their own professional choice of materials and activities and which, in an overview, also presents explicitly their personal theory of teaching and learning as related to their choice of course focus. This work occupies the whole of the spring term and one-third of the summer term, files are presented in July and examined viva voce by internal and external examiners. Once again this is seen as the essential ground-work for the student to undertake a professional project — in their own school in the autumn term following the full-time year of study.

The professional project is the final item of work submitted for honours classification in the professional degree of BEd. It is given this name rather than 'dissertation' to indicate that it must be focussed on a problem in the student's own professional setting; library studies are not admissible. It follows that the range of topics open to any student will relate to their professional position; a class teacher will have a more limited range than a headteacher, for example. For part-time students this exercise occupies the third year of the course — for the full-time student it occupies one-third of the summer term of the full-time course and the autumn term following, when students are back in their own schools.

Objectives, assessment criteria and tutorial approach are identical in the two programmes. The objectives are:

Students will:

(a) demonstrate competence in surveying, extracting and contextualizing appropriate theories and concepts in a chosen field of academic enquiry;

(b) demonstrate orally and in writing an understanding of educational issues and problems which are confronted in the student's professional situation;

(c) demonstrate skill in the application of theoretical insights to selected professional problems;

(d) demonstrate skill in the identification, selection and application of an appropriate methodology for the investigation of a professional problem;

(e) formulate coherent recommendations for ameliorative action in relation to a selected professional problem;

(f) report on the work done in 12,000–15,000 words.

The final element builds upon the skills developed in class discussions and in case study presentations, whilst at the same time requiring greater depth and range of insights to be brought to bear upon the solution of the selected problem. The whole is undertaken in the light of the knowledge available through the appropriate professional literature.

The professional project is approached via a guided study programme in which the student, with tutorial help, identifies a problem area and through selected reading refines this to a specific problem or question and identifies an appropriate methodology for its investigation. In the part-time programme this occupies the autumn term of the third year and students are expected to start their fieldwork in the spring term; in the full-time programme this element occupies one-third of the summer term. In each case there is a weekly tutorial associated with this work. It is assumed that the project will occupy one school term (spring for part-time students and autumn for full-time students). Where students are undertaking a more extensive piece of work they would normally be expected to submit their report upon progress at the end of one term. It is also assumed that the work undertaken for the project will not be entirely self-contained and that students will, at the viva voce examination, be able to discuss developments subsequent to the writing of their project report.

The assessment criteria, available to students from the outset, guide not only the marking of the report and the viva voce examination but also the focus of tutorials, to ensure that students remain aware of the range of skills and standards required through self-evaluation in the light of the criteria. Project assessment criteria are:

(a) the student's methodical, coherent and systematic approach;

(b) a comprehensive analysis of the chosen situation with significant and relevant insights;

(c) a comprehensive rationale for decisions taken and action adopted;

(d) awareness of key issues related to the chosen area and insights in discussing these issues;

(e) application of appropriate theory synthesized with relevant professional experience (apt and explicit reference to relevant material in books and journals is expected);

(f) a careful critical analysis rather than a descriptive account of practical work with evidence of the exercise of sound judgments throughout;

(g) appropriate clear style and presentation making a coherent project.

It has been claimed that the early studies in both programmes lead to the development of the skills and attitudes necessary for undertaking the project and that the project is the natural culmination of the work of the whole programme. The intention, and perhaps the likelihood of this actually being achieved, can be demonstrated by reference to the programme objectives — the attainment of which should be visible in the project:

Analysis	— the analysis of a professional issue and the recognition of material relevant to associated practice, decisions and judgments; the analysis of previous work in the field, including an awareness of its point of view, bias or line of thought.
Synthesis	— the synthesis of knowledge of previous work in the field, and its incorporation and development in the project; the organization and presentation of any new data, evidence and opinions collected during the course of the project.
Evaluation	— the awareness of, and the ability to apply, procedures and standards appropriate to the issues examined in the project.
Communication	— the effective communication of the material of the project in accordance with the criteria relevant to the procedures, studies and practice involved.

The course team sees all its activities from the introductory summer school onwards as leading to the development of these abilities.

Students in their evaluative comments on the programmes talk in terms of increased confidence in their own ability as teachers, greater willingness to get involved in innovative work and greater willingness to cooperate with colleagues in development work and to take a leading role. Headteachers' evaluative comments support the student view. The course team views this as evidence that students are moving towards achievement of 'professional behaviour' as defined to them in the introductory summer school.

These comments and judgments were supported by the evaluation exercise carried out in 1984–85. The evaluator found that the declared intention of creating a dialogue between theory and practice, and enabling the participants to engage in the process of professional reflection on and enquiry into their practice, was successfully put into effect at numerous points in the course. In the taught units of both the core and pathway modules students were encouraged to use their experience and practice as a means of illuminating and extending their insight into the theories presented to them. The same attributes were expected and demonstrated in the school file and especially in the professional project. The students readily accepted and valued these central characteristics of the course. As one of them commented: 'The course has stimulated not rethinking but starting to think.'

11 The Role of Placements in In-service Education

M.E. Stevens

The Diploma

The Diploma in the Education of the 14–19 age group is a one-year full-time in-service training course for professionals involved in the education and training of the age group. It is validated by the University of Wales and is now in its fourth year at the North East Wales Institute of Higher Education, Connah's Quay, Clwyd.

Without going into detail about the course itself, it is perhaps appropriate for me to mention four features of it that are typical of its design and methodology.

First of all the course is *experiential*. This is typified, above all, by the course module known as the Professional Day. For one day a week, throughout the course, participants work out of College on placements which I shall describe shortly.

The course is also *inter-agency*. From its inception, it has always been the intention that teachers, lecturers, careers officers and youth workers should exchange views and learn from each other, primarily as course participants, but also by means of the two out-of-College days (Professional Day and Study Day).

Thirdly, the course is *self-directed*. Although we, as a team, are responsible for the running of the course and the choice of our material, we always stress that the participants shall take responsibility for their own learning. The placements are obvious opportunities for this, and there is no party line. We are neither left-wing trendies nor agents of the Manpower Services Commission (MSC).

Last of all the course is *developmental*. We are concerned with changes in society, in education and in the personal growth and professional development of our course members.

Rationale for the Placements

The Evangelical Model

Teachers go out on placement as ambassadors; for a while they represent the education service, and there is a dialogue between representatives, between teachers and industrialists, between teachers and social workers, between teachers and other teachers. Occasionally this may involve an element of disagreement, or argument or confrontation, but we hope that there will develop a breakdown, at least, of long-held and ill-supported stereotyped views of each other.

The Deficiency Model

We acknowledge that there is not enough liaison between schools and workplaces. Teachers may indeed forget that the difficult fifth-former on the way out is the employers' new recruit. Teachers are comparatively unaware of current industrial developments and practices. Industrialists too may be naive in their views of the complexities of the education service. Everyone who has been to school can set him/herself up as an authority on schools which teachers, while on the premises, can challenge.

The Structural Model

We are setting up a form of work experience for teachers and lecturers. The placements are task-centred. We want to encourage active participation, not simply looking on from the outside.

The Economic Model

We are all being encouraged to look more closely at the relevance of education. Does the education service go far enough to meet the demands of industry? The placement can be seen as a way of enlightening the teacher and helping to produce, eventually, that much sought after commodity, value for money. My own experience of placements suggests, however, that generalized needs of industry remain elusive. One employer wants initiative, another a compliant workforce, one demands metric, the other pleads for feet and inches.

The Status Model

The placement can become an arena for a debate on the comparative virtues of education and training. The argument is acted out, before your very eyes. There is a conflict, however slight, between education and training, and a struggle between ideologies. On a placement, it is possible to see the meeting of minds of dissimilar kinds.[1]

The Placements

There are four placements on the diploma course, three forming part of the Professional Day module and a separate industrial placement.

The Industrial Placement

Course members spend a fortnight (ten working days) at a place of work which is not an educational establishment. 'Industrial' is taken to mean both manufacturing and service industries (British Steel, Theatr Clwyd, Hotpoint, a local leisure complex, for example), and both large and small concerns. These may or may not have training programmes for 16–19-year-olds. A 'day' is loosely taken to mean the normal working day experienced by a typical employee. However, we usually stipulate six hours' attendance, because a hospital or a bottle-making factory may be open twenty-four hours a day. Some course members have been on employers' premises to see shift work in action and one at least has spent time with the night shift.

Course members experience a range of activities on the industrial placement. These include:

(i)   work experience;
(ii)   a 'Cook's' tour of departments;
(iii)   attachment to a key member of staff;
(iv)   small projects or assignments;
(v)   attendance at meetings as an observer;
(vi)   opportunities to interview personnel.

The placement is linked closely to an assignment which forms part of the assessment procedure of the diploma, and occurs very early on in the course (currently week 5).

The Professional Day Placement

Alternative setting.
The second placement, also in the first term of the course, is a nine-day attachment to a professional, agency or institution having some responsibility for the education and/or training of the 14–19-year-old. Because we want course members to broaden their experience we stipulate that this placement should be in a setting with which they are *not* familiar. This may be at a TVEI centre, a Youth Club, an FE college (for schoolteachers), or a comprehensive school (for lecturers); with Social Services intermediate treatment workers, probation officers, or careers officers and so on. Again a 'day' is six hours, but obviously this has to be interpreted in various ways. At a youth club, for example, it may mean two evenings a week.

This placement began life on the course as a one-day a week attachment. For various reasons we have changed this, and currently operate a block placement. We have chosen nine days, because it enables course members to spend the first day of a fortnight in the field and return to College the second day for review, before returning to the placement to complete the two weeks.

Familiar setting.
This placement occupies a central position in the course, being a one-day a week attachment for the whole of the second term. On this occasion the schoolteacher returns to school, the lecturer to College, the careers officer to the service.

Usually this means a course member returning to their present school or college where they will often, but not necessarily, return once the course is over.

This placement has several objectives: we want to relate theory to practice, we want to enable teachers and lecturers to maintain contacts with colleagues, to be seen to be back at the chalk face and not on a holiday camp known as a course. Above all we want them to conduct some research into their own practice.

Some members return to a familiar setting but not their former place of work. This may be because they will never return to their former workplace or perhaps because they wish to extend their experience. There are advantages and drawbacks in this arrangement.

We expect course members to work a normal timetable for up to half a day, but this may not necessarily be with groups they are accustomed to teaching. A teacher of Welsh, for example, moved into the Careers Department, a PE teacher worked on CPVE courses. Both of these placements provide material for two further assignments which are assessed.

Negotiated.

In the final term, each course member negotiates a placement with a host who, once again, is involved in the education and/or training of the 14–19 age group. Within this broad definition it is the course member's responsibility to choose, negotiate and set up the placement. In 1985–86 course members were attached to tertiary colleges and special education centres, for example. Some chose to return to their own schools, perhaps because they had been given a new role for the forthcoming year. This placement lasts for eight days and does not form part of the assessment process.

The Choice of Placement

Should the course member select and set up his or her own place-ment? Our experience suggests that there is perhaps less resistance to a placement when the student/teacher has been involved in its selection. For example, this year for the first time we have given incoming students a choice as to whether they find their own 'industry' or let us do it for them. Each one has chosen to go it alone. In previous years, we have looked for the placements, set them up and then allocated them ourselves bearing in mind such factors as proximity to home, possible subject compatability, links already made with a school and so on. Allowing course members the choice relieves us of this burden, and also enables them to find what they want. But is it what they need?

In the case of the professional day (alternative setting) place-ment students can often opt for a cosy life. A college lecturer, given the choice, may not choose to work in a comprehensive school, but the insight may be most important if she/he does and may well be appreciated afterwards. A comprehensive school teacher with a for-mal, perhaps rigid background, might not deliberately choose the flexible informal setting of a youth club. But working alongside other professionals who adopt a very different approach can be salutary and also illuminating. On the whole I am inclined to encourage course members to choose for themselves, as long as we too can have a say if need be.

There is however the problem that allowing up to sixteen people to approach hosts can lead to some overlap, particularly if the placement is negotiated before the course begins. And one industrialist at least is unhappy about this, and would prefer us to nominate rather than be approached by perhaps several teachers.

Placement Preparation

Before each placement begins, we naturally devote a significant amount of course time to preparation. This is particularly true of the industrial placement, partly because it is the first one and also because there are more unknowns when you are not working with professionals who are like-minded colleagues committed to education.

Accordingly I will give a brief synopsis of the work we arrange for our course members in the fortnight before they go out into industry.

The course begins with a week's residential, which is in itself an induction period and also an opportunity to develop ways of working together. As a result course members are used to working in pairs and groups and have had the experience of trusting and sharing with each other. The next two weeks are therefore a form of 'crash course' for the industrial placement. Apart from inputs on industrial and economic developments (Government policy for example, YTS Schemes and the MSC), we try to sharpen three aspects of the student/teacher's own behaviour: observation skills, interviewing methods and record-keeping.

Observation Skills

At this point I would like to describe one session which occurs on the first day. As the activity coincides with the first day in College, we use their arrival fresh at NEWI as an example of the way in which sensitive observation of new surroundings can form the basis of a study of a workplace. We use the activity as a form of College induction.

Activity: All course members are asked to go to a particular section of the College premises and observe what happens there (the Resources Centre, for example, or the foyer). Secondly they are asked to make notes on what they see. Thirdly they are invited to approach someone unknown to them and engage them in conversation in a way that will help them elicit more information about the use of the area, its shortcomings or its attractions. Next, they are asked to jot down a hypothesis which could be checked out at a later date (for example, this area is not being used primarily for the purpose it was intended). Finally they return to base and talk to another course member who has also been engaged in observing the same locality, in an attempt to see how far perceptions are unique or shared. They are then asked to write up from their notes a short account of the area visited and to hand in both notes and the final (short) piece.

It will be apparent that we are also trying to include features of a process important in other ways. For instance the activity incorporates an early opportunity at writing (many teachers may not have to write much in the course of their working lives — even those who expect their pupils to be able to) and by asking them to *hand in* their first piece of work we are preparing them for the inevitability of assessment. We try to return the pieces the following day and therefore reduce anxiety.

The activity also introduces many vital components of placement practice. It:

(i) Rehearses the 'first day at work' syndrome.

(ii) Reinforces the fact that initial observations are the most acute. Employees (and students) quickly become inured to noise, smell and lack of ventilation or light.

(iii) Involves both descriptive *and* interpretative writing and observations.

(iv) Demonstrates the, perhaps obvious, point, that we each see things differently and certainly interpret things differently.

(v) Emphasizes the need to be proactive in engaging others in talk. One of the main sources of information and insight on the placement will naturally be the people who work there. But these individuals will themselves be waiting to be approached. Rarely will they initiate exchanges about the nature of, to them, a familiar and perhaps tedious workplace. Teachers too, by the very isolation of their working role, isolation that is from other adults, are often not used to developing casual working relationships with other adults. I realize, of course, that this is a sweeping generalization but my experience of schools is that teachers mix predominantly with other teachers (in some cases, such as scientists who brew up together in a laboratory, even with a small like-minded group). They rarely see each other at work or have opportunities to work *with* each other on a regular basis. Accordingly we are aiming to encourage our student/teachers to extend the range of their contacts.

This part of the activity also leads naturally to another 'skill', that of interviewing. At this stage I do not intend to describe in detail the sessions on interviewing and record-keeping. One other feature of the 'crash course', however, which I think is worth mentioning is the industrial visit.

The Industrial Visit: An Assignment in Miniature

Half-way through the crash course which precedes the industrial placement, course members make a half-day industrial visit. They are expected to incorporate practices they have already developed, particularly *observation, interviewing* and useful *record-keeping*. On their return to the group they are expected to share their experiences. Issues and trends will begin to emerge (the role of women in management, for example, or attitudes of employers to teachers and schools). The purpose of the visit, therefore, is to give an early opportunity to put theory into practice, to have a 'dummy run' before the placement begins, to learn how colleagues have coped with a multitude of situations (absence of a key figure for example, or being imprisoned in an office) and to begin to gain insight into current industrial systems and practices.

Placement Progression

The model in table 1 is taken from Borzak and Suelzle (1981) *Stages of Fieldwork*.

Table 1: Placement Progression

Stage	Role	Features	Strategy
Entry	Stranger	1 Ignorance 2 Slowness 3 Details noticed 4 Greater impact	1 so, asking questions is allowed 3 record details
	Guest	1 Given admittance 2 Shown how 3 Treated with courtesy and concern	1 so gain knowledge 2 gain insight into structural relationships 3 reciprocate
Initiation	Novice	1 Expectations of you increase 2 Privileges decrease 3 Negative comments surface 4 Attempts made to form alliances 5 Ribbing and teasing	1 meet them 2 develop self-directing approach 3 show tact 4 avoid cliques 5 good humour needed
Competency	Co-worker	1 Entrusted with tasks 2 Increased awareness of issues 3 Awareness of possible alternatives to current practices 4 Enhanced ability to ask the 'right' questions	1 avoid 'going native' 2 note and review 3 avoid voicing too much apparent criticism 4 opportunity to develop competency in problem-solving
Completion	Student	1 Withdrawal 2 Regret (perhaps!) 3 Acquired routine again disrupted 4 Tendency to compensate	1 prepare for this 2 look back and structure experience 3 prepare for what is to come 4 do not make promises you cannot keep

Supervision

The supervision of student/teachers while on placement is obviously important. Each member of staff is responsible for three or four course members both in College (tutorials) and out of College (supervision).

Each supervisor will visit the course member for about three hours during one placement and this may be a single visit although it is usually two, and in the middle term more.

What should a supervisor do on such a visit? On one level it is a courtesy call, ensuring a smooth passage for the student and maintaining cordial relations with employers. Obviously it is also important to find time to be alone with the student, for an honest appraisal of the situation. Too often it can seem that the supervisor, like the student, is being sucked into the system. Often the value of the visit may come later, back at College, when the supervisor uses the encounter as an aid to a better understanding of the course member's situation and by sharing the dynamics of the placement.

Inevitably it will appear that the supervisor is operating a checking procedure: checking that the student is coping with the placement on one level, although it may also seem that it is the host who is under scrutiny.

Sometimes supervision becomes a matter of *rescuing*. A course member can sometimes employ self-defeating tactics which block progress. For example, a teacher can avoid contact with young people in a youth club by spending too much time with the leader and not even leaving his office. A teacher's negative perception of the MSC or the Careers Service can prevent them from being open to the real nature of the work that is being undertaken by young people. Sometimes the student/teacher is over-programmed and s/he needs help in abandoning the strict schedule in favour of a self-directed one. Too rigid a plan before the placement can cause problems when reality fails to live up to expectations. For example, the person who negotiated the placement with the student/teacher turns out to be away for the duration and a less well briefed and perhaps less motivated contact takes over.

Occasionally, too, supervision takes on the form of a *damage-limitation exercise*. Some problems loom larger than others, and it may be necessary to move in early and prevent a rapid deterioration. One student was looking at intermediate treatment methods for coping with young offenders. It soon became apparent that intermediate treatment was jointly managed by Social Services and the

Probation Service, and before long the course member became seriously embroiled in the problems of joint management. On another occasion a course member was asked to tackle a project which involved him in more work than had been agreed. He was in fact replacing a member of staff.

A member of the tutorial staff is perhaps best able to retrieve such situations, but by and large the supervision process is there to help student/teachers to make the most of the opportunity. I suggest, however, that we need to look more closely at supervision; it is not enough to drive along, meet the course member, tour the premises and have lunch. A constructive engagement means focussing on the student/teacher's skills in penetrating the experience of the placement rather than being swept along by it.

'Placement Exchange'

Even though each course member writes an assignment arising out of each placement, it is important, I feel, that experiences should also be shared. We have therefore included a 'placement exchange' in which reflections and observations are shared.

Two course members were placed in a youth centre and talked about their experiences of 'drop-in' centres developed there for the unemployed. These are some of my notes made during their presentation:

The Centre:	A SHELTER (warm, dry and free)
	A SECOND HOME (friends, games, meeting)
	TERRITORIAL DEFENCE BEHAVIOUR
The young adults:	MAJORITY UNEMPLOYED
	HARD CORE of REGULARS with fleeting NEW MEMBERS
	CONCERN about OTHERS (for example, took handicapped children swimming)
	SHARING (for example, no squabble about order of play on pool table, cf. youth club behaviour)
	DEPRESSION (not enjoyment centres)

Some issues:

(i) Drop-in centre *at odds* with YTS schemes — is it a rival attraction?

(ii)   There is WORK and then there is EMPLOYMENT —
       not synonymous.
(iii) Moral implications on discovering the BLACK ECO-
       NOMY (on the dole and making money; crime).
(iv)   Political implications: what do I, as a casual observer,
       think should be done/can be done?

Statements such as these naturally provoke discussion and develop issues which are not necessarily addressed in the more formal
assessed assignments.

Issues

I would like to conclude by raising some of the problems that seem
to be faced by teachers and lecturers while on placement.

Perception

How the course member perceives the placement is naturally crucial
to its success. Some are dissatisfied with the choice of placement.
Perhaps it was not their own first choice, and, if chosen by course
tutors it may be seen as irrelevant, failing to meet their needs. This
can often result in a complex process of projection. The host is seen
as difficult or antagonizing, or the course member is continually
waiting for direction from someone in the agency or workplace.
This behaviour is probably a symbolic way of responding to us:
'you put me here: you get me out of it.'
    How the host perceives the student teacher also affects the
progress of the placement. More than one industrialist has been
known to treat teachers in a negative way. It is almost as if the one
person before them is felt to be responsible for all the shortcomings
of young employees, and the student teacher can be blamed for
David Jones's appalling maths or even violence in the streets. This is
made worse if the host sees the teacher as ignorant of the real world,
and in dire need of exposure to the harsh climate of 'proper' work.

Research Contamination

The need to find a topic to research or an issue to share with
colleagues just because the course demands you should, can affect

the experience of the placement and even appear to contaminate it. On the other hand it can sharpen the focus and help the student/ teacher to concentrate on specifics and look beneath the surface. Sometimes, however, panic sets in. The researcher changes direction midway or spends too much time gathering information and runs out of time to evaluate the process. Sometimes, again, the student/ teacher blames the course or the course tutors for colluding with a process which makes writing it up outweigh the placement itself. This reminds me of the pupil who said to me that he did not want to go to the pantomime because 'they' would only make him write about it afterwards. It seems to be crucial in the preparation for the placement that negative feelings are allowed to surface; and if possible to reinforce the argument that the placement provides an opportunity for learning and is not a straitjacket imposed by the demands of the course.

Personal Agendas

I remember one student/teacher with strong anti-military feelings who faced a period with a firm which, among other things, contributed to the nation's weapons manufacture. Another with strong feelings about the value of democratic and shared decision-making found himself face to face with an autocratic training officer. Such a mismatch between individuals and placements is inevitable. In this respect it is also important to note that hosts have their own agendas when agreeing to accept student/teachers. Why do hosts say yes to a placement? Is it altruism, publicity, a genuine attempt at developing links or self-interest? A headteacher may well see the return of a member of staff, who had apparently gone off on a course but was now in fact suddenly available to teach four periods a week in the second term, as a bonus too good to miss, and seek to extend the number of periods taught or use them unashamedly to ease the substitution list.

Lack of Reality

One of the complaints voiced most frequently and one that is laid at our door as tutors is that the placement is unreal. It is only a fortnight (we are told), and does not give the full flavour of working in a hospital or a factory or a theatre. This can be a defensive mechanism, used where a placement has failed to live up to its expectations, but there is, of course, considerable truth in it. In fact the whole point about a placement is that it is by definition temporary, it is not something you *have* to do to earn a living. Nevertheless, rather like role play and simulations, the placement gives some opportunity at least to experience other worlds, however vicariously, and this may, in turn lead to a reassessment of an established position or a slight shift in attitude. As one student/teacher remarked, 'The factory was clean; not at all what I expected.'

Note

1   I am indebted to my colleague, Mr J. Aled Williams, for permission to include this model.

References

Borzak, L. and Suelzle, L. (1981) 'Stages of fieldwork', in Borzak, L. (Ed.) *Field Study: A Sourcebook for Experiential Learning* Sage.

12 Desperate Straits with the Micro: Do Enquiry-based Courses Provide the Answer?

Bridget Somekh

Introduction

This chapter describes work undertaken during 1985/86 when I was Curriculum Development Officer at Netherhall Educational Software, a post which entailed an in-service brief as part of the Micros Support Team for Cambridgeshire LEA. It reflects on the contribution which enquiry-based courses can make to the in-service education of teachers in the use of micros in education. It is a product of my background in school-based research (CARN and the TIQL Project[1]), because it assumes the central importance of the teacher as researcher, the blurring of the line between the teacher trainer and the teacher learner, and the Stenhouse (1975) model of the curriculum with its inevitable gap between what is intended by the teacher and what is received by the children in practice. It draws on the knowledge I gained over eighteen months by visiting schools and working with teachers across the full age range, supporting them in taking on the major innovation of micros in education. After describing the context of micros in education, the chapter describes two short enquiry-based courses I ran on 'Using a computer in the primary classroom'. It then goes on to evaluate these courses as a possible model for future in-service in micros in education.

Problems with Micros in Education

It is my contention that there are particular problems associated with micros in education as an innovation, and in particular with the in-service education of teachers in their use. I have described this elsewhere (Somekh, 1986a) but would like to expand on some points:

(i) micros are part of the world of high technology and are perceived by most teachers as being beyond their comprehension, and therefore alien;

(ii) computers have a science fiction image of high intelligence, yet in reality the educational micro is limited in its capacity (memory) and its software; it often depends on the person using it adopting a trial and error approach, and is adept at making you feel stupid if you like to get things right first time;

(iii) micros have been introduced to schools extremely rapidly, largely through the Department of Trade and Industry's Micros in Schools scheme, and there is great pressure from parents and the community for teachers to use them;

(iv) because of their rapid introduction, for at least the first two years (1982–84) there was very little good software to translate the machinery into educational reality — indeed, designers and programmers had to carry out research alongside teachers to determine the very criteria for good educational software;

(v) micros are expensive and have to be shared by large numbers of children — teachers are, therefore, involved in transporting them about the building, setting them up and dismantling them, and sharing software with colleagues;

(vi) teachers' unfamiliarity with micros clashes unfortunately with the traditional assumption that they should be seen by their pupils to be knowledgeable;

(vii) the presence of a micro in the classroom can distract the focus of attention away from the teacher, particularly when software is interactive and the child is controlling his/her own learning experience;

(viii) the presence of a micro in the classroom has an influence on teaching style: for example, a single micro enforces group work, and moving to a specialist computer room (now the norm in secondary schools) makes it difficult to integrate the computer work with the 'normal' work.

The resulting situation, as one would expect from the substantial body of literature on innovation (admirably presented in Fullan,

1982), is that many teachers are resistant to using micros, expressing anger openly and feeling anxiety inwardly. Those few who have embraced the new technology have tended to make their colleagues even more resistant, both by their own enthusiasm and by the feelings of inadequacy they inspire. It has not helped that micros have been introduced at a time of cuts in education spending in this country. Teachers have resented seeing money spent on hardware while other more urgent priorities are being shelved.

Paradoxically, however, some of the points listed above as problematic for teachers constitute the micros' greatest strength as an educational tool. My research on using Quinkeys for word-processing with a small group of teachers (see Somekh, 1985) persuaded me of their potential as a catalyst for changing teaching and learning styles. This initial interest led to my involvement with the Netherhall software group and resulted in my running the two short courses described in this chapter.

Two Courses, Each Constituting Six Two-hour Sessions and Following Very Similar Lines

Using a Computer in the Primary Classroom: A Practical Exploration of its Strengths and Weaknesses in Supporting and Extending Children's Learning

The publicity material set out the aims to 'explore and discuss ... by collecting observations from classrooms and opening these for discussion ... the strengths and weaknesses of the computer in supporting and extending children's learning ... different types of classroom organization when a computer is in use ... related issues, such as extra strains which may be imposed on the teacher and the ways in which these can be changed to support the teacher ... and a small number of software packages.' It promised also, 'At least one visit will be made to each participant to give support in using the computer in the classroom.'

The gathering of data was of central importance, despite the shortness of the course and the limitations which this inevitably imposed.

There were also several implicit aims underpinning the course philosophy:

(i)   course members should become a mutual support group

in which it was safe to admit to lack of knowledge and expertise;

(ii)   the micro should be presented neutrally as a subject for exploration, to be accepted or rejected by course members on the basis of classroom trials;

(iii) discussion of educational issues should be given precedence over the teaching of technical skills and/or familiarization with software;

(iv)   experimentation should be encouraged, particularly with different patterns of grouping children for work with the micro;

(v)   the micro should be seen as an opportunity for children to engage in discovery learning, and this should be emphasized as a counterbalance to anxieties about the need for extensive lesson preparation in an unfamiliar context;

(vi)   there should be an emphasis on substantial pieces of software, such as word-processors and adventure games/ simulations, capable of supporting the best educational practice in all areas of the curriculum;

(vii) there should be an emphasis on the central role of the teacher in choosing the software, determining how it should be used, and enhancing the children's learning experiences with the computer.

Although the two courses were substantially similar, in the second there was greater emphasis on supporting those members of the group who had a role as micros support teachers in their schools — if you like, more of a sense that I was 'training trainers' as well as developing the skills of the individual.

The courses were run at the Cambridge Education Development Centre (Teachers' Centre) which provided an informal setting.

The course members varied in their previous experience with micros, about half of them having previously attended one of the two-day DTI training courses, but several of these having had little practical experience since that time. The first group tended to be more homogeneous (by and large lacking in confidence), the second had a wider 'ability' spread.

The main constraint of the course was lack of time. When translated into practical terms, the broad aims of the course necessitated finding time for:

(a)   Allaying fears.

(b)   Discussing general issues.
(c)   Teaching data collection techniques.
(d)   Discussing data collected during the previous week.
(e)   Giving confidence in 'hands on' use of the micro.
(f)   Teaching disc handling techniques, i.e. how to format a disc, copy software from one disc to another and load a program into the micro.
(g)   Familiarizing course members with the available software.
(h)   Teaching word-processing techniques.

The situation worsened when I discovered at the first session that some people had only expected the sessions to last for one-and-a-half hours.

I employed what strategies I could to overcome the problem. For example:

1   In the opening session, I made some points didactically and allowed discussion to follow from a direct lead, rather than letting points emerge from the group. My previous experience made me fairly sure of the most common problems, as outlined above, so I assumed they would be shared by the group. Thus, to allay fears and build a safe context for sharing problems, I was at pains to demystify the micro by reminiscing about my own bad experiences and expounding on the problem of 'the micro being too stupid' (see (ii) under 'Problems with micros' above).

2   I cut corners shamelessly on teaching research techniques, working on the principle that if they gathered some data, however roughly and inaccurately, the process itself would be enough to change the nature of contributions to the discussion: from generalizations subject to prejudices and assumptions to anecdotes from which we could draw implications about real situations.

3   After the first session discussion itself was closely linked to follow-up of data collected, or arose from practical sessions.

4   Software was not introduced at all until the second session but was gradually given more time as the course progressed. I worked on the principle of introducing four major types of software, including word-processing, one in each of the four middle sessions. In the last session course members were free to explore any of the available software.

5   Word-processing was demonstrated in a report-back session from group discussion in which I acted as scribe for the

ideas. This enabled me to introduce it in a real context. During the second half of that session I was able to teach the basic procedures of word-processing and still leave time for a short practical session working in twos and threes.

6 In several of the sessions time for practical work was included after the opening discussion; and every week the session continued informally for an extra hour (two-and-a-half hours in all) to enable individual teaching of disc-handling, copying of discs, viewing and borrowing of software, and time for 'hands on' experience. In the last week this informal, practical session took up the entire time.

7 I relied on the school visit to sort out individual problems and give more specific advice. Although this was not compulsory it proved a popular option.

Course Evaluation

A Document Written by the Course Members

On both courses the strategy employed in the opening session (see 1 above) resulted in lively discussion which opened up many important issues. In the following weeks, discussion following classroom observations was fed directly into a collaborative document which was copied to all members of the group. These documents reflect the quality of the discussion and the one from the first course is quoted here in full:

POINTS MADE BY MEMBERS OF THE GROUP AFTER THE FIRST WEEK OF OBSERVING CHILDREN USING THE COMPUTER

1 The extrovert child was in rather a rush and the more timid child was calmer and found the keyboard easier to handle.

2 Girls lack the confidence initially but once they succeed they cope as well as the boys.

3 The computer encourages discussion and when they were using it they were less inhibited about working with children of the opposite sex! Because the computer is a new medium it helps the children to get over the habits of working separately.

4 I felt strongly that they weren't getting nearly as much

out of using the computer without an adult as they would have with an adult. There were opportunities for learning which they missed.

5   A lot of programs demand that the children use self-discipline. They are often alone. They could lark about if they wanted to.

6   They really enjoyed it. I don't think they learned anything more than from other activities, but they certainly enjoyed what they were doing .... They commented on the fact that it was great .... It was the second most popular thing after the Wendy House.

7   What they are getting is instant feed-back. Children said they liked to know if they were right or wrong.

8   The computer tends to encourage the idea that there is such a thing as right or wrong. This is very narrow. (Note: this refers to software of the 'skill and drill' type.)

9   You've got to be on top of what they are doing all the time to make sure they are being stretched.

10 It seems to waste rather a lot of time with children writing laboriously. On the other hand, the computer helps to encourge discussion and reading without them having to write anything down.

11 It's important to ask children to write in their books sometimes alongside their work on the computer.

12 It is important to match the program with the ability of the children, but it is important not to feel you always have to prepare too carefully so that you find it too burdensome preparing. Sometimes it is best to 'have a go'.

FURTHER POINTS MADE BY MEMBERS OF THE GROUP AFTER A SECOND WEEK OF OBSERVATION (MAINLY WORKING WITH WORD-PROCESSING)

13 When using a word-processor the children are more prepared to study what they have written, and revise and correct willingly.

14 The types of corrections which they make are — spelling, punctuation, vocabulary and style.

15 The availability of the computer might influence the way the teacher uses it and the children's reaction to it.

16 When children typed their own work it helped them with capital letters, spaces between words and full stops.

17 One girl actually made spelling mistakes so that she could correct them.

18 The 5-year-olds were very keen to type their work even though it took a long time.

POINTS MADE BY MEMBERS OF THE GROUP AFTER TWO WEEKS OF OBSERVING CHILREN WORKING WITH WORD-PROCESSING

19 One group (of 9-year-olds) wrote, 'He had black hair' and then changed it to 'He had matted black hair all over his body'. The teacher encouraged this kind of editing by saying to the children, 'If you could have written your sentence at the age of six it is not good enough.'

20 Because the writing is exposed on the screen does it prevent them from being imaginative? Maybe you have to present the task as a group story, so that they don't feel it is personal.

21 But are we right to ask children to write committee stories? They might not want their stories interfered with by other people.

22 I had a group who were rather poor at writing and they were propping each other up in a very helpful way.

23 One group joined together writing poems and discussing words (the teacher acted as their typist). They were so enthusiastic after writing two pieces on the screen that, after their session was finished, they all went off and wrote with enthusiasm in their books.

24 We looked at sentences and how we could improve the style of them ... I found it a very unusual opportunity to look at the way they were writing and discuss it with them.

25 It took far longer than it would to write in books. I thought it was worth it, but wouldn't want to do it too often.

26 Keyboard skills I consider as another activity — different from language development — and I wouldn't mix the two. (So it might be more appropriate to type for

the children sometimes until they are able to go a little faster themselves.)

I think it is possible to extrapolate from this document the value of adopting an enquiry-based approach to even a short course of this kind on Micros in Education. The document is not finished and is often self-contradictory, but it is reflective and exploratory and clearly based on experience of real situations. At the end of the discussion on the first day of the course the big question from at least two teachers had been, 'Do we *have* to use the computer?', yet only two or three weeks later one of these same teachers contributed point 19, showing how word-processing was becoming important for the editing of children's writing in her class.

Evaluation Interviews with Three Course Members

The three were chosen to be reasonably representative of the two course groups: all three were women (only two men attended altogether), one described herself as a 'lay person', neither of the other two had used a disk drive before coming on the course.

All three stated clearly that they had learnt more or less all their technical skills and knowledge of software from coming on the course.

All three said that at the present time (six months after the course for two, and three months after for one) they were using the micro as much or more than they were during the course.

Two of the three singled out my visit to the school as 'very positive'.

Two of the three, when asked for any 'positive comments about the course', mentioned the supportive, friendly group first: 'very friendly so you didn't worry about asking about things you didn't know ... people were willing to help each other ... you were willing to help.'

As a result of coming on the course two of the three have unofficially become the person in their schools with responsibility for micros. For example, they have taken responsibility for choosing the software coming free from the DTI offer, and for 'campaigning for things at the PTA'. Of these two, one offered as a positive comment, 'The support given by you and the people attending the course to follow up work at school.' She has developed a strategy for INSET for her colleagues: 'It's a shared role — I'm anxious that it doesn't become mine.' She said that not only had *she* learnt how to copy discs, 'the others can do it as well' .... She has suggested documenting the school software and sees this as a strategy for keeping everyone involved: 'I've made myself sit back and wait for other people, although it would have been quicker to do it myself.' As an extension to this she has organized for staff to take turns in presenting a piece of software to the others at staff meetings — she herself doing the first presentation, the Head doing the second, and someone else now lined up to do the third. She saw the course as having been of fundamental importance: 'Without that course we wouldn't be doing what we are doing in our school.'

The enquiry dimension of the course seems to have been important in developing the group dynamic outlined above. It also emerged more directly:

One said, 'I liked the homework ... it was good to hear what other people thought of the programs.' She had, however, noticed the problems of sharing raw data (a result of the lack of time on the course): 'I think it should have been stressed to people to choose about a minute's worth ... but to select would have involved quite a bit more work.'

Another said, 'I purposefully set aside a time for observing ... it was valuable to do it, but I wouldn't have done it unless you had asked.' She went on to explain that she frequently used a tape-recorder to record children's talk but had found observation better than taping when children were using the computer, because of needing to know what was happening on the screen.

There was also evidence of a substantial change in the way they used the micro in their teaching, which I would maintain was the result of the enquiry process:

One said, 'You made me realize the computer's potential — if you get a program you can use it in different ways —

develop it to fit the special needs of your group.' and 'I wasn't very keen on maths games. I prefer to use it as a word-processor. I feel children get more from it when using it for some considerable time.'

The second said, 'I think it did point out using a micro with a big group — or a whole class of infants for story writing. I wouldn't have dreamt of doing that sort of thing.'

The third (referring to the strategy she is using to involve the staff with using micros) said, 'Part of (the ideas for practical classroom organization) came from sessions talking to each other on the course — but more from staff meetings at school.' She added that both computers were now used, whereas they 'sat more or less unused' before.

The Micro and the Primary Curriculum: 'Added On' or Integrated?

From my visits to primary schools I can report that often the micro is isolated within the classroom, sometimes even outside the room altogether. Typically, children visit it in pairs to spend fifteen minutes working at a simple program which requires them to practise a skill such as multiplication. Sometimes the software has little of interest to offer, other times it clearly has possibilities but the teacher is unaware of the work and unable to help the children make the most of the learning experience. My course members confirmed that initially their own classrooms reflected the same common pattern. When, in the first session, they drew diagrams of their rooms showing the position of the computer in relation to people and furniture, one person commented, 'A psychiatrist would have something interesting to say about this — the micro's about as far away from me as it could be.' We discovered on the course that with relatively little effort the computer can be used more flexibly with varying sizes of group; and that when a larger group is working with the computer it becomes acceptable for the teacher to leave the rest of the class and spend time working with that group (the teachers saw this as an issue of dividing their time equally among class members).

It seems to me that the main problem with micros in education is that they have been 'added on' to the curriculum which already exists, instead of being integrated as part of it. There is nothing new about this statement: attempting to combat the phenomenon has been a central concern for teacher trainers running micros courses. However, it has proved difficult to effect any real change. It is almost as if teachers have instinctively anaesthetized or emasculated the micro: in setting up a system by which pairs of children take turns and tick their names off the list before calling the next pair when their time is up, they have isolated it from the main stream of classroom experience. In effect they have abrogated their profession-al responsibility to judge the quality of the learning experience provided by the software. Pressured to use the computer before they were adequately prepared, they have allowed themselves to believe that 'hands on' (jargon for touching the computer keyboard) must be a good thing because it gives something called 'computer awareness'.

In any case, the advice to integrate the micro into the curricu-lum is not easy to follow. For most teachers it conjures up pictures of acquiring a large quantity of software, viewing it, deciding on its suitability for age and ability ranges, and then planning to have appropriate pieces to back up each learning activity which occurs. It does not help that this software is often thought of in terms of specific content so that it does not have general applicability. Such a massive amount of preparation is clearly impossible on top of the ordinary work load, so teachers have had to come up with a painless alternative. Having established a routine in which the computer is used as an 'extra' activity, they don't seem to like what it has to offer but are prepared to believe that it may do some good and probably doesn't do much harm. At least little Johnny will go home and report that he has used the computer.

It is the rushed and pressurized arrival of the micros which has forced teachers to take defensive action and established habitual patterns of bad practice. The encouraging thing is that, given the enormous gap between what teachers value as good learning experi-ences and the reality of what children are doing with computers, it only takes a little observation to bring about a marked change in a teacher's approach and consequent enthusiasm for the micro as a useful aid to children's learning. Of all the enquiry-based courses I have run over the years these two gave me the greatest sense of course members successfully changing their practice.

In the meantime, software has improved greatly, to the point in summer 1986 where there is quite a large amount of really good software. In particular, word-processors are completely open-ended and can be integrated into the curriculum with very little extra preparation. Instead of being a burden in the classroom the micro can begin to feel to the teacher like an assistant helper. Paradoxically, one of the best and easiest ways of integrating the micro with the curriculum is to make it central and design a whole topic around it. An adventure game/simulation, for instance, can become the springboard for a wide range of work in science, art, writing, maths and music. Substantial planning will be necessary but no more than for other wide-ranging topic work normally carried out in primary schools.

The Case for Enquiry-based Courses Dealing with Micros in Education

There are already some courses on Micros in Education which include a requirement for a dissertation based on practical research. A particularly forward-looking one is 'Computers in the changing curriculum', which will be run in 1986/87 jointly by the Advisory Unit for Computer-based Education and Hatfield Polytechnic. My own interest, however, is in courses which make enquiry an integral part of the learning process from start to finish, rather than seeing it as a discrete part of the course. So far I do not know of any other enquiry-based courses of this kind which have specifically dealt with micros in education, although I know that work is being undertaken by individuals choosing micros-related topics of study within more general courses. The latter is not really satisfactory because of the level of INSET needed to institutionalize the innovation of micros in education and establish good practice. I believe that there is a need for courses building on my experience as described here. With six short sessions I was able to make an impact but not really able to involve teachers in more than very rudimentary enquiry in their classrooms. A longer course would provide time to teach research methodology and enable course members to engage in the cycle of data collection, analysis, changes to practice, data collection ... writing up. However, to establish a whole Advanced Diploma in Educational Computing would probably be a mistake, tending to reinforce the unfortunate division between the micro and the curriculum as a whole. Ideally, at the advanced diploma level, I think micros should be dealt with in a substantial unit within the context of a general course.

As I have stated elsewhere (see Somekh, 1986b), case study/action research has a great deal to offer micros in education. Some valuable work has already been done, notably the Hertingfordbury Project under the direction of John Levett at the Advisory Unit for Computer-based Education in Hatfield (see Levett, 1986) and the work of Pauline Minnis at the Cambridge Institute of Education (see Minnis, 1986). However, this has only served to prove the strength of the case. In a nutshell, there is an urgent need for research which looks at the way in which the micro can act as a catalyst for changes in teaching styles by encouraging collaborative group work and autonomous learning. Meanwhile, the urgent 're-medial' job which needs to be done to eradicate bad practice in the name of the micro can best be effected by teachers carrying out research in the context of in-service courses.

Acknowledgements

I should like to thank Ann Holt, Warden of the Cambridge Curriculum Development Centre, for her help in running the courses described in this chapter.

I should also like to thank all the course participants, in particular Margaret Gates of Milton Road Junior School, Jean Lawrence of Isleham Primary School and Hilary Clarke of Coton Primary School, all in Cambridgeshire, for their help in the evaluation.

Note

1 CARN is the Classroom Action Research Network founded by John Elliott in 1977, based at the Cambridge Institute of Education and incorporating the follow-up work of the Ford Teaching Project; TIQL was the Schools Council Programme Two Project, Teacher-Pupil Interaction and the Quality of Learning, directed by John Elliott at the Cambridge Institute of Education between 1981 and 1983.

References

FULLAN, M. (1982) *The Meaning of Educational Change*, Columbia, Teachers College Press.

LEVETT, J. (1986) *Pursuing Pathways*, Hatfield, Advisory Unit for Computer-Based Education.

MINNIS, P. (1986) 'Use of a microcomputer in a primary school: Research diary', *CARN Special Bulletin: Action Research and the Micro*, Cambridge Institute of Education.

SOMEKH, B. (1985) 'An enquiry into the use of quinkeys for word-processing in secondary english teaching', unpublished MA dissertation available from Cambridge Institute of Education.

SOMEKH, B. (1986a) 'Microelectronics in education: The teacher's perspective', *Secondary Education Journal*, autumn.

SOMEKH, B. (1986b) 'Editorial: Micros and action research', *CARN Special Bulletin: Action Research and the Micro*, Cambridge Institute of Education.

STENHOUSE, L. (1975) *An Introduction to Curriculum Research and Development*, London, Heinemann Educational.

Part 4

Continuing to Change

A feature of the 'Developing Enquiry-based Courses: Further Concerns' conference, from which the material for this book was principally drawn, was the extent to which the participants saw the opportunities for continuing development. As teacher educators they saw themselves primarily as practitioners, they shared innovatory ideas, proposed forms of change, examined critically and attempted to make more intelligible features of their own practice. Particularly, they created a climate in which each was encouraged to treat contradictions as a means to gain further and more profound insights.

Each of the three chapters here is quite distinctive in its orientation. What binds them together is that quest for improvement which was so central to the conference.

Whitaker's evaluation of the uses made of the Open University pack, *Curriculum in Action* (a course which has already met with some success in facilitating teacher enquiry), is one which is bound to generate some controversy. The learning stages of users, nominated by Whitaker, will certainly be met with some interest and no doubt will be contested. The stages described as: zero learning; diffident pragmatism; inspiration; committed innovation; undiscriminating use; and rejection, articulate with the fundamental question which the evaluation seeks to answer. The question is posited thus: 'Does new and reflective knowledge lead to the "unlearning" of hitherto unquestioned knowledge?' Interestingly, the stages are not characterized as a smooth and upwardly proceeding continuum, but rather as a path of uncertainty along which the learner both progresses and lingers. The evaluation does not claim to be of a summative kind, but rather purports to raise issues in ways which will lead the users of the materials to regard them afresh.

The second chapter in this section explores some issues in practitioner research by investigating thirty projects related to parent/teacher/parent communication. Again these were undertaken as part of an Open University course which was strongly oriented to teacher enquiry. Three issues are identified as a result of examining the projects: ethicality, methodology and researcher roles. They are discussed with respect to the ways in which they affect the main stages of the research process i.e.:

(a) selection of topic;
(b) access;
(c) choice of methods;
(d) fieldwork;
(e) recommendations; and
(f) dissemination.

The intersections of the issues with the research stages are presented as a matrix and discussed by way of a number of examples drawn from the projects.

In contrast, Winter's chapter is a proposal rather than an actuality. It provides a powerful theoretical basis for the notion that teachers may become more reflexive in their thinking if they create fictional accounts of practical experience. The chapter argues that having written the account the learner reflects upon the experience of having written the account. As a means of concretizing the argument Winter offers a piece of his own writing and evolves his own critique. Significantly, for Winter, the action does not rest here. Following personal introspection the account is then proffered to fellow practitioners for continuing interrogation. This process allows those taken-for-granted features of the writer's educational understanding to be challenged and confronted. Indeed this is true of all the pieces of work outlined in this section; we are encouraged by these writers to tolerate uncertainty a little longer.

13 Curriculum in Action:
An Approach to Evaluation

Jean Whittaker

Issues relating to the in-service education of teachers are receiving a great deal of attention in the UK. These issues are political and professional; it is not easy to separate them, the one affects the other as circumstances change. Factors like smaller school rolls, tighter control of the ways in which monies are allocated and spent and the changes in the economic circumstances of teachers relative to other professions have resulted in a less mobile and more stable teaching force so that changes to schools have to be brought about largely from within by involving existing staff rather than through new appointments to the staff. This situation exists at a time when the introduction of major changes to the structure of secondary public examinations taken at the age of 16 years (the end of compulsory schooling) is imminent. In addition, societal and professional pressures are demanding a different kind of secondary school curriculum — one which is seen to be more relevant to life out of school and after pupils have left school. The primary school curriculum is also being placed under the microscope, as part of the same call for greater accountability. For both phases of schooling, this is manifest in the current pressure for a national curriculum which all children would study.

These are only some of the factors and it would not be appropriate to discuss them and the accompanying host of important issues here. It is, however, sufficient to indicate that teachers are looking for in-service activities locally, regionally and nationally to help them make changes to their practice in their schools and classrooms. These needs, therefore, are the starting points of a study which will evaluate teachers' learning from in-service education, the progress of which this chapter reports.

Cane's (1969) definition of in-service education, 'those courses and activities in which a serving teacher may participate for the purpose of extending his professional knowledge, interest and skill', is pertinent. The courses and activities are, therefore, potentially valuable means for improving the quality of teaching and learning in schools through upgrading and updating the knowledge and skills of teachers.

It is important to include both 'courses' and 'activities'. The former term is well known and the latter makes legitimate those forms of in-service which may be undertaken independently, for example, *The Curriculum in Action: An Approach to Evaluation* (Ashton *et al.*, 1980) pack of teacher materials. They encourage teachers to examine their practice by investigating the processes taking place in their classrooms through focussing on the six, apparently simple, questions that underpin *Curriculum in Action:*

1　What are the pupils actually doing?
2　What are they learning?
3　How worthwhile is it?
4　What did I (the teacher) do?
5　What did I learn?
6　What do I intend to do now?

to guide the teachers' observation, reflection and action. These questions form a structure and, as the users work through them, skills of evaluation are developed using 'progressive focussing' procedures. A strength is that the teachers choose what to observe, when to do so and for how long. Focussing on the process is not content-free but is sufficiently flexible to be applicable to the curriculum of all classrooms and lectures; workshops and seminars; primary and secondary schools; colleges and universities.

Curriculum in Action recognizes that teachers evaluate as a regular part of their working day even though much of the evaluation is intuitive and not recorded. It is clear, however, that teachers can find time to record observations, and that, for some, this leads to increased reflection. Subsequent analysis of these recordings permits teachers to think about and learn from their practice so that decisions about changes of practice are likely to be more informed and less haphazard:

> This helped them to make discoveries that increased their understanding of their pupils and led to changes in their teaching. (Unit 2, Block 2, page 6)

Eraut (1985) examines 'knowledge creation' and 'knowledge use' by school teachers and other professions:

> The teacher has no time at all to reflect. Choices made during the preparation of teaching may be decision-governed, but those made during the course of, teaching are largely intuitive. The pressure for action is immediate, and to hesitate is to lose. The whole situation is far less under control. To adapt a metaphor of Marshall McLuhan's, action in the classroom is hot action, while action in the consulting room is usually rather cooler.
>
> Where the action is cool, the consideration of new ideas is much more feasible. There will still be pressures of time, but there is less direct interference between deliberation and action. There is more scope for limited trial and experiment. Personal style is less pervasive than in performing occupations like teaching, though still not unimportant. Where the action is hot, however, people have to develop habits and routines in order to cope; and self-awareness is more difficult as there is little opportunity to notice or think about what one is doing.

It is my contention that experience gained as a result of using *Curriculum in Action* in:

> developing evaluation and self-awareness skills;
> analyzing observation;
> assessing learning;
> stating and testing hypotheses;
> developing the curriculum;

brings about a 'cooling' of action and produces a more thoughtful reflective teacher, through this additional and 'new' knowledge and understanding. Cronbach *et al.* (1980) suggest that new ideas affect decision-making indirectly, often without acknowledgement. They are used interpretively rather than applicatively and influence people by introducing new perspectives.

This links with those parts of the evaluation processes of *Curriculum in Action* which encourage deliberate reflection over a period of time. These are essentially pragmatic and emphasize the part played by first-hand experience and subjectivism along with the individuality of each, that is, classrooms and events. On other occasions the impact is immediate, where adjectives like 'earth-shattering' and 'mind-bending' are appropriate and accord in intensity with the profound experiences Foshay (1986) describes. In a recent paper he compares his 'spiritual' components of the curriculum with Maslow's (1968) and Bloom's (1981) 'peak' experiences, after which teachers are never quite the same.

It is a tenet of the IT-INSET (Initial Training and In-Service Education and Training) project whose personnel were also course writers of *Curriculum in Action* that we

> learn how to do something by doing it ... and that it is vastly more powerful than listening to lectures on curriculum theory. (Ashton *et al.*, 1983)

This was written with reference to teachers evaluating and developing the curriculum of their classrooms. In their subsequent analyses teachers define categories and progress to making judgments of value about the curriculum. These, too, are the beginnings of personal theorizing through which some teachers make 'better' sense of their classroom practice. If this goes alongside a propensity to change practice, it will affect the quality of children's learning. For those enrolled on award-bearing courses, to fulfil requirements of written assignments, support is then sought from published theory. This theory is derived from practice and the level of learning and understanding is likely to be 'deeper'.

The report which follows represents the progress of the evaluation to date. The emphasis is upon the research strategies and the reason underpinning their application. Some early data are also presented.

The Study

This study, which has its roots in 'illuminative evaluation' (Parlett and Hamilton, 1972), starts in the practical mode by helping teachers to evaluate their own practice and classroom curricula, from which 'theory' is gradually and systematically being derived and refined or 'grounded'. The study's objective is to help them become more effective teachers and is examining three key questions:

1   What are the effects on the thinking and learning of teachers of observing, recording and analyzing their observation of the curriculum of their classrooms?

2 What is the nature of their thinking and learning?

3 What are teachers' perceptions of the effects of their observation, recording and analyses and of their subsequent thinking and learning on their classroom practice?

The study has two additional, specific objectives:

4 To see whether it is possible to describe the stages (and the possible links between them) of teachers' professional development, gained through in-service courses and activities;

5 To develop and explore the use of interactive video as a research tool, particularly in its contribution to the examination of the three research questions.

The Sample

This study draws on the reactions and experiences of many teachers and students who have used the *Curriculum in Action* materials and their evaluation processes. In some cases they had the opportunity to meet regularly in groups to discuss the progress of their evaluations and other related issues. These may be regarded in the nature of a pilot study. The main study, which is not yet completed, is based on three groups:

(i) the first group of teachers has been convened by an LEA (local education authority) adviser: it is a non-award-bearing course;

(ii) the second is using *Curriculum in Action* under the guidance of a convenor from a higher education institution and is also non-award-bearing;

(iii) the third group of teachers is using *Curriculum in Action* as part of an award-bearing course (In-service BEd) which has been convened by a teacher educator.

These distinctions are important because of:

(a) the demands of submitting written assignments (as part of award-bearing courses) and their effects on sustaining commitment to the activities associated with the course or group, as well as those of a full-time teaching post and personal and family life;

(b) the status and professional role of the convenor of the course or group;

(c) the nature of written comments and discussions at group meetings, where honest reporting by teachers of the curriculum in action in their classrooms can be threatening. They could affect future career opportunities.

The categories of data being collected and which reflect the research questions are:

(i)   indicators of teachers' perspectives and the curriculum of their classrooms;

(ii) indicators of their thinking, learning and studying styles and habits;

(iii) indicators of teachers' personal, professional and biographical characteristics; previous and present career details and future aspirations; their propensity for and ability to change practice.

Indicators of Teachers' Perspectives

The teachers have *written comments on three pieces of pupils' writing and three photographs taken in classrooms.* All the teachers wrote about the same pieces of writing and then commented on the group of photographs appropriate to the phase of schooling in which they are currently working. This task was undertaken at the beginning of the study in order to provide some base line information on each teacher's initial understanding and perceptions before the effects of the evaluation processes of *Curriculum in Action* have become internalized. This information will contribute to means whereby changes of 'perspective' (Becker *et al.*, 1968) are detected. A similar task will be undertaken when the teachers have completed working through the *Curriculum in Action* materials and applying the six questions to their work in school.

A *video recording* has been made as each teacher, in the sample and taking the part-time In-service BEd degree course, talked to the group about his/her work in school. The teachers chose the precise aspects of their work which they wished to present; whether or not to include photographs of their classrooms and schools and/or examples of their pupils' work and, if so, which. The teachers were asked to prepare this towards the end of the bridging course which precedes the commencement of the degree course, so that they were given adequate time to collect together appropriate materials and examples. Apart from the contribution that it makes to this study as additional base line information, the activity served as a means of teachers getting to know each other and the schools in which the course members worked.

As the teachers apply the six *Curriculum in Action* questions, their recordings and analyses of their classroom observations, in effect, form a diary and thus provide a rich souce of data for this study. Fulwiler (1978) encourages the keeping of 'journals or intellectual diaries' which contain records of what has been taught, writers' feelings and values as they reflect about concepts and issues, and ideas for applying what has been learned.

Each teacher will be *interviewed*, during which an interview guide will be used to explore the teachers' perceptions. An interview guide (Patton, 1980) permits an easy conversational style of interviewing and ensures that the same topics are raised for discussion in each interview. It is 'especially useful in conducting group interviews', these may be used with two groups of teachers in the study sample. The items in the interview guide probe the changes of practice which have already been implemented and the justifications for retaining established practice. All teachers will be interviewed again at the end of the study. The items in both sets of interviews and the analysis of comments and discussions take cognizance of the facts that teaching is a 'creative' activity and that the teacher is a 'manager' of pupils' learning. Schon's (1983) concept of the 'reflective practitioner' (a term which includes teachers: see Eraut, 1982) is relevant here:

> Managers do reflect-in-action, but they seldom reflect on their reflection-in-action. Hence this crucially important dimension of their art tends to remain private and inaccessible to others. Moreover, because awareness of one's intuitive thinking usually grows out of practice in articulating it to others, managers often have little access to their own reflection-in-action.

It is acknowledged that reliance is placed on self-reporting and what the individual teacher chooses to make 'public'. Early results suggest that the latter may be a significant criterion in the construction of operational definitions of the stages of professional development.

Indicators of Teachers' Thinking, Learning and Studying Styles and Habits

Various means are being used to elicit teachers' ways of thinking and learning (including aspects of 'unlearning') and their approaches to studying. Their views about the purposes of in-service courses and activities, that is, what in-service *is* and its effectiveness, provide a link with their reported changes in practice.

The Approaches to Studying questionnaire (1983) derived from the work of Pask (1976), Svensson (1977) and Entwistle and Ramsden (1983) has sixteen factors which permit the identification of groups of teachers with similar profiles on the following criteria:

approaches to learning and learning strategies;
levels of thinking;
attitudes to, motivation for and styles of studying.

These groups will be used as a basis for the analysis of other indicators. Another comparison for those teachers in the sample taking the award-bearing courses is the degree class awarded. The questionnaire has been developed from work concerned with the prediction of academic success. Norms are available for students taking first degree courses on a full-time basis and either immediately or shortly after leaving school. Teachers taking part-time, award-bearing courses, for example, In-service BEd degree courses, are different. Besides being older, their professional experience should contribute to the degree results gained. A separate part of the study is a comparison of this group, on the factors of this questionnaire, with a larger group of teachers who have taken the part-time In-service BEd degree course: it will attempt to establish norms for teacher students and to assess whether they perform differently from younger, pre-service students.

Interactive Video

The use of interactive video as a research tool is novel. For the purposes of this study, a computer assisted interactive video (Rhodes, 1984) has been made using extracts from videos taken in classrooms and focussing upon questions which are derived from *Curriculum in Action.*

All teachers will be asked to work through the program and, apart from teachers' responses to the set of questions about each of the four video extracts, the computer will track how each teacher uses the program, for example, which parts are viewed again and, perhaps, several times. It will provide additional insights into their study habits, learning styles, their disposition to take action and their reflexive processes.

This interactive video has potential for other in-service purposes. It is sufficiently flexible to form the basis of group discussion in a staff development programme. All four video extracts selected for this particular program would have value as gentle induction into the appraisal process, whether as appraiser or appraised.

Teachers' Personal and Professional Biographies, Their Career Achievements and Future Aspirations

The use of personal biographies provides another set of base line information. Elliott (1982) quotes Spencer Hall who suggests that personal biographies give insights into priorities and preferences, partly because of what the teacher chooses to include. These details will provide another basis on which teachers will be grouped for analysis of other data. They will also contribute to the operational definitions of the stages in professional development.

Stages of Professional Development

In this part of the study, a series of descriptive statements derived from relevant literature and from information given and collected is being used to construct operational definitions of the different stages of professional development which are beginning to emerge. They represent the degree to which teachers have been affected by the processes of evaluating the curriculum in their classrooms (those processes which are implicit in the *Curriculum in Action* materials). Extensive use of qualitative data in interviews with teachers, their comments on photographs and pupils' work, and their responses to questionnaires, is being made. Entwistle and Ramsden (1983) report these methods as being acceptable and cite Marton, Pask and Perry in support,

> No explicit theoretical framework is imposed on the data ... explanatory constructs are hypothesized to facilitate understanding of (in their case) students' approaches to learning.

The method of analysis puts responsibility on the researcher to be guided by the data without preconceived interventions. All the above sources, as well as Elliott (1982) and Foster (1984) recommend that independent judges check analyses; accordingly a validating group to provide this 'second opinion' has been formed. The data are also being used as sources of items for questionnaires and interview guides. Six stages of professional development are identifiable. They describe:

teachers' pedagogical style;

perceptions of their professional role in facilitating pupils' learning;

ability to reflect on what they see in, and record of, events taking place in the classroom;

ability to learn from this new 'practical', and 'craft' (Eraut, 1982) knowledge to change practice.

They draw on and extend the 'levels of implementation' used in the IT-INSET project and, more recently, the work of Peeke (1984) and include:

levels of and their view or definition of thinking, learning and of creativity;

teachers' perception of the effects of in-service courses and activities;

measures of teachers' ability to make judgments and to listen;

teachers' views of what constitutes theory and their ability to theorize.

They derive from reading teachers' comments, scoring their responses to the *Approaches to Studying* questionnaire and applying the six *Curriculum in Action* questions to my work with them and other groups, outside the scope of this study, but who are using the *Curriculum in Action* materials. First, a word of caution, these stages and their characteristics are tentative and represent no more than an intuitive and informal impression. They are derived from numerous statements and, therefore, represent mere summaries. They also await more rigorous and systematic analysis when all stages of the research are completed.

Zero Learners

These teachers on in-service courses appear to be going through the motions, quick to hand back, in this case, the *Curriculum in Action* materials as if to move on to the next in-service courses and activities. They are not likely to have made any visible changes in their classroom practice or the way they relate to their pupils. 'I know my pupils and I know when they understand ... and have learnt something' are typical statements. As group members, there are those who are good contributors with much to say and those who say little unless asked directly.

They view teaching as a directive didactic activity, 'making' pupils fit a 'correct' mould and requiring 'right' answers. In marking and analyzing pupils' written work, they focus immediately on errors. This critical characteristic is difficult to dislodge even when, as part of an in-service activity, they were asked to focus directly on rewarding aspects of good quality in their pupils' work and on 'being positive'. Further, the analyses of these activities revealed little evidence of listening to pupils, much more teacher-talk than was expected and which was of either a procedural or disciplinary nature.

As learners themselves, they like a tight structure and to be in receipt of information from an expert. They rely heavily on description, reproducing the ideas of others, and rote learning. They use anecdotal evidence frequently but rarely analyze or make connections between theory and practice. These teachers are surface thinkers and are likely to judge their own and pupils' learning similarly.

Diffident Pragmatists

This group display willingness to learn and change. They are diffident because the willingness is hindered by actual or perceived lack of the necessary skills and knowledge. They are likely to describe the essential parts of learning tasks by working on small chunks, step by step, until a logical order is achieved. Concentration on guidelines, procedures, anecdotes and description in discussion with colleagues enables these teachers to understand new knowledge. There is still uncertainty, as expressed in typical statements like 'haven't found the answer yet' and in seeking 'cues', when preparing for examinations.

These teachers talk to others about changes in practice and the reasons for doing so. They are able to quote theoretical sources but often the practical and theoretical strands are perceived as being separate. This apparent inability to conceptualize is manifested in inability to recognize the increased understanding gained during classroom observations.

Given time for deliberation and discussion, competence develops through increased confidence which is rooted in successful implementation of changes; thus pragmatism begins to overcome diffidence.

Inspirers

These teachers have made significant changes to their teaching as a result of analyzing their practice. They may have firm views about which aspects of their work might benefit from further evaluation and of the criteria to judge effectiveness. Their view of the task of the teacher is unlikely to be one of prescribing, making, moulding, forcing. They perceive learning tasks as a joint responsibility of teachers and pupils, listening to the pupils' point-of-view, encouraging experimentation and work of quality. What is important is that these teachers believe that they have made changes, and then, 'I realized that my pupils were learning nothing from the course that I had devised specifically for them, so I abandoned it and started again . . . .' From that point onwards, the quality of this teacher's thinking, ability to conceptualize and articulate the links between thinking, theory and action in the classroom was of a different order. These teachers are flexible and make time for others.

They are enthusiastic learners possessing a wide range of skills and abilities including the qualities of being able to abstract, conceptualize and offer imaginative and novel approaches to situations. It is likely that they will think quickly and also 'on their feet' where necessary, switching rapidly from one situation and problem to another. They use experimentation and reflection to create structure and to understand interconnections between theory and practice. As such, their thinking and learning are at a deeper level than that of the 'diffident pragmatists' which in itself is a motivator and helps them motivate others.

These teachers encourage others to participate in in-service courses and activities, often acting as contributors to courses themselves.

Committed Innovators

These are sensitive, highly committed teachers whose personal learning and understanding of pupils' learning have been changed radically as a result of progressive focussing on the processes which take place in classrooms.

They see the role of the teacher as a facilitator of learning, an encourager, a helper, colleague and friend ... they see the act of teaching as an interaction between two equal selves, teacher and learner, in which the more experienced serves as the gentle guide. Teacher educators, therefore, might emphasize the uniqueness of children and should do the same for teachers — whether at the pre-service or in-service stage. Their education should allow them to develop in their own terms, from where they are at present.

Their classroom-based work ensures continuity and progression yet the thinking and purpose of these teachers have changed in a dramatic way — similar to a religious conversion — their professional view will never be quite the same.

This group of teachers are highly motivated and deep thinking. They are capable of abstract, as well as concrete and practical thinking. They can apply lessons learned in one situation to another different one and extend these lessons as part of 'developing theory' based on practical experience.

The next two groups are distinctive: they have used the *Curriculum in Action* materials and rejected them. Their reasons for this are different from those who joined in-service courses and activities but who for a variety of personal circumstances were unable to continue.

The Undiscerning

These users of the *Curriculum in Action* materials share some of the characteristics of the zero learners and rejectors. They apparently have secure notions of what is 'right' and 'wrong'. They expect their pupils to complete work quickly, follow 'correct' procedures, follow instructions and are likely to attribute their lack of success to pupils' lack of concentration or interest, rationalizing that some pupils are 'more responsive' than others.

Some of these teachers are likely to be teaching in a phase of schooling different from that of their initial training. Evidence indicates that they will continue to teach ineffectively and, in some cases, inappropriately even when their *Curriculum in Action* observations present them with indications of 'bad' practice. When questioned, they justify this with comments like, 'well, they (the pupils) get something from it ....' An examination of their *Curricu-*

lum in Action journals reveals responses to some of the *Curriculum in Action* questions with brief literal and often tense comments, for example,

   3 'How worthwhile was it?' (that is, what the pupils were learning), to which a typical response is, 'Very worthwhile.'
   5 'What did you (the teacher) learn?', elicited the response, 'I learned nothing, everything went as expected ....'
   6 'What do you intend to do now?', resulted in, 'Continue as before.'

As learners they will go out of their way to make a favourable impression on the lecturers who teach them to try to find out, obliquely, the details of examination questions. They are likely to push arguments about procedures to trip up lecturers. Being surface learners, they lay emphasis on factual learning and the effort required to memorize facts. They prefer courses to be highly organized and clearly structured because they have difficulty in connecting details and ideas to form an overall pattern.

Rejectors

The final group have used the *Curriculum in Action* materials and rejected them fairly quickly. The process in not for them. 'I can't see the point of knowing (and recording) all these details about limited aspects of my work ... no day is typical ... no observation period is typical ...' is an honest and characteristic comment.

These teachers are likely to be in a position of high status; to have initial training in a phase other than the one in which they are currently working; to admit to having strong principles, which may, in fact, appear to be prejudices rather than principles; to hold strong views of which they can justify only some on logical grounds and to have no time for research or research findings. Their views on the value of in-service courses vary but an extreme position is represented by, 'I don't believe in in-service', a response written across an LEA questionnaire.

They are very honest. They are often regarded as good teachers, good disciplinarians and are respected by their colleagues, their pupils and parents for these qualities. Others do not like them:

children and young people, other teachers, teaching, and they certainly do not wish to be promoted.

To keep the classroom door firmly closed and to hold strong views on the best way of teaching ... are representative of this group of teachers. They see mornings as time to do the 'hard work', like a quiet atmosphere with no movement in the classroom and prefer to stick closely to syllabuses and guidelines.

They reported difficulty in managing to arrange time to make recordings of observations of their pupils and, when they achieved this, the observations were invariably of sedentary activities. Some reported changes which have not, in fact, taken place, others drew upon theory at the planning stage but the actions in the classroom did not match it.

The last point was revealed initially in group discussions but, when challenged, the probing of the group, though genuinely interested, proved to be too threatening and they left. Others' leaving was more prolonged. They unsettled other members of the group by re-echoing such comments as, 'I can't understand what is going on ...' and 'I'm giving it up.'

The information contained in these stages of professional development may be of use to coordinators and providers of in-service courses and activities, particularly as future activities are likely to be increasingly school-based and focussed. Evidence indicates that the evaluation processes of *Curriculum in Action* encourage deliberate reflection in teachers to different degrees (for example, the teacher's statement quoted in the fourth description, inspirers, and those teachers in the fifth, the undiscerning, who report changes which have not taken place). These latter accord with previous research to which Ashton and Merritt (1979) drew attention in the findings of Goodlad *et al.* (1974) and Keddie (1971). In the former, teachers genuinely believed themselves to be employing innovatory practices, when they were not and, in the latter, 'The teachers drew explicitly upon current educational theory in planning their work but their practice in the classroom was so at variance with their stated beliefs and understandings that Keddie described them as operating in two different contexts, the educational and the classroom.'

The experience of convenors working with groups using *Curriculum in Action* has permitted a deeper analysis of teachers' perceptions of the craft of teaching. Their everyday actions appear to be related to routine and intuitive responses which are embedded in 'principles' but which are rarely explicit. To do things in certain ways becomes part of their 'principles' and therefore their 'theories in use' or their 'espoused theories', though, when asked, the teachers may not, at first, be able to articulate the theoretical principles underpinning their actions.

Differences paralleling the stages are discernible, though progress need not be through all the stages in a sequential manner. Rather there may be leaps forward. A tentative explanation rests on factors like:

(i) teachers with different starting points and past experience;

(ii) their different constructions of good teaching, their ability to make sense of their own teaching and then make changes to improve its quality;

(iii) their different understandings of what learning is and how they know if and when it has taken place.

For the first, above, starting points should be an appraisal of what each teacher does well. This approach builds positively on strengths rather than presenting teachers' in-service programmes as 'deficit models' to be rectified. The second point encourages an examination of the components of good teaching. But, would this reflection on the processes of classrooms lead to learning and changes of practice? A subsidiary question which cannot be ignored is whether, and the degree to which, some teachers will experience 'unlearning'. Day (1981) suggests,

> Changing one's teaching style involves deskilling, risk, information overload and mental strain — as more and more gets treated as problematic and less and less is taken for granted.

'Unlearning' is not easy to detect and relies on teachers' honesty in reporting.

From the evidence available, it is clear that there are not commonly agreed definitions of what 'learning', 'knowledge' (to be taught or learned) and 'teaching' are. There are links with these and teachers' styles (and levels) of and ability to think.

Differences emerge when, in developing evaluation skills, some of the activities in the *Curriculum in Action* materials focus on how teachers interpret the action observed in their classrooms: the materials emphasize the dangers of making unsubstantiated inferences. There is evidence from their writing about the photographs and their comments on pupils' work that some teachers continue to make these inferences even after undertaking the *Curriculum in Action* observation and analysis tasks.

There are items on the *Approaches to Studying* questionnaire, teachers' responses to which corroborate these more informal qualitative data. Entwistle and Ramsden (1983) define 'deep' and 'surface' learning approaches, the categories from which these items are taken:

> Students adopting a *deep approach* . . . use meaningful learning strategies, directing their attention towards understanding what is being learnt by relating it to previous knowledge and their own experience in an active and critical way . . . . Deep approaches are related to more complex learning outcomes, better grades and degree results, and higher self-rated performance . . . . By contrast, a *surface approach* involves an emphasis on reproducing facts and ideas — a narrow strategy of rote learning with the limited aim of 'getting by' . . . . The non-academic and reproducing (surface) orientations are related to poorer outcomes.

These provide insights which may contribute to explanations of the observed differences. There are teachers in this study who adopt deep approaches and some who adopt surface approaches. Perhaps a significant consideration for in-service providers and the teachers of such groups should be whether it is possible to move those who adopt a surface approach to a deep one and, if so, how this change might be achieved. Further, is it reasonable to expect teachers who habitually adopt a surface approach, with its implicit view of knowledge, to be able to promote deep approaches in the pupils they teach? Abilities like abstract thinking and being able to conceptualize are not characteristic of surface approaches and, if these have not been experienced by teachers themselves, can they recognize their existence in others (their pupils)?

Currently, there is pressure to improve the quality of education. One such improvement would be for pupils to be exposed to more and more 'content'. Another would be for pupils to adopt deep approaches and acquire the understanding and insights that result from raising the level of thinking and conceptualization.

A dimension which cannot be ignored is the effects on pupils of teachers using the *Curriculum in Action* materials. Some of the reports of observations written by teachers reveal that pupils have gained knowledge and specific skills, and increased in confidence, motivation and independence. All these were attributed to teachers applying the six *Curriculum in Action* questions to their work over a period of time. They also reported changes in the balance of individual, whole class and group teaching and, therefore, a more effective use of their time. They also reported: fewer teacher interventions; more pupil talk; less concern about noise levels; less time spent on repeating instructions as they moved from one group to another; novel and completely unexpected solutions to problems and changes in classroom layout. They appear to be managing and organizing themselves, the teaching/learning process and the classroom environment differently. It is anticipated that further analysis will reveal that their teaching is more effective and that there is an improvement in quality. An urgent need is to find a language which will allow the articulation of these personal testimonies to a wider audience.

References

ASHTON, P.M.E. and MERRITT, J.E. (1979) 'INSET at a Distance', *Cambridge Journal of Education*, 9, 2 and 3.

ASHTON, P.M.E. *et al.* (1980) *Curriculum in Action: An Approach to Evaluation*, Milton Keynes, Open University Press.

ASHTON, P.M.E. *et al.* (1983) *Teacher Education in the Classroom*, London, Croom Helm.

BATESON, G. (1972) *Steps to an Ecology of Mind*, St. Albans: Granda Publishing.

BECKER, H.S. *et al.* (1968) *Making the Grade: The Academic Side of College Life*, New York, Wiley.

BLOOM, B.S. (1956) *Taxonomy of Educational Objectives I: Cognitive Domain*, London, Longman.

BLOOM, B.S. (1981) *All Our Children Learning*, New York, McGraw Hill.

BRUNER, J. (1964) 'Some theories on instruction', in STONES, E. (Ed.) (1970) *Readings in Educational Psychology*, London, Methuen.

CANE, B. (1969) *In-service Training of Teachers*, Slough NFER.

CRONBACH, I.J. *et al.* (1980) *Toward Reform of Program Evaluation*, San Francisco, CA, Jossey-Bass.

DAY, C.W. (1981) *Classroom-based In-service Teacher Education: The Development and Evaluation of a Client-centred Model*, Occasional Paper 9, University of Sussex, Brighton.

ELLIOTT, J. (1982) 'School focussed Inset: Some issues', *British Journal of In-Service Education*, 9, 1.

ENTWISTLE, N.J. and RAMSDEN, P. (1983) *Understanding Student Learning*, London, Croom Helm.

ERAUT, M. (1982) 'What is learned in in-service education and how? A knowledge use perspective', *British Journal of In-Service Education*, 9, 1.

ERAUT, M. (1985) 'Knowledge-creation and knowledge use in professional contexts', *Studies in Higher Education*, 10, 2.

FOSHAY, A.W. (1986) 'A humanistic approach to curriculum theory: One aspect', unpublished discussion paper presented to School of Education, University of Birmingham.

FOSTER, D. (1984) 'Common sense explanation for the educational development of individuals', unpublished paper presented to the British Educational Research Association.

FRANSSON, A. (1977) 'On qualitative differences in learning IV — Effects of motivation and test anxiety on process and outcome', *British Journal of Educational Psychology*, 47.

FULWILER, T. (1978) 'Journal writing across the curriculum', paper presented at the Conference on College Composition and Communication, Washington DC, cited by GLATTHORN, A.A. (1985) in LINK, F.R. (Ed.) *Essays on the Intellect*, Alexandria, VA, ASCD.

GLASER, B. and STRAUSS, A. (1967) *The Discovery of Grounded Theory*, New York, Aldine.

GOODLAD, J.I. *et al.* (1974) *Looking Behind the Classroom Door*, Worthington, Ohio, Charles A. Jones Publishing Co.

KEDDIE, N. (1971) 'Classroom knowledge', in YOUNG, M. (Ed.), *Knowledge and Control*, London, Collier-Macmillan.

KELLY, A.V. (1977) *The Curriculum: Theory and Practice*, London, Harper and Row.

MASLOW, A.H. (1968) *Toward a Psychology of Being*, New York, Van Nostrand.

PARLETT, M. and HAMILTON, D. (1972) 'Illuminative evaluation: A new approach to the study of innovative programmes', reprinted in TAWNEY, D. (1973) (Ed.) *Curriculum Evaluation Today: Trends and Implications*, London, Macmillan.

PASK, G. (1976) 'Styles and strategies of learning', *British Journal of Educational Psychology*, 46.

PATTON, M.Q. (1980) *Qualitative Evaluation Methods*, Beverley Hills, CA, Sage.

PEEKE, G. (1984) 'Teachers and curriculum changes', *Journal of Curriculum Studies*, 16, 1.

RHODES, D.M. (1984) 'Computer assisted video instruction in the high tech academy', paper presented at the Sixth International Conference on Higher Education, Lancaster.

RHODES, D.M. (1985) 'Some observations on designing, producing and implementing computer assisted interactive video', paper presented to the Association for Educational Communications and Technology, Anaheim, California.

SALJO, R. (1975) *Qualitative Differences in Learning as a Function of the Learner's Conception of the Task*, Gothenburg, Acta Universitatis Gothoburgensis.

SCHON, D.A. (1983) *The Reflective Practitioner*, New York, Basic Books.

STENHOUSE, L. (1975) *An Introduction to Curriculum Research and Development*, London, Heinemann.

SVENSSON, I. (1977) 'On qualitative differences in learning III — Study skills and learning', *British Journal of Educational Psychology*, 47.

WALKER, R. and ADELMAN, C. (1975) *A Guide to Classroom Observation*, London, Methuen.

14 Practitioner Research in School Management: An Analysis of Research Studies Undertaken for an Open University Course

Margaret Preedy and Colin Riches

'While in recent years there has been a range of research activities in the field of education ... there is a dearth of literature on *how* research is conducted in educational settings' (Burgess, 1984, p. 7). To help remedy this deficiency Burgess asked a number of people to write autobiographical accounts of what 'doing research' meant to them. This discussion is an exploratory biographical examination of the research process engaged in by a number of students who completed short research studies, with a managerial focus, on teacher-parent communication in secondary schools.

The course for which these studies were produced is the final part of the Open University's Advanced Diploma in Educational Management. Each student is required to write reports on three small-scale investigations undertaken over an academic year. Students have to select their topics from within four main areas (management of the external environment, leadership and organization, management of the curriculum and the management of human and material resources) and, with tutorial guidance, decide on the scope, objectives and methods of each particular project. The project reports under examination here are within the area of managing external relations. The topic was to 'investigate the written and/or face to face methods of communication used in contacting parents of pupils (or students) in an educational institution', but the title could be modified in consultation with the tutor. Students engaging in this (and other) projects were assisted by a methodology handbook (Open University, 1984a), a project guide (Open University, 1984b) and two associated course readers (Bell *et al.*, 1984; Goulding *et al.*,

1984). They had also studied at least two courses related to educational management as part I of the Diploma.

Burgess required researchers to give an account of 'the formal and informal processes of doing research alongside technical procedures — what actually happens in terms of success and failure and discovery during a research project' (Burgess, 1984, p. 9). They were given key questions to answer such as: 'What was the origin of the project?', 'What were the research aims and objectives?', 'What form did the research design take?', 'How was access obtained?', 'What methods of social investigation were used?', 'What form did field relations take?', 'What was the relationship between data collection and data analysis?' 'What was the role of theory in the project?', 'What ethical problems were confronted?', 'What form did data dissemination take?'

Students doing projects for this Open University Diploma are encouraged to conduct a similar evaluation in the process of planning and conducting their investigations. Our examination of students' research and their comments on the research process consists of interpretations and analysis at second-hand, but has certain advantages (over Burgess's accounts) of comparison, a broader overview and distance from the research setting. The students worked with some special opportunities and advantages, particularly as regards institutional access (nearly all were teachers in the schools they studied). They also had a number of constraints and difficulties — some of which will be explored below — notably limited time and resources. Despite these restrictions, some very useful studies were produced which caused the researchers and others in their respective institutions to look more closely at management practice relating to teacher-parent communications.

The aim of this study is to explore some of the issues which arose for practitioners engaged in small-scale research projects, conducted within quite tight time schedules. In our investigation of some thirty projects, we have identified three broad but overlapping issues: (i) *ethical* issues, i.e. the consideration of moral questions centering on duty and conduct in relation to the various stages of research; (ii) factors relating to the *research paradigm* and/or approach used. The particular approach to research and the style employed — ethnographic, survey, experimental — will reflect the researcher's operation within a particular research tradition — positivism, naturalism or reflexivity (or the implications of the fact that 'the researcher is part of the social world which he studies' (Hammersley and Atkinson, 1983)). This has relevance to the selection of a field of study, the research process and its outcomes; (iii) the *researcher's role*: this is closely related to the notion of reflexivity. 'All social research is founded on the human capacity for participant observation. We act in the social world and yet are able to reflect upon ourselves and our actions as objects in that world' (*ibid.*, p. 25). By including the researcher's own role within the research focus we can reflect on the impact of the investigator's involvement in that research process. If these three areas are arranged on a vertical axis and the various stages of the research process on the horizontal axis this gives a matrix in the following form:

	Stages					
Issues	*(a)* Selection of topic	*(b)* Access	*(c)* Choice of methods	*(d)* Fieldwork (data collection)	*(e)* Recommen- dations	*(f)* Dissemi- nation
1 Ethical 2 Research paradigm 3 Researcher's role						

The rest of this chapter will examine how the issues identified affect the main stages of the research process on teacher-parent communications. These issues have important implications for the conduct and outcomes of small-scale practitioner studies in general as well as for research undertaken in connection with a particular course.

Ethical Questions

Selection of a Topic for Investigation

At various stages in the selection and development of a research project a number of ethical principles need to be observed. Simons (1984) has identified the following criteria in relation to studies of school self-evaluation, but they apply generally to all topic areas: participants need to be assured of impartiality and confidentiality linked to some participant control, to have a measure of collaboration and negotiation about the way data are to be selected and used, and to know that the researcher will be held accountable to them in agreed ways.

Deciding a topic or 'problem recognition' (Verma and Beard, 1981) presents ethical as well as practical problems. One may identify an area of investigation which is feasible and related to practice (a requirement for our students), but it may be too sensitive to pursue because it touches on a known problem area in a school or entails criticism of particular policies or colleagues. Fortunately, teacher-parent relations is a less sensitive research area than some others, for example, the effectiveness of senior management. However, a number of ethical problems did confront students: staff and parents were often asked to evaluate the quality of home-school communications. Although confidentiality of data and anonymity might be assured there can be real difficulties in asking staff/parents to make judgments on the effectiveness of communications which they may initiate or receive (or otherwise!). At the time when this project topic was selected there was the particular problem of asking for parent views when parent-teacher relations were under stress because of teachers' industrial action.

Access

While it is comparatively easy to identify a suitable area of enquiry this does not necessarily ensure that participants will cooperate or that access will be given unconditionally and without any contamination of the evidence. 'Even the most friendly and cooperative gatekeepers or sponsors will shape the conduct and development of the research' (Hammersley and Atkinson, 1983, p. 73). Once physical access has been gained, the investigator is often faced with a moral dilemma: cooperation is a moral necessity but this can lead to restrictions on the focus of the investigation. The projects which we have examined often refer to their reliance on the goodwill of immediate colleagues, the head of the school and parents, and the importance of gaining access to respondents' time and openness. Few accountable authorities can give completely open access to privileged/confidential information within a school: the boundaries of the enquiry have to be negotiated with participants, who usually need to be convinced that there is some pay-off for them in giving access. While most of the project reports on teacher-parent communications identified the school used but preserved anonymity for those within it, many participants must have realized that, in practice, actual personnel identification of some data could not be ruled out. One strategy for encouraging access — particularly to parents — was to try to explain that the exercise was part of the school's effort to make home-school communication more effective (in one case the head rather than the researcher wrote an introductory letter to parents). Although almost all researchers mentioned that the exercise was also for their own purposes, the identification of possible outcomes in order to gain access can have ethical implications as well as contaminating the evidence. 'Doing the right thing', but perhaps giving the wrong or selective reasons for doing it, is an unresolved ethical problem in this type of research. 'Negotiating access is a balancing act. Gains and losses now and later, as well as ethical and strategic considerations must be traded off against one another in whatever manner is judged to be most appropriate' (*ibid.*, p. 72).

Selection of Method

Generally speaking, the greater the use made of qualitative methods of research, such as in-depth interviews, detailed observation (for example, of colleagues' interactions with parents) and diary exercises, rather than quantitative ones, such as anonymous questionnaires, the more acute are the ethical issues which arise. The face-to-face accosting of reality which takes place in the use of qualitative methods may expose sensitivities. For example, how fair is it to ask parents to comment critically on teachers' abilities to communicate effectively through school reports on their children's progress, when good relationships remain important after the research has ended? It requires great faith on the part of the interviewees to believe that nothing of what they say will be passed on. A number of the studies mentioned that questionnaires were used to protect anonymity and thus to encourage truthful responses. The need to be sensitive to the concerns of participants was highlighted by one researcher who was asked by a newly-appointed head not to interview parents as school-home relations were under particular strain because of industrial action by staff.

Fieldwork

A sensible approach to engaging in fieldwork is to recognize the weaknesses as well as the strengths of a particular research process in the field. A special difficulty (as well as opportunity) for 'insider'-researchers is that they have a wider knowledge of colleagues and of the background factors which would be unknown to researchers from outside. During the fieldwork, confidential, sensitive or revealing information may come to light which could affect future relationships with colleagues, for example, a strong view expressed by a senior member of staff to his head (who was doing the research) that if parents were kept closely informed by staff about what was happening in the school then parent teacher meetings or 'drop ins' should be unnecessary. By the same token, respondents faced problems of tempering the truth in the knowledge that fruitful professional relationships had to continue after the research had been completed. Problems of personal ethics arose again in dealing with parents especially those who were disadvantaged or who may have seen the school and researchers as being in positions of power, and thus were vulnerable in the context of the interview. Johnson (1984, p. 15) suggests that 'respondents become vulnerable during the course of extended sympathetic interviewing . . . . The writer makes it a rule . . . when conducting home interviews with parents, not to leave respondents in a worse state than that in which she found them.'

Recommendations

One gains the impression from reading the reports that those in authority in the schools involved were genuinely looking for findings which would result in helpful recommendations for improvement. Many suggested changes were proposed on the basis of evidence from the research, for example, 'instructions on how to prepare for parents' evenings to be devised by senior management in consultation with the teaching staff'; 'the one worrying sign of tension was the respondents' [parents'] feeling that they should have more say in what goes on in the school; this definitely requires an examination in depth' (a comment on a primary school by an 'outsider'-researcher); 'a significant number of parents found the complexities of option choices difficult to comprehend . . . face-to-face contact with parents is essential if complex information is to be communicated successfully'. Some recommendations were critical of colleagues and school policy, or were out of line with the ethos of the school or with generally accepted notions about the professional role of teachers and the extent to which there should be parent participation, for example, on curriculum matters. Other types of recommendation on administrative and practical areas of teacher-parent communication (for example, more frequent parents' evenings, better organization of these meetings) are subject to fewer ethical problems than proposals for change which entail more radical criticism of school policy or staff performance. The frankness of the recommendations made is likely to be related to the extent to which the findings of the report are to be disseminated.

Dissemination of Findings

Most project reports mentioned dissemination in the school concerned, though sometimes only the head would see the findings — and often the report provided a useful input to management decisions about increasing the effectiveness of home-school communications. Restrictions on the communication of findings to local education authorities (LEAs) and parents were usually imposed. Only one of the projects mentioned, in its letter to parents about the research, that the study findings would be available for them to see; another said the report would be available to the LEA as well as the school. The question of the moral/professional accountability of the researcher applies here too, but the ethical issues are less acute if all parties have agreed beforehand on the degree of dissemination. However, this does not overcome the personal frustration for researchers who feel that findings have application and relevance to some who have been kind enough to take part, but have not had the benefit of seeing the report.

Research Approaches and Paradigms

Selection of Topic

Researchers work within a framework of fundamental concepts and structures (paradigms) which help to define what will count as problems in research. The very categories of research are fixed by the paradigm. For example, those taking a positivistic approach have a view of the importance of scientific method, with standardized procedures which put various hypotheses to the test. There will be a tendency for such researchers to choose topics which are most capable of quantitative analysis through the use of survey methods and other relatively rigorous types of measurement. The study of parent-teacher communication proved popular for a variety of reasons. A model questionnaire on the topic was presented in the course, quantification of results was encouraged for enquiries in this field, but in reality the method chosen could well have been a function of more practical constraints such as limited time and re-sources, school term dates and Open University cut-off dates for assignments. Useful, if limited, data could be obtained using the positivistic approach, although some students presented a critique of the paradigm within which they worked (see below).

Access

The effect of selecting the teacher-parent communication topic with considerable use of survey methods meant that access was easier than if students had gone for in-depth ethnographic studies involving long-term intensive observations of colleagues/parents. Students adopting such a methodology did not face major pro-blems of gaining access to sensitive data. Some project reports, though, noted that the parents' 'grapevine' as a channel of informa-tion about the school was an important but relatively inaccessible source of data (see also East Sussex LEA/University of Sussex, 1980). Questionnaire methods of investigation also leave out of account the role of pupils in influencing the parents' interpretations of communications from school. The pupil messenger acting as a gatekeeper is a particularly elusive variable in home-school com-munications, and is not accessible by quantitative approaches.

Methods

We have already hinted at the tension which exists in the reports under review, between positivist/quantitative and relativist/quali-tative approaches, although the research approach is not always made explicit. Detailed considerations such as sample size, represen-tativeness, validity and reliability, objectivity and subjectivity are all related to the methodological stance which is taken, but there are strategies for checking and counterbalancing weaknesses in particular procedures. For example, students are reminded that 'though interviews and observations and even the selection of documents for study, are all likely to be influenced by subjective judgment or personal bias, it is possible to achieve a degree of objectivity by bringing bias into the open' (Nisbet and Watt, 1984, p. 74). Nisbet and Watt also point out the value of using a variety of methods and cross-checking different sources of data (triangulation), but in a small-scale, limited time-span study, this may be at the expense of in-depth application of a single and valuable method. One wonders, too, about the representativeness of small samples. There is also a problem of pupil-stereotyping in the selection of samples, for example, 'the alienated disruptive student', 'the highly motivated cooperative student'.

A major methodological issue is the extent to which the researchers' case studies are relatable to similar situations in other schools. A project report on written communication between school and parents gives a balanced view of this problem:

> It is hoped that the study will fulfil one of the suggested benefits of single event, as opposed to generalizable, research by being of some immediate use, and while not allowing generalization, it may allow staff in [other schools] to relate to the problem and recommendations.

Fieldwork

Multiple variables impinge on the fieldwork process and the researcher has little control over many of them, but they will influence the way in which methodology is applied. Some projects noted the need to modify methods during the fieldwork phase, for example, in the light of time constraints or because events were cancelled due to industrial action. The issue of objectivity/subjectivity was sometimes bought into sharp focus when inexperienced researchers had to engage in fieldwork. The problem of the interview is one example. One student, after commenting upon the difficulty of planning an interview, wrote: 'Throughout the interview it proved almost impossible for the interviewer to remain neutral. I was aware that my choice of question, the use of my voice, the pace of the interview, the physical circumstances and the time of day all affected the interviewee and interviewer.' Researchers encountered problems, too, in the delivery and return of questionnaires to parents by pupils (older boys were the most frequent offenders here!), the only feasible method because of the cost of postage. The problem of bias in the response group thus emerged.

Recommendations

The weight given to different forms of evidence was affected by the research paradigm used, for example, the extent to which respondents were seen as representative of the groups from which they were drawn, and what the researcher saw as legitimate and possible areas for change. Most students were cautious in making recommendations on the basis of limited evidence, and those suggestions which were made tended to focus on organizational and administrative remedies, leaving deeper issues untouched, for example, management style, school ethos, personnel, attitudes towards parents.

Dissemination of Findings

The degree of dissemination of research findings will depend upon the relevance and credibility attributed to the evidence and upon the effectiveness of the machinery for distribution. Critics of either positivistic or ethnographic approaches can be expected to be somewhat doubtful about each other's methods and hence about the conclusions and recommendations based on the use of these methods. However, no matter what the research perspectives might be, the findings of many of the research reports should be disseminated so that their relevance can be assessed and their evidence be made available to a wider research community. There is a need for discussion among researchers about the most appropriate methodologies for investigating management issues in educational institutions. This could lead to the formulation of methodological approaches which can be replicated using similar instruments in different schools (probably on an area basis), and drawing on the research expertise which is developing among practitioners in the schools. Such developments could provide the basis for fruitful comparative studies in school management issues by groups of researchers. They would also be of benefit to individual researchers working alone, who may spend much time in investigating ways of

proceeding which have already been developed and applied elsewhere.

Role of the Researcher

Choice of Topic

The researcher is involved in a two-way relationship with his/her
own institution and the Open University. Researchers need to produce studies which have academic quality and rigour and which also
make an input to management decisions within their own schools.
In choosing a topic researchers have to consider their own current
and future professional agendas, aside from the research study, and
also the perceptions of colleagues. The topic selected may influence
how the researcher's concerns as teacher and his/her broader,
perhaps managerial, role are seen by other staff. The extent to which
senior staff help with or have control over a project focus will vary
with the post occupied by the researcher. There is plenty of evidence from the enquiry that topic choice can be influenced by the
head's own agenda rather than necessarily the researcher's own
interests. For example:

> From the outset the headmaster has taken an active interest
> in the project, seeing it as an opportunity to test parents'
> reactions to the school and also hoping to find out from the
> completed project methods by which parent-teacher com-
> munication could be strengthened.

Access

Here again, the nature of the status position in the school occupied
by the insider-researcher influences the extent of access to colleagues. The researcher has (as we have already seen) an ambivalent
and problematic role vis-à-vis parents. He/she occupies a boundary
position, being seen by parents as a representative of the school, but
also a researcher. This ambivalence is reflected in the letters to
parents, inviting cooperation in the project, which stressed the dual
function of the project: to contribute to a review of school practices
and to project work for the Open University Advanced Diploma.

Methods

The role of the insider-researcher in the school may lead to the use of less sensitive data collection methods, for example, questionnaires and documentary analysis, rather than, for example, in-depth interviews. Elliot (1984) suggests that teacher-researchers tend to do this 'because the latter methods involve "personalised" situations in which colleagues and pupils observed or interviewed find it difficult to mentally divorce a person's position and role as researcher from his/her other positions and roles within the school' (p. 66). Similarly some members of staff acting as respondents in one teacher-parent project 'expressed difficulty in separating the researcher's role from that of the teacher's'.

Fieldwork

This enquiry has revealed the problems of respondents giving answers which they feel they ought to give because of the researcher's role within the school. Parents and staff may give socially and/or professionally acceptable answers and tend to over-report their actual and preferred involvement in home-school contacts. The frankness of respondents and the degree to which they reveal sensitive data, which are not within the public domain of school life, may depend on the researcher's authority/power within the school hierarchy (for example, as senior or junior staff member), and in relation to parents (for example, whether he/she is involved in teaching their child). A particular problem related to the researcher's dual role arises in fieldwork associated with multi-purpose objectives. One such example was an action research project which collected information from parents on third year option choices of their child (requiring pupils' names), as well as asking their views on how the school managed the process. This must surely have an impact on the response rate and the views expressed. There is a need to identify the micropolitical processes which are in operation in such research because they may affect the conduct and outcomes of the research. The collaboration of colleagues may be associated with the extent to which they 'owe the researcher a favour', and participation in the project may give rise to later reciprocal demands on the researcher in his/her day-to-day professional role in school.

Recommendations

Simkins (1985) argues that, 'A worthwhile management project' should go beyond 'the collection and interpretation of data to the development and ideally the implementation of strategies for changing patterns of behaviour' (p. 72). In this course student projects are not engaged in an in-depth analysis of 'strategies for changing patterns of behaviour' for two reasons; first the time-scale does not allow it, and secondly, although most students are based in schools or colleges, the course requirements do not demand this. Students are, however, required to recognize the management implications of their research findings and to make recommendations for management action. There is evidence from these projects that the researcher's role/post in school may impede the frankness of recommendations made. Obviously a junior member of staff is dependent on the cooperation of senior members in setting up the project and may not find it easy to be as frank as he or she would like to be, whereas senior management team members may find it easier to make more radical proposals for change.

Dissemination of Findings

Students have produced evidence that their work has been disseminated fairly widely in their schools; indeed senior staff have often been keen to take up points made in the recommendations, although this is not a guarantee that action will be taken. There is prima facie evidence that when those making recommendations are in a position of considerable power effectively to manage interpersonal relationships then dissemination is likely to be widespread and successful. Conversely, work by more junior staff is less likely to receive a great deal of attention.

Conclusion

It is evident from the teacher-parent communication projects that, in spite of all the limitations of time for fieldwork, recording and analysis, many useful data have been unearthed on which positive management action can be taken. Though one can criticize specific aspects of some of the work, the role of the project work in highlighting the awareness of factors which have management implications makes the activity well worthwhile. The project work has led students to reflect critically on management practice in their own institutions and to develop their research skills in this field. The work has also provided a stimulus to institutional review and analysis of management policy and process.

The discussion in this chapter, centred on the model matrix on p. 218, is a preliminary exploration of issues confronting practitioners undertaking research. Obviously there is considerable overlap between the three broad issues of ethics, paradigm and role. But perhaps this attempt may encourage more sophisticated accounts of research practice in the field of educational management based on a closer examination of the process, which will produce fuller 'confessional accounts' (Burgess, 1984, p. 267) leading to a greater understanding of the particular skills required in educational management research.

Note

This chapter has also been published in Simkins, T. (Ed.) (1986) *Research in the Management of Secondary Education*, Sheffield Papers in Education Management No. 56, Sheffield, Sheffield City Polytechnic.

References

Bell, J., Bush, T., Fox, A., Goodey, J. and Goulding, S. (Eds) (1984) *Conducting Small-Scale Investigations in Educational Management*, London, Harper and Row.

Burgess, R.G. (1984) *The Research Process in Educational Settings: Ten Case Studies*, Lewes, Falmer Press.

East Sussex LEA/University of Sussex (1980) *Accountability in the Middle Years of Schooling: Final Report of the Sussex LEA and University of Sussex Research Project*, Falmer, University of Sussex.

Elliott, J. (1984) 'Implementing school-based action research: Some hypotheses', in Bell, J., Bush, T., Fox, A., Goodey, J. and Goulding, S. (Eds) *Conducting Small-scale Investigations in Educational Management*, London, Harper and Row, pp. 58–71.

Gibson, R. (1984) 'Teacher-parent communication — Holbein' in Goulding, S., Bell, J., Bush, T., Fox, A. and Goodey, J. (Eds) *Case Studies in Educational Management*, London, Harper and Row, pp. 7–33.

Goulding, S., Bell, J., Bush, T., Fox, A. and Goodey, J. (Eds) (1984) *Case Studies in Educational Management*, London, Harper and Row.

Hammersley, M. and Atkinson, P. (1983) *Ethnography: Principles in Practice*, London, Tavistock.

JOHNSON, D. (1984) 'Planning small-scale research', in BELL, J., BUSH, T., FOX, A., GOODEY, J. and GOULDING, S. (Eds) *Conducting Small-scale Investigations in Educational Management*, London, Harper and Row, pp. 5–26.

NISBET, J. and WATT, J. (1984) 'Case study', in BELL, J., BUSH, T., FOX, A., GOODEY, J. and GOULDING, S. (Eds) *Conducting Small-scale Investigations in Educational Management*, London, Harper and Row, pp. 72–92.

OPEN UNIVERSITY (1984a) EP851: *Applied Studies in Educational Management, Approaches to Small-Scale Investigations in Educational Management: A Methodology Handbook*, Milton Keynes, Open University.

OPEN UNIVERSITY (1984b) EP851: *Applied Studies in Educational Management, Project Guide*, Milton Keynes, Open University.

SIMKINS, T. (1985) Review of BELL, J. *et al.* (1984) 'Conducting small-scale investigations in educational management', *British Journal of In-Service Education*, 11, 3, summer.

SIMONS, H. (1984) 'Ethical principles in school self-evaluation', in BELL, J., BUSH, T., FOX, A., GOODEY, J. and GOULDING, S. (Eds) *Conducting Small-scale Investigations in Educational Management*, London, Harper and Row, pp. 123–32.

VERMA, G.K. and BEARD, R.M. (1981) *What Is Educational Research? Perspectives on Techniques of Research*, Aldershot, Gower Press.

15 Fictional-Critical Writing: An Approach to Case Study Research by Practitioners and for In-service and Pre-service Work with Teachers

Richard Winter

Introduction

The following chapter consists of two main sections: an argument suggesting a method of organizing research materials[1] which, it is claimed, is appropriate for case study research in general, and then an attempt to exemplify the method, where I write as a practitioner-researcher engaging in the first stage of formulating a line of enquiry for a piece of self-evaluative action research, an enquiry which has, in fact, since the writing of the chapter proceeded along the lines indicated in this section.

Narrative, Imagination and Theory

> The dialectic between proposition and critique which is personified in the relationship between artist and critic is integrated in the scientific method. (Stenhouse, 1975, p. 124)

This comment by Stenhouse had, until recently, struck me as intriguing but rather mysterious. It seems to link up with what John Elliott (1978) suggests:

> In explaining 'what is going on', action-research tells a 'story' about the event by relating it to a context of mutually interdependent contingencies .... This 'story' is sometimes called a case study .... Case study provides a theory of the

situation, but it is a naturalistic theory embodied in narrative form. (p. 356)

But what I wish to consider in this chapter is: how could telling a story be analogous to providing a theory? Certainly we can see the nature of the problem which 'narrative form' is intended to solve: when practitioners carry out research, the aim is both a description, which will seem plausible because of its richness of 'contingent' detail derived from the situation itself (hence 'naturalistic'), and the creation of a theory, which we may take to be a structure that in some sense lies behind those details and gives them a pattern and a significance in relation to other situations. There is thus a tension for the case study writer between achieving validity through the exhaustive accumulation of details and through the selective organization of those details. Now, given that practitioners writing case studies have limited time and resources, attempts at exhaustiveness will never seem sufficient, so we will always face the question: how can our inevitable selectivity be more than a personal opinion? What procedure might give 'selection' the status of 'theory'? Elliott's answer is: embody theory in narrative form. And it is this idea which I wish to explore: how is writing a story an act of theorizing?

First of all, we may note that telling a story is not merely recounting a chronological sequence, but a skilful process of organizing material to make it 'interesting'. And Elliott is not alone in recommending these skills to the writer of case studies. Kemmis (1980) reminds us that 'case studies work by example rather than by abstract argument ... just as Tolstoy's theory of history is embedded in the story of *War and Peace*' (pp. 136–8). Similarly, MacDonald and Walker (1975) declare:

Case study is the way of the artist, who achieves greatness when, through the portrayal of a single instance, he communicates enduring truths about the human condition. (p. 3)

The notion of an enduring truth within the specific instance is focussed in the idea of the 'typical', and they go on to cite the novelist Zola, who, they say, worked by 'carefully researching the factual settings ... (and) creating characters to represent the social type' (*ibid.*).

But to suggest that a single instance can 'represent' a general type is merely to restate the problem: we need to know: how? And anyway, most case study writers will not be much encouraged by suggestions that they should emulate Tolstoy or Zola; case study writers are not setting out to 'achieve greatness' but to develop fresh and significant insights into their experience. Is it possible, then, to recover aesthetic form from the realm of 'Great Literature' so that we can make it generally available as a method? And if so, by what means?

Walker himself has written an article with the encouraging title 'On the uses of fiction in educational research' (Walker, 1981). He says: 'A story sets limits, it controls what the writer lets the reader see. In this sense a story is analogous to a theory' (p. 157). Here again: theory 'equals' selectivity. But he goes on to say, 'The attraction of fictional forms . . . is that they offer a license to go beyond what, as an evaluator/researcher, you can be fairly sure of knowing' (p. 163) and to propose that fictional forms can be 'adopted' by case study writers as 'a means of disguise' (p. 159) so that they can report their data while protecting the confidentiality of their sources. Walker gives a useful example of this process; but in presenting fiction as a disguise and as a licence to go beyond what one knows, he does not show how the aesthetic structuring of material can constitute a method for theorizing, rather than merely a format in which theory (created by some other process) can be presented; he does not show how a fictional narrative can be a way of exploring the meaning of one's data, a way of understanding. For this we need to turn to other sources.

First of all we can remind ourselves of the long tradition of argument concerning the role of fiction in the development of children's understanding. In the 1960s, David Holbrook's work, based on Freudian theory, recommended 'creative writing' as a quasi-therapeutic process of self-understanding. For James Britton, in the 1970s, one of the three basic 'functions' of language involved in the development of 'writing abilities' was the 'poetic', i.e. the self-conscious and careful arrangement of words, feelings, events, and ideas into a satisfying pattern (Britton *el al.*, 1975, p. 90). And in the 1980s Donald Graves wrote that it was important for children to write about what they knew, though what some children know can best be expressed in fiction. Marion Whitehead (1980) suggests that fairy stories are 'an allegory of the long process of growing up' (p. 50) and 'a clear example of the way in which a culture gives its young, through the medium of the story, an explanation of the way things are in the world and a formula for living and coping in that world' (p. 57). She concludes: 'The conventions of narrative (are) a set of strategies for organizing and reflecting upon experience' (p. 59).

At this point, though, it is clear that the whole argument is not just about children, but about the process of understanding in general; about the way in which a culture makes available symbolic resources for the development of understanding. Thus, Whitehead's theory of fairy stories may be seen as an application of Propp's analysis of folk tales as a finite system of 'functions' (he lists thirty-one) within which any given tale articulates the ultimate overthrow of evil, the remedy of lack or misfortune and the themes of escape, reward, and success (Propp, 1968, p. 92). Further, when Propp says that a folk tale can be studied 'according to the functions of its dramatis personae' (p. 20) — explaining that 'a function' is 'an act of a character defined from the point of view of its significance for the course of the action' (p. 21) — his suggestion is equally true for *any* piece of fictional narrative. For example, a broadly similar argument is presented by Lukács concerning the 'realist' novel: the author's 'perspective' is embodied in a 'typology' of significant ('typical') actors (the characters of the story) who thus act out the 'meaning' of the narrative as the 'plot' of their interaction (Lukács, 1971, pp. 55–6).

Any fiction can be approached in this way. Jane Austen's novels can be thought of as exploring a perspective on feminine destiny: they show how a young woman (character 1), rendered emotionally vulnerable by the weakness or absence of a father-figure (2), is tempted by a glamorous but propertyless young man (3), contemplates the romantic and matrimonial fates of other female characters (4, 5, 6 ...), and finally comes to appreciate the worth of an older, less attractive but economically more stable suitor (7). In A.A. Milne's *Winnie the Pooh* books, each toy/character represents a problematic emotional and moral dimension (piglet: cowardice/bravery; kanga-roo: maternal oppression/independence; rabbit: bossiness; owl: intellectual snobbery ...). The stories explore the relationship between these qualities as Christopher Robin comes to terms with them, so that at the end he is emotionally prepared to leave Pooh (his infant self) behind, and go to school. A similar analysis could be made of a *Grange Hill* book or of an episode of *Kojak*. In this way 'thinking up' a plot and a range of characters in a certain context is analogous to formulating a theory of that context as a set of hypothetical possibilities which are examined by the development of the story (see Winter, 1975).

But stories are not the exclusive realm of 'the novelist'. On the contrary, Barbara Hardy suggests that 'narrative imagination is a common human possession' (Hardy, 1975, quoted in Factor, 1984, p. 35): we do not 'store' experience as data, like a computer; we 'story' it — in anecdotes, jokes, dreams, ambitions and gossip. And we regularly explore experience by playing with its possibilities and varieties in our response to the fictions which so largely make up our 'entertainment', i.e. films, TV, radio and novels.

Barbara Hardy's phrase reminds us that the link between 'storying' and 'theorizing' is the process of imagination, and it is at this point that we can begin to see a truly crucial relevance for aesthetic structuring in the process of practitioner research. What a researcher wishes to do above all is to generate new insights — insights which only the research process has made available — and this is not so easy: it is quite hard to avoid merely documenting one's old, familiar insights with another layer of data, especially given the limits on the range of data imposed by resourcing constraints. And here is the contribution of imagination. For the imagination works by playing. And it does not need a representative sample to play with. It plays with what it has (see Levi-Strauss on art as 'the science of the concrete' — Levi-Strauss, 1966, pp. 16–25). There is nothing frivolous about the 'play' of imagination; on the contrary, as theorists of child development have been saying for decades, play is the mode of innovative understanding. What imagination plays with is the actual and potential discontinuities within experience, using the metaphorical processes of language to manipulate and to reorder our sense of similarity and dissimilarity between the elements in a state of affairs. 'Imagination' designates the process of thinking by which the familiar patterns of experience can be both deconstructed (familiar linkages broken) and reconstructed (unfamiliar linkages made); it is the fundamental notion which refers to the human capacity for thinking new thoughts. In other words, fictional form can set free the case study writer's imagination, to roam, to explore and to discover. It is to this theme — imaginative play as the restructuring of the familiar — that I now turn.

The difficulty with the approach to fiction outlined above (based on an author's perspective as the origin of a typology of characters) is that it seems to perpetrate a number of oversimplifications: (i) it makes a fiction into a sort of allegory, a unified schema of abstractions which ignores the ambiguities, the contradictions and the ironic complexities which characterize both any interesting fictional text and any thoughtful understanding of a situation or series of events; (ii) it makes a fiction into the expression of an author's point of view concerning an external reality; it suggests that the text is an attempt to 'represent' reality; (iii) this in turn seems to claim that meanings are worked out in advance and 'put into' a text, so that what the text means is what the writer intended, which would deny the possibility of creative interpretation by readers. All of these simplifications are inimical to the purposes of case study research by practitioners. Let us try to remedy them one by one.

The Plurality of the Text

A fictional text embodies a plurality of voices — various characters, various voices within a character, various levels of authorial comment (implicit and explicit) — and these voices interact as the play of a dialectic between their inconsistencies: the unity of a fiction is its overall irony. Bertholt Brecht makes this implicit tendency in all fiction quite explicit in his own work. His aim, he says, is 'to make dialectics into a source of enjoyment. The unexpectedness of ... zigzag development, the instability of every circumstance, the joke of contradiction, and so forth: all these are ways of enjoying the liveliness of man' (Brecht, 1974, p. 277). Hence he describes his own texts as 'epic', in the Aristotelian sense that they do not maintain the unities of time, place and character, but constitute a 'montage' (*ibid.*, p. 37) of separated scenes which are related 'in a contradictory manner ... without an ending in which everything is resolved' (p. 279). Brecht argues that a full understanding of *any* phenomena must entail understanding the dialectical play of their contradictions.[2] The 'realist' view of fiction works towards unity, resolution and a comforting sense of how everything of necessity 'fits together', which makes it difficult to think in terms of historical change or of the possibility of things being otherwise. In contrast, the contradictions of non-unified 'epic' fiction show the play of possibility and contingency; its impact is to undermine the familiar sense of necessary cause and effect, and that commonsense unity we attribute to personal motivation. Its effect is to surprise and to shock (*ibid.*, p. 71). But this is not exclusive to Brecht's work: other clear examples would be Shakespeare's plays, *Catch 22*, and any episode of *Cagney and Lacey*. In other words, a fictional text is not to be taken as imparting knowledge about reality but as raising questions about reality, through the unresolved plurality of its meanings (see Belsey, 1980, pp. 91–2).

The Reflexivity of the Text

The complexity and the plurality of the fictional text do not originate only in the contradictions of the real world. Contradictions and non-rational inconsistency are also characteristics of the human personality, i.e. of the writer. And, furthermore, language does not function as a neat logical labelling system but rather as an elusive web of overlapping meanings, metaphors and many-layered symbols. Writers therefore always face two questions: firstly, who is the 'I' that writes? (Consider the psychic mystery glossed over in the following sentence: 'I¹ didn't know how I² was going to write that until I³ found that I⁴ had written it.') And secondly: how do my words — with all their manifold references — relate to my experience or to anyone else's? In other words, the rational unity of the subject who writes, and the transparent clarity of the medium by which my words appear to relate to an external world are comforting, commonsense oversimplifications (*ibid.*, chapter 3). My argument is that, in contrast, unity and clarity are strictly impossible goals for the writer: writing is a struggle — with one's own consciousness and with words — and one that can never fully or finally 'succeed'. Writing is therefore never simply *about* an external world, but always (implicitly at least) also about the writer, and about the writer's attempt to write. The act of writing is always *self-exploratory*, i.e. 'reflexive'.

For this reason, novels are frequently written about writers, musicals about staging a musical, films about film-producers. V.S. Naipaul writes in his introduction to the two apparently descriptive autobiographical sketches in *Finding the Centre* (significant title!): 'Both pieces are about the process of writing' (p. 9). Similarly, in the TV series about a Los Angeles newspaper (*Lou Grant*) the point of each episode is that the newspaper people, whose job is to write about the events of an external world, find that the weekly problem is not merely an external issue but one in which (they come to realize) they are personally involved. To sum up, a piece of writing is always an act of self-exploration: what it 'means' is not known beforehand and 'put into' the text, rather it is discovered by being written. The problem with apparently descriptive writing is that it perpetuates the commonsense idea that writers could and should simply reflect reality; the fictional form, in contrast, draws attention to its inevitable reflexivity, and can thus help to make writers more aware of their own processes of understanding through writing.

Richard Winter

The Creative Reader

Catherine Belsey says: 'The interrogative text . . . invites the reader to produce answers to questions it implicitly or explicitly raises' (Belsey, 1980, p. 91). In Brecht's terms, when readers or viewers appreciate the disunity, the contradictions in a text, they are forced to respond critically, to distance themselves from the momentary emotions of the fictional characters by appreciating the irony of the overall process in which the characters are enmeshed. This, the 'alienation' effect, 'is necessary to all understanding' (Brecht, 1974, p. 71). The implicit contradictions and ironies of the fictional structure provoke an intellectual response, which makes explicit that structure and thereby grasps its implications, possibilities and limits. In this way the reader is called upon to answer the questions raised by the text, and to do so the reader must ask, in Macherey's striking phrase: 'What is it that the text does not and *cannot* say?' (Macherey, 1978, p. 87). In other words: what does the text conceal; and what do those concealments conceal?

But the reader's critical response is more than an imaginative play with the *text*; it is, as it were, also a reformulation of the self. Wolfgang Iser describes the process as follows: the ironies and contradictions within any fictional text mean that there are 'gaps' and 'blockages' in the flow of the text which force readers to collaborate in maintaining its meaning, by attempting to remedy the gaps and apparent inconsistencies from their own experience. Thus 'we have the apparently paradoxical situation in which the reader is forced to reveal aspects of himself in order to experience a reality which is different from his own' (Iser, 1974, pp. 132–3). The ironies, the discontinuities of the multiple-voiced text 'draw us into the text, compelling us to conduct a creative examination not only of the text but also of ourselves' (*ibid.*, p. 141). This is 'the dialectics of reading', which requires the reader 'to formulate the unformulated' (*ibid.*, p. 145).

The idea that formulating a response to an aesthetic structure is a process of self-formulation is neatly exemplified in the following incident. My daughter, aged 2½, was listening to the opening bars of the slow movement of a piece of classical chamber music.

She said: 'What's that music saying?'
RW: 'I don't know. What do you think it's saying?'
Child: 'She's all alone.'
RW: 'Who's all alone?'
Child: 'That little girl.'

238

Conclusion

Let us return to the case study and its problem of imposing form on its data. I began this chapter with a comment by Lawrence Stenhouse:

> The dialectic between proposition and critique which is personified in the relationship between artist and critic is integrated in the scientific method.

We can now expand this. Once the data from a case study have been collected, they will have the form of a plurality of 'voices'. Rather than attempting to synthesize these voices into prescriptive, 'logical' unity — instances classified under 'concepts' — the writer should (I suggest) organize them as a montage, to bring out their ironies, contradictions, discrepancies. In order to do this, an initial structuring is carried out, as an act of 'storying'.[3] This does not call upon readers to accept it, but rather anticipates a continuing analytical response from a group of readers — collaborators, therefore, in the research process — as a critical commentary to be included, later, in the text of the report — a commentary which makes explicit what the fiction leaves implicit, and which seeks to identify what the fiction conceals. In this way practitioner research can be true to its collaborative spirit. Alternatively, the critical commentary may be written by the original writer in the light of reactions to the work from others. In the latter case we have a powerful two-step procedure for 'self-evaluation'. This two-step process — fictional structuring followed by analytical critique — may take place before, during, or after the familiar data-gathering processes of case study research. Furthermore, and irrespective of when or with whom the work is carried out, the procedure is true to practitioner research's spirit of developing professional practice: it returns the research process to the realm of writing, and thus (it has been argued) of a developing self-awareness. Donald Graves says, 'We need to have teachers who write themselves. I just can't stress the importance of that enough' (Graves, 1981, p. 6). And by 'writing' he means that process of taking responsibility for one's words, without which they are not 'owned' but merely 'rented', i.e. controlled by others. (Perhaps this throws light on why practitioner researchers sometimes seem to 'take refuge' in questionnaire returns and transcripts, as though the latter could speak for themselves.)

Finally, I would argue (following Stenhouse's hint) that this fictional-critical procedure can enable writing about a single situation to achieve a theoretical status, in the sense of transcending the familiar pragmatic meanings of day-to-day professional life. To theorize, in this sense, is to address directly the ways in which these familiar meanings (opinions, ideologies, convictions that there can be no alternative) conceal the contradictions, the ironic inconsistencies, in which they are inevitably based. And it is also in this sense that (again following Stenhouse's hint) it can be a central element in a 'scientific method' for small-scale social science research — as long as we accept that social science cannot plausibly aim to make 'accurate objective' descriptions of reality; that social science's project is one of innovative, critical theory.

An Example: Defining a Focus for an Enquiry

The following piece does not explore the results of a study; instead it is an exploration to try to find a focus for a projected study, a focus that would be located, as it were, at the leading edge of my professional anxieties, and not — as can so easily occur — in a 'safe', well-mapped area of interest.

I initially spent some days reviewing possible themes, i.e. those which seemed 'interesting' because they seemed to embody a contradiction. The two which seemed most promising were: (i) the lecturer whose teaching belies his actions; and (ii) the 'theorist' lecturer v. the 'practical' teacher-student. I then had a dream in which I seemed to be involved in a situation of racial conflict surrounding a student union election. This bore no direct relation to any experience whatever, but it was a dream which seemed to be about my professional life — an extremely rare occurrence — and I immediately made a connection between the dream and some rather tense moments during a recent teaching session on 'multicultural education'. Since, in general, dreams are a well-documented starting point both for creative work and for self-analysis, I decided to start there. In the interval between the dream and the writing (about a week) two further incidents — conversations with colleagues — took place, which seemed highly relevant although I was not sure in what way; so they found their way into the text, as well as triggering a memory from about eight years previously.

'INTERFACE'
(*An Everyday Story of Pedagogical Folk*)

(1)   Alan Finkelstein became aware of an elegant hand, fringed with white lace and tipped with red fingernails, waving urgently at the back of the room. He looked up from his lecture notes on 'The concept of multicultural education' and sighed. 'Look, Margaret, I think all this might become clearer towards the end, when I've shown

(2)   how the different factors and arguments fit together.'

     Margaret Richardson smiled sweetly, but was not deterred. 'I just wondered where individual merit comes in.'

     Alan nodded encouragingly. 'Good point. Individual merit *is* very important — as an *idea* that people believe in ....'

     'Oh, good! Because it just seemed from what you were saying that there was no such thing, and I, personally, feel that ...'

     'Listen, man!' On the other side of the crowded lecture-room Winston Edwards punched a black leather-clad arm into the air. 'Sure, it's great for Margaret living in her smug little village to talk about "individual merit", but where I grew up, the first merit a black boy had to have was to keep his head down. Otherwise: *big trouble!*' Winston drew an expressive finger across his throat. 'Man! You guys don't know what the *hell* you're talking about. This whole thing is CRAP.'

(3)   'Okay, okay, Winston; I think I see the point you're trying to make.' Alan felt the perspiration break out on his forehead. 'But can we just get a little more explicit: what do you mean by 'this whole thing?'

     'This lecture, this discussion. It's just words. The real problem

(4)   is out there. It's a problem of power and politics. Talking is okay for people like you and Margaret, because you don't *have* the problem.'

     'Oh, but that's *terrible!*' Margaret Richardson shook her head, as though to dislodge the alien thought. 'Surely, education is all

(5)   about solving problems through reasonable discussion, not power. Otherwise what are we doing here?'

     Alan perked up. 'Great! Now, that puts the whole issue perfectly: what is the relationship between Winston's point about power and Margaret's point about reason? Now, if I can draw your attention back to the lecture notes I gave you, point three is: the

(6)   theory of ideology. "Ideology is a set of social practices which *inserts* us into our life situation ..."'

     His sense of relief was to be short-lived.

(7)   'No, but Alan,' came Richard Evans' broad Welsh tones, 'you

(8)   can't just ignore this. What about *this* situation here? Where do *you* stand? What's the point of this lecture? You're always going on about theorists being "marginal men" but is that enough? Like Winston said: you can't just stand to one side. Otherwise education is just a cop-out.'

Margaret Richardson gave the knife a delicate twist: 'I mean (9) you're the lecturer here because of individual merit, surely?'

Winston groaned. 'This — is — just — un — believable!'

❖   ❖   ❖   ❖

At coffee-time Alan displaced a little emotion by distributing a circular to all the members of the Course Committee, calling a lunch-time meeting at two days' notice.

'Look at this bum', he observed aside to Joanna Summers, as he wrestled to insert yet another sheet of paper into a pigeon-hole from which documents and envelopes of various sizes and hues were cas-
(10) cading like the boughs of a weeping willow. 'Clearly a persistent non-emptier. What the hell do these people do all day? How are we supposed to get in touch with them?'

Joanna laughed. 'Watch it, Alan; that sounds like a bureaucrat talking. Whatever became of that high-minded oppositional radical we used to know?'

'He's just been beaten into a pulp. That "multicultural education" thing was a disaster. It's all your fault, you know: I said all along that *you* should do that session. It would have been so much more *meaningful*.'

'Meaningful! *What* meaning? I've no wish to be a professional *black*. I'm an economist. You find me an economics class and I'll teach them economics, be they white, black, brown, or green with pink spots — fascists and all. But you can't *teach* anti-racism.'
(11)   Listen, Joanna: that is totally depressing. Surely education stands for a set of *values*, not just bodies of knowledge.'

'Oh, sure; education can *stand* for values — like an Annt Sally! Maybe you can take having things thrown at you: you're on the winning side — you only have a Jewish *name*. My black, female head has got too many bruises getting me to where I am. They'll take a long time to heal. Until then I'm keeping out of the firing line.'

'But as an educator you *can't*. Education is the interface between a society and its ideals. Educators *have* to be critics.'

'Not necessarily. They can become bureaucrats. I've got a class. See you.'

✻   ✻   ✻   ✻

At the end of the day, Alan gave his pigeon-hole a last check before leaving, and found two memos. One was a circular:

From: Alec Johnson (Teaching Practice Coordinator)
To: Teaching Practice Supervisors
Dear Colleague,

A lot of second year students seem to be rather confused concerning arrangements for the Teaching Practice Feedback Day on 20 June. In part this seems to be because of poor notice-board discipline. Could you please stress to your students the importance of checking the TP Notice Board *at regular intervals*, so that they do not miss crucial announcements.
Thanks.

A.J.

(12) Alan snorted. The other memo was personal:

To: Mr A.W. Finkelstein
(13) *From*: James Assington-Marshall, BEcon, MSc, LLB
(Registrar, School of Education)
Dear Alan,

I've just had a somewhat disturbing complaint from one of the ladies in your third year curriculum studies group, who alleges that your session today became overtly political, and that she was subjected to personal abuse from another student, without any critical reproof being offered by yourself in response to what she saw as a breach of academic standards and of elementary good manners.

I'm sure you realize how important it is that controversy be carefully circumscribed within reasonable bounds at all times, especially when the local press are so keen to print anything vaguely 'scandalous' about the College on the slenderest of evidence. I know I can rely on your future co-operation in this — we all have our moments of inattention! Please feel free to drop in at any time to discuss matters, if you think it might help.

Jim.

✻   ✻   ✻   ✻

An hour later, Alan slumped in an armchair, sipped a beer, and looked out through the French window into the garden. Thank God his daughter had brought a friend over to play after school: he should be able to relax for a bit before he was summoned to skip, play hopscotch, or make tea.

Suddenly a small black figure in a brilliant yellow dress emerged from behind the shed, and slouched across the lawn. Her face was set in a scowl.

'What's the matter, Edwina? Have you and Rebecca had a quarrel?'

'Rebecca says I can't be the teacher, and it's my *turn*. I've been the little girl for ages and ages and *ages!*'

Alan called out sharply: 'Rebecca, come here!'

As Rebecca, stout and blond, stumped grimly over to the French window, preparing her defence en route, Edwina continued, 'Rebecca says, teachers aren't black people, so it wouldn't make sense for me to be the teacher. It's not *fair.*'

Alan patted Edwina's curly head, and shouted, 'Hurry up, Rebecca!'

＊　　＊　　＊　　＊

Harmony, and the overriding principles of social justice and taking turns having been once more restored — at the domestic level — Alan made scrambled eggs and retired once more to his armchair.

At the far end of the lawn the two girls were playing a skipping game, and the sounds of shrill enthusiastic chanting wafted over to him:

'Javinda! Javinda!
Javinda is a smelly cat!
Javinda! Javinda!'
Alan groaned, and shut the French window.

Analytical Critique

The point of the critique is *not*, of course, to evaluate the literary quality of the story, but to focus on the professional issues expressed, in order (a) to make explicit the contradictions which are implicit in the story; and (b) to identify what the story seems to be attempting to *conceal* (see quotation from Macherey, 1978, p. 87).

The following comments are based on the responses of two readers, as well as my own reflections. The figures refer to those in the margin of the story.

(a) Making the Implicit Explicit (i.e. the elaboration of details from the fictional text to show how they articulate general themes — limitations of space permit only a few examples of the approach.)

(1) 'White lace' and 'red fingernails' suggests that Alan has a suppressed sexual awareness of Margaret, which brings out her ambiguous function in the story: at one level she and Alan are opposed — it is she who precipitates the Registrar's reproof — but when one compares (5), (9) and (11) it is clear that Margaret is nevertheless closely aligned with Alan's stance concerning 'Education'.

(2)(6) Here Alan is trying to escape from the real threats posed by the debate to the power of his role as lecturer, which is ironically related to (4) and (8). Similarly at (3) Alan thinks he can contain the 'political' forces within the framework of 'a discussion', and somewhat ludicrously adopts the stance of the 'neutral chairperson', without discarding his power ('the point you're *trying* to make . . .').

(7) Welsh-ness. The 'ethnic' theme is broader than Alan realizes.

One of the central contradictions is that Alan does not see that his theory of ideology (6) undercuts his own position, and the rest of the story shows the ironic relation between his ideas and his own circumstances (at work and at home). This is the contradiction which lay at the centre of the text and organized it during the process of writing. The story, then, embodies a 'theory' of ideology in terms of a set of dilemmas (see Winter, 1982), i.e. the problematic relationship between education and politics, between what one says and the social position from which one says it.

(b) What the Text Cannot Say

(13) This is the only name in the story which is not a version of one of mine ('Richard-John-Edward-Winter') and I spent a long time constructing it: 'ASSington-*Marshall*' = foolish controller. And yet the contradictions revealed in the story show that this difference (education v. bureaucracy) is not one that can be simply asserted. (Note, for example, the inconsistency between Alan's responses at (10) and at (12).) The carefully constructed naivety of Assington-Marshall's bland tone conceals a deep affinity with Alan's own role, and the other 'bureaucratic' memo is written by *Alec* (cf. *Alan*) *John*son (cf. Richard *John* Edward Winter). This link, then, seems to indicate a contradiction which the text cannot articulate, and therefore the point at which 'new thinking' needs to be done. In other words, it defines a potentially valuable topic for empirical enquiry.

Richard Winter

Towards the Formulation of a Research Topic

The original thought was the contradiction between what one teaches and what one does, and the resistance of social problems to purely educational processes: hence the last scene, where the two children — their own racial tension temporarily resolved — start an implicitly racist chant against an absent schoolmate, 'Javinda'. These were fairly familiar ideas, and, as such, perhaps did not teach me very much. But much less familiar were the contradictions surrounding one's executive power as an educator, one's activities as a course organizer, examiner and rejecter of applicants. This dimension of the story, which had been secondary to the 'race' theme when I started to plan it, grew during the writing, especially in response to the two conversations with colleagues referred to (new 'data'!). This theme now seems much more pertinent, and a point at which investigative work may usefully be developed.

It is interesting that the ending of the story has a wholly negative neatness: Alan closes the window to shut out the sounds of a social problem he now realizes he is powerless to solve. But the problems of my own executive actions as a power-wielding member of an education system cannot be shut out: the role of the bureaucrat cannot simply be distanced by means of a comic name; the bureaucrat too has to be recognized as an internal voice, an inevitable dimension of my own professional self. Another reader has suggested that the memo from Assington-Marshall seems less 'convincing' than the rest of the story, being uneasily poised between realism and farce. This seems to support the suggestion that this passage embodies an unspoken contradiction, and thus points to where further analysis and research could usefully start. This is, indeed, the line of enquiry which I have since begun to undertake, as a piece of self-evaluative/collaborative action research into 'bureaucratic' aspects of my work, namely assessing coursework, and accepting/rejecting applicants for courses.

Acknowledgements

I should like to thank Claudine Nutley, Roy Widgery, Susan Hart, David Ball and the students on the MEd course at the Essex Institute for their contributions to the development of these ideas.

Notes

1 This argument is an elaboration of part of a longer general analysis of the methodolgy for small-scale social inquiry, published as *Action-Research and the Nature of Social Inquiry* (WINTER, 1987a).

2 See WINTER (1987b) for an account of dialectical structure as a characteristic of practitioner research.

3 Although I am concerned in this chapter with the construction of a fictional narrative, much of the argument would be relevant to the constructing of a 'documentary' format, also recommended in MacDonald and WALKER (1975, p. 9).

References

BELSEY, C. (1980) *Critical Practice*, London, Methuen.

BRECHT, B. (1974) *Brecht on Theatre*, 2nd edn, London, Methuen.

BRITTON, J. et al. (1975) *The Development of Writing Abilities (11–18)*, London, Macmillan.

ELLIOTT, J. (1978) 'What is action-research in schools?', *Journal of Curriculum Studies*, 10, 4.

FACTOR, J. (1984) 'The role of the arts in child development', in McVITTY, W. (Ed.) *Children and Learning*, Rozelle, NSW, Primary English Teaching Association.

GRAVES, D. (1981) 'Renters and owners', *The English Magazine*, 8.

HARDY, B. (1975) *Tellers and Listeners: The Narrative Imagination*, London, Athlone Press.

ISER, W. (1974) 'The reading process: A phenomenological approach', in COHEN, R. (Ed.) *New Directions in Literary History*, London, Routledge and Kegan Paul.

KEMMIS, S. (1980) 'The imagination of the case and the invention of the study', in SIMONS, H. (Ed.) *Towards a Science of the Singular*, Norwich, University of East Anglia.

LEVI-STRAUSS, C. (1966) *The Savage Mind*, London, Weidenfeld and Nicholson.

LUKÁCS, G. (1971) *Realism in Our Time*, New York, Harper and Row.

MACDONALD, B. and WALKER, R. (1975) 'Case study and the philosophy of educational research', *Cambridge Journal of Education*, 5, 1.

MACHEREY, P. (1978) *A Theory of Literary Production*, London, Routledge and Kegan Paul.

NAIPAUL, V.S. (1984) *Finding the Centre*, London, Andre Deutsch.

PROPP, V. (1968) *Morphology of the Folktale* (2nd edn) Austin, TX, University of Texas Press.

STENHOUSE, L. (1975) *An Introduction to Curriculum Research and Development*, London, Heinemann.

WALKER, R. (1981) 'On the uses of fiction in educational research', in SMETHERHAM, D. (Ed.) *Practising Evaluation*, Driffield, Nafferton.

WHITEHEAD, M. (1980) 'Once upon a time?', *English in Education*, 14, 1.

WINTER, R. (1975) 'Literature and sociological theory', *Cambridge Journal of Education*, 5, 1.

WINTER, R. (1982) ' "Dilemma Analysis" — A contribution to methodology for action-research', *Cambridge Journal of Education*, 12, 3.

WINTER, R. (1987a) *Action-Research and the Nature of Social Inquiry*, Aldershot, Gower.

WINTER, R. (1987b) 'Collaboration? The dialectics of practice and reflection in action-research', *Classroom Action-Research Bulletin*, No. 8, Cambridge, Cambridge Institute of Education.

Part 5

Some Conclusions

It has not been possible, here, to reproduce all of the exchanges, the talk, the debate and argumentation which occurred at Newnham College, Cambridge in September 1986. Plenary sessions, while allowing maximum participation, made recording difficult and at best partial. The presentation by Rob Walker and Ron Lewis, from Deakin University, Australia, dealt with the difficulties of distance education in a context where the distances may parallel those between London and Moscow. We have only fragments left from this lively account. These follow below as a series of points derived from Walker and Lewis's notes:

1   Our experience tells us that establishing and maintaining an orientation to enquiry and research-based teaching is not simply a question of ideas and ideals. It is one thing to get the philosophy straight, to aspire to the general educational values implied by enquiry-based or research-based teaching; but holding the right values is not enough to ensure implementation in practice. Finding the form for a curriculum which makes its expressed values operational, as Lawrence Stenhouse pointed out, is often not as simple as it might seem.

2   In attempting to assemble any curriculum it is clearly important to pay attention to the sub-text as well as to the text. If our aspiration is to establish enquiry-based and research-based courses we need to keep more than one eye on the hidden curriculum, while at the same time attempting to create a surface curriculum that is coherent and consistent in its own terms. The Deakin experience has been that this is a very difficult thing to do, as there seems to be a distinctive entropy in the process of curriculum assembly. Indeed it may be the case that in trying hard to create the conditions that allow for an enquiry mode for the learner we may destroy the very things we are trying to create.

3   Without some effort and degree of vigilance any teaching programme we design will tend to settle back into the patterns we customarily recognize as conventional.

4 Distance education generates its own distinct problems. Courses tend to be planned in advance at a considerable level of detail and students tend to have restricted access to each other and the course group; with students as far afield as New Guinea and Western Australia the possibilities of collaborative learning are constrained. Consequently, distance learning tends to be individualized and the teaching more of an instructional/transmissional kind. Nonetheless, students can be introduced to concepts related to the ecology of their own classrooms and can raise and explore a wide range of issues.

As well as plenary sessions small groups met throughout the conference to discuss papers in some depth and with some intensity. David Hopkins, in reporting back to the plenary session, asked the fundamental question, 'How do you develop reflective competence?' From this question seven suggestions were generated:

1 reflective competence is developed through risk-taking on the part of both teacher and taught;
2 conditions for collaboration cannot be left to chance, they must be built into the course design;
3 interaction of a critical kind must be highly valued by members of the group and the providing institution;
4 teaching itself must be a collaborative practice involving a team rather than an individual;
5 assessment cannot be of a normative kind;
6 a dialectic between knowledge and experience must be promoted and sustained; and
7 shelter conditions need to be created which will allow for failure as part of the process of learning.

Two participants, Colin Biott and Susan Groundwater-Smith, formed further and fuller accounts following the conference. Their insights follow and act as the concluding chapters of the book.

16 The Quest for Authentic Description: Shared Reflections on Teaching Enquiry-based Courses

Colin Biott

This brief summary outlines the common concerns which emerged during discussion of a set of papers addressed to the topic 'Developments in enquiry-based courses'. It is not possible here to do justice to the subtleties of three days of discussion, but the intention is to draw out two main questions which are currently occupying experienced tutors. These two questions are related to the use of description in professional enquiry and to the extent to which such enquiry is politicized.

The processes of the conference did, themselves, become a focus for reflection and for comparison with tutors' own pedagogical practices. This reminded me of how, as a young boy, I had been intrigued by a lemonade bottle label on which was a picture of the bottle itself. On that picture of the bottle was a label on which there was a picture of the same bottle. On it there was a label .... There was a feeling of frustration about the eye not being able to see any more images of the bottle. A toy magnifying glass was of little help.

There is something similarly intriguing about a group of tutors from different institutions talking about its collective experience of running enquiry-based, teacher-education courses. This is especially so when the group reflects critically on its own attempts to improve its pedagogical knowledge of how to run pre-service and post-experience courses which, in turn, help students to understand the processes by which they enhance their pedagogical knowledge as school-teachers. In this case, however, the complexity of the task was being celebrated, as enthusiasts exercised their own reflective competence.

Much attention was focussed on the shape and function of the conference itself. How can the participants get the most value from the three days together? Can the conference sponsor genuine enquiry and discourse? What kind of preparation and materials, if any, would speed up the discovery of common themes of interest and the pooling of the collective experience of those present. The task for the group is to try to read the interests and expectations of its participants. There is a fine balance between spending too much of the time pursuing the preoccupations of those whose concerns are not shared by others, and allowing sufficient time for others to find some sense of engagement with those ideas. The group I worked with did favour the use of pre-conference papers and brief presentations for this purpose.

In the main, these presentations and supporting papers were accounts of course rationales and programmes, with variable attention paid to the institutional and sociopolitical contexts, and to some of the key issues to have emerged during the design, implementation and evaluation stages. There were, at least, two agendas running simultaneously during the group's discussion of the papers. On the one hand there were the descriptions of institutional contexts and the course designs themselves, fed by the questions others asked about such things as the number of students, number of assignments or forms of assessment. The information helped them to achieve a sense of place and at the same time to reconstruct their own experience. On the other hand there were the more abstract reflections on fundamental and generic issues of course development. Both in my experience of teaching an in-service MEd course and in being a group tutor at previous Cambridge conferences I have found that the interplay and tension between the quest for authenticity of the description. and the power of abstract ideas is characteristic of the enquiry-based approach to learning through discussion. It would seem that the contextual knowledge gained from authentic description is essential in sponsoring debate about the significance of institutional structures and environments in shaping courses and in causing problems in innovative approaches. There is an engagement of professional imagination as well as intellect.

Some saw the priority for progress as the need to change structures whilst others focussed more on the task of changing the expectations of tutors and students about teaching and learning. There was some exploration of the extent to which 'changing people' is a process of politicization and some dispute about the degree to which pre-service students should be politicized. A related question referred to the extent of uncertainty, doubt and sense of insecurity which can be tolerated by novice and experienced professionals. Both of these questions led to consideration of the common ground and the distinctions which might be drawn between pre-service and in-service teacher education. It was useful to have presentations and discussion about both kinds of courses within the same group.

The questions which held the group together across the fields of pre-service and in-service courses were:

1   How can we avoid enquiry-based courses becoming procedural or mechanistic?
2   How can tutors allow or encourage students to pursue genuinely felt professional questions?
3   Can groups find ways of making their own sense and meaning of their experience rather than taking on ready-formulated ideas from the library shelves?
4   Can a group find its own language of description, analysis and support?
5   Who owns the process of discovering, conceptualizing and limiting the scope of the problems?
6   What are the roles of first-hand experience and 'literature' in finding and defining the issues?
7   How can the course tutor sustain a role which is recessive, supportive, encouraging and analytical?
8   In the case of award-bearing courses, is there congruence between the assessment criteria which are appropriate to the students, the tutors, the institution and validating body?

Early in the conference Hugo Letiche, of Erasmus University, Rotterdam, outlined the principles of 'interactive experiential learning'. He pointed out how this form of learning is about solving practical problems. He emphasized that there can be no standard procedures, techniques, classes or curricula for this purpose. The message which the group found apt was to 'define your course's non-values; make it clear what the students aren't supposed to do' (see Chapter 1 in this collection):

do NOT forget the complexity of experiential investigation;
there is NO one privileged approach to circumstance;
do NOT prematurely achieve closure, or unwanted limitations of scope;
do NOT try to transcend description;
do NOT try to determine content;
do NOT say what knowledge is.

The avoidance of mechanistic, procedural formulae became a negative imperative which bound the group together. Much of the talk revolved around the difficulties of achieving genuine enquiry-based courses within the existing culture of higher education. The task was seen, in part, as the generation of appropriate, qualitative criteria. However, at the same time there was the recognition that more appropriate and realistic goals may need to be set.

It was felt that too much emphasis has been placed on analysis of data even to the extent of inhibiting the problem definition, the data collection process and the kind of data which have been sought. At worst, those who have been trying to improve their professional knowledge and practice have felt that they have had to justify their enquiry strategy to validators whose own research efforts have a less immediate and personalized application.

There was a danger of underestimating the place of student consciousness in courses. Robottom indicated the value of narrative reporting by the students at Deakin University, Australia. After a period of time the students are challenged to describe the rationale of the reflective pieces in their own journals. Ryan at King Alfred's College, Winchester, and Ashcroft and Isaac at Oxford Polytechnic were pursuing similar intentions, the latter being particularly interested in the way in which the reflection might be achieved collaboratively. Letiche's notion of 'not transcending description' was followed by the need for students to discover the framework which predisposed them to select and order the features of their accounts. They were asked to make meaning of the way that they have rendered their experience describable. This process was being seen as a way of giving students insight into the complexities of experiential learning. It is the antithesis of trying to reduce ambiguity through a quest for an efficient set of procedures. To say that a course is established is not to allude to established procedures. On the contrary, what was being implied was that a 'mature' course would have kept the complexity going.

Bell of Sheffield Polytechnic alerted the group to the distinction between 'action research' and 'case study', and to the complementary potential values of these as part of 'action enquiry' (see Chapter 2 in this collection). Action research, which develops practical intelligence, requires an extended time scale for the cycle of investigation, reflection and action. This, along with its political or emancipatory dimension, raises doubts about its value for pre-service courses. Perhaps the task of portrayal in a case study, which builds critical intelligence, is more appropriate for the pre-service course. Case study, unlike action research, does not imply change.

This issue was approached in another way during discussions about the politicization of change. A key question related to the 'ownership' of the problem. Does the host teacher, the school, the LEA or the student have the right to define the problem and the approach to enquiry? Robottom described how the participant-research tasks for Deakin University pre-service students do adopt a politicized view of science education. Issues such as sexism in science and science teaching, negotiated curriculum and activity-based learning require students to adopt a politicized perspective. The tasks involve the preparation of an initial position paper, some actual teaching, action research and the presentation of evidence and a final critique.

An alternative view being expressed in the group was that to politicize students was, in a sense, to give them an apprenticeship for not 'getting on'. Their concern for survival, for being on display and for being judged could also mean that the politics of change was too demanding a challenge for them. On the other hand descriptive accounts or 'critical portrayals' in case studies are not apolitical either. When students collectively gain some reflective distance from their own descriptive accounts the process is seen to contain within it the capacity to change expectations about pedagogy in an authentic way. Participants at this conference were left asking themselves whether the three days had confirmed this view.

17 Credential Bearing Enquiry-based Courses: Paradox or New Challenge?

Susan Groundwater-Smith

Enquiry-based courses, as they have been described in this book, are predicated upon a fundamental assumption about the nature of knowledge — that knowledge is a personal invention. The argument is that for knowledge to be truly authentic it requires the knower more than merely to assimilate the information which is available to him or her. A positive act of construction is required whereby the knower tests the information against the yardstick of personal experience. The quality of the emerging understanding is dependent upon the ability of the knower to evaluate the information in a prudent and exhaustive fashion. Each person's knowledge is the next person's information. In transmitting information we should not be persuaded that we are fabricating identical forms of knowledge.

This view permits us to see that we are involved in a never ending stream of judgments which themselves are transformed as we are challenged by new and contradictory information. Thus knowledge is personal, dynamic and never complete. To use Polanyi's (1958) view of knowledge we 'dwell' personally in a world of clues and sense impressions which we create and recreate in meaningful wholes (Prosch, 1971). The lived experience of becoming knowledgeable is cognitive, social and sensory. It is not catalogued in our minds in neat, verbal formulations but is organized as a series of complex maps, pictures and semantic tokens.

I have already indicated that there is a qualitative question attached to knowledge. Formulations based upon hasty and unreflective judgment will be less authentic than those which are predicated upon careful, systematic and rigorously interrogated evaluations. There is little doubt that educational practices are conducted as a consequence of judgments made by practitioners; the problem is that these judgments are too often based upon habit, precedent and tradition and are organized into what might be described as 'ersatz' knowledge structures. Contributors to this book have argued for the provision of conditions which will allow the process to remain fluid and be based upon continuous critical reflection.

There is, threaded through the preceding chapters, a second fundamental assumption regarding enquiry-based courses and their relation to the formulation of knowledge. That is that there is an inextricable link between 'knowing' and 'acting'. Professional knowledge is not seen as an end in itself, but as the propellant which moves the knower forward to consolidate, improve and possibly radically change practice.

Thus far, there is agreement among those who have seen themselves as advocates for enquiry-based courses regarding three issues:

(i) that the knower is engaged in his or her world in ways that are inseparably sensory, cognitive and affective;
(ii) that the knowledge which is personally crafted via such involvement is never complete;
(iii) that action is predicated upon the individual's personal knowledge, so constructed.

But from hereon a thread of dissent begins to emerge. For there is a third assumption, both in this book and the wider field, which is explicit in the work of some and not of others. This assumption is that action, to be worthwhile, must carry within it the seeds of emancipation. That is to say, there should be a continuous, relentless interrogation of sedimented social practices with the intention of changing those which result in inequality and injustice. Emancipation is seen as a moral imperative.

Stenhouse (1983) reminds us that while the appeal to personal judgment is fundamental, its effect must be expressed in emancipatory terms:

> The essence of emancipation, as I conceive it is the intellectual, moral and spiritual autonomy which we recognize when we eschew paternalism and the rule of authority and hold ourselves obliged to appeal to judgement. (p. 162)

Stenhouse's work has been greatly influential in the generation of enquiry-based courses. It rejects the view that practitioners should be dependent upon the work of academic researchers who aspire to a position of detached objectivity. He argues that it is not possible to separate facts from values, for if we should attempt to do so we shall also separate the possibility of examining the normative structures which 'produced' those facts. The teacher enquiring into his or her practice should recognize, first of all, and above all else, that he or she operates within a number of institutional norms, and that these norms have their own sociohistorical antecedents.

Knowledge, in this emancipatory sense, functions to free the knower from taken-for-granted constraints. Knowledge is not only intensely personal but also morally purposeful. Knowledge, then, in these terms, is not some sort of portable self-contained thing which may be transmitted by technically controlled conduits, or by reference to the wisdom of self-declared authorities, but is personally constructed and itself located in sociohistorical space, and is the basis for prudent and constructive action.

A number of writers who have contributed chapters in this book have indicated the influence of those identified with the Frankfurt School of Critical Theorists, most notably Jurgen Habermas. This influential contemporary thinker has argued that knowledge about social reality carries with it certain ideological, political and evaluative convictions. All social knowledge, for Habermas, is infused with 'politically relevant values' (Farganis, 1975, p. 483). More explicitly, Habermas makes connections between logical-methodological rules, i.e. ways in which knowledge is derived, and knowledge constitutive interests. He proposes that there are three levels of knowledge interests, with each level transcending the one which came before. These interests are expressed as technical-cognitive interests, practical interests and emancipatory-cognitive interests (Habermas, 1978, p. 308).

Habermas argues that the technical-cognitive knowledge interest is dominated by an unquestioning acceptance of the tenets of enquiry in certain branches of the physical sciences, although perhaps less so in the study of physics itself. An attempt is made, in much conservative science, to create behavioural laws. Habermas sees this, when applied to the social sciences, as not only illusory but also as the basis for manipulation of sociopolitical practices which assume specialized competencies, thus allowing one group to manage and control another. It is this set of knowledge interests which Popkewitz *et al.* (1987) have argued has been served by conventional teacher education courses at both the pre-service and in-service levels.

Practical knowledge interests, on the other hand, provide for understanding to be derived by seeking for meaning rather than by being dependent upon surface level observation. The knower is a reasoning interpreter of the action. However, those social norms which lie in the very bedrock remain unexamined, unchallenged and unaltered. It may well be argued that a number of the descriptions of practices offered in this book fall into this category.

The third, and final knowledge-forming interest, that which is described by Habermas as emancipatory-cognitive, addresses closely the matter of intersubjectivity, self-reflection and reflexivity. The impetus is towards the empowerment of the knower to perceive the genesis and evolution of ideas in sociohistorical space, and having thus identified them to understand their consequences upon individuals and groups, students, teachers, parents . . . .

> It (emancipation) is based on reflection and self-recognition by reasoned beings of the historical and social location of their own reasoning and results in the practice of emancipation from dogma. (Young, 1983, p. 9)

Arguably, several chapters in this book may be seen as attempts, albeit imperfect, to realize this ideal. However, a severe constraint exists and one which is highly problematic in the face of all this rhetoric. That is the matter of facilitating emancipatory action-oriented enquiry within award-bearing courses. In order to meet institutional demands, there is a considerable pressure for work to be presented for assessment purposes which is of an individualistic, rather than a collaborative, kind. Even the York Outstation Program for teams of teachers, which was outlined by Ian Lewis, rewards individual effort at the end of it all. As Holly (1986) points out, 'this approach extends the "cult of the individual" the acquisitive, self-centred competitive strain of autonomous professionals' (p. 1).

Herein lies the conflict. On the one hand, the argument favouring emancipatory-cognitive knowledge interests insists upon conditions which will allow for open communication within collaborative communities of interest, on the other, award-granting institutions require evidence of individual academic effort resulting in assessable products. Alongside this difficulty lies another to do with the asymmetry of power relations within enquiry-based courses. Even given a situation in which group work might be judged as such, what of relative status within group membership? If enquiry-based courses aspire to take a truly emancipatory form then the provision of a collaborative critical community whose members hold equal status and rights is essential.

Why do I assert this so strongly? To answer this question in part we need to return to Habermas and his notions of communicative competence which lie at the heart of critical social theory as he sees it. Habermas' central endeavour is directed to developing the ideals of freedom, equality, companionability and rational public discourse. Through his various writings he has evolved the notion of the Ideal Speech Situation (ISS) which proposes that each time we speak, the claim is made that what we have to say is intelligible, true, correct and sincere. Furthermore that claim rests upon a background consensus about what these terms mean and a mutual recognition that they actually prevail. This means, necessarily, a set of ideal conditions. There is to be no domination or coercion and all speakers are to have equal rights to assert, to question and to discuss. The extent to which the ISS varies from the actual speech situation is the extent to which communication, and from it emancipatory knowledge, are smoothly shaped or distorted.

Habermas sees the ISS as counterfactual, i.e. that it is a formulation which stands in contradistinction to reality. The plea is for a commitment *towards* its realization. In all of our exchanges and discourses wherein we are creating policies and practices which will affect the lives of others we need to be continually alert to the extent to which the ISS does *not* exist. The most systematically distorting feature for Habermas (1984) is the desire of participants, in such discourses, to succeed in socially competitive situations as opposed to an authentic desire to reach understanding. Award-bearing courses, by their nature, have embedded within them elements of competitiveness. Habermas says: 'Such communication pathologies can be conceived of as the result of a confusion between actions oriented to reaching understanding and actions oriented to success' (p. 332). It may well be that individual teacher-initiated research will gain short-term benefits for that teacher and his/her class, but militate against more enduring long-term benefits for that community.

Certainly this view of enquiry-based courses, kindled by emancipatory knowledge interests and requiring collaborative reasoning and collegiality (an almost impossible condition to meet), is not without its critics. The most colourful and trenchant of these is to be found in Gibson's (1985) critique of *Becoming Critical* (Carr and Kemmis, 1986), a work which has been cited by a number of writers in this book. Gibson's criticisms rest very much upon the concern he has that action research, as a particular form of teacher enquiry, has moved beyond the interpersonal and institutional and into the structural. It is this very aspiration to influence the structural which impedes, perhaps even prohibits, its realization. And yet it is this very aspiration which is also truly emancipatory. Without question the provision of award-bearing courses is itself deeply embedded in structural practices; are those who offer such courses both willing and able significantly to question and challenge the institutional mores of which they are themselves a part?

How then does a critical community form? Does it exist only in the imagination of the academic theorist? And, if so, does it then become the ultimate paradox? One thing which is clear to me is that enquiry-based courses of the ideal, emancipatory kind, free of coercion, with participants holding symmetrical relationships, one with the other, are not possible within the confines of award-bearing courses. Indeed, it might be argued that the conduct of teacher enquiry within award-bearing courses may have contributed to the reification of certain practices in complete contradiction to the intentions of those offering such courses. It may well be that some enquiry-based teacher research has become a strategy for reproducing technical behaviour more expertly.

For example, the Action Research Planner (McTaggart and Kemmis, 1981) was designed to assist those undertaking enquiry-based teaching, often within Deakin University's own award-bearing courses offered to off-campus students. It was intended as a means of facilitating teacher research, but became seen as a set of technical rules for the conduct of the action research game complete with a snakes and ladders spiral which would allow movement around the board, leading ultimately to the granting of a credential. (Indeed, Bell, in an earlier chapter in this book, refers to the spiral having gained iconic properties.) The credential game exists in time and space, it has well-defined boundaries, a start, a finish, winners and losers. It has its umpires and referees, both on and off the field. No matter how congenially the game is run, no matter how democratic its management, the award-bearing course cannot provide the truly symmetrical conditions which would lead to collective emancipation.

All of which leads me to wonder whether teacher research, serving emancipatory-cognitive knowledge interests, is a chimera, mythological rather than possible. In Greek mythology the chimera is characterized as a fire-breathing monster with a lion's head, a goat's body and a serpent's tail. Figuratively it is used to characterize a mere wild fancy, an unfounded conception. Is the assembly of an award-bearing course based upon teacher enquiry such a beast, an attempt to bring together such disparate and contradictory ideas that it becomes an impossibility?

I think not. I believe that emancipatory teacher research is possible and that award-bearing courses can create conditions which, while not *directly* resulting in such emancipation within the course itself, can set in motion small disturbances, awkward unanswered questions, unsettled conditions, irritations and scratchiness. These might lead to both the participants themselves and those around them beginning to question profoundly their own certitude. What must remain unanswered is how enduring such changes in the individual psyche will be and the extent to which transformed individuals can themselves enable others to re-examine their knowledge and actions. Perhaps then, at the end of the day, enquiry-based courses can be a powerful means of bringing us to the very threshold of emancipation. That part of the journey, alone, is a difficult and challenging struggle. To step over, however, goes beyond the bounds of that which any course can promise.

References

CARR, W. and KEMMIS, S. (1986) *Becoming Critical*, Lewes, Falmer Press.

FARGANIS, J. (1975) 'A Preface to critical theory', *Theory and Society*, 2, pp. 483–508.

GIBSON, R. (1985) 'Critical time for action research', *Cambridge Journal of Education*, 15, 1, pp. 56–64.

HABERMAS, J. (1978) 'Appendix "Knowledge and human interests: A general perspective"', *Knowledge and Human Interests*, 2nd edn, translated by J.J. Shapiro, London, Heinemann Educational Books.

HABERMAS, J. (1984) *The Theory of Communicative Action. Vol. One: Reason and Rationalization of Society*, London, Heinemann Educational Books.

HOLLY, P. (1986) 'Action research: Teacher based, teachers based, or staff based?', paper presented at the International Symposium Concerning Theoretical Models and Strategies for Educational Innovation, University of Murcia, Spain.

McTAGGART, R. and KEMMIS, S. (1981) *The Action Research Planner*, Geelong, Deakin University Press.

POLANYI, M. (1958) *Personal Knowledge*, Chicago, University of Chicago Press.

POPKEWITZ, T. (1987) *Critical Studies in Teacher Education: Its Folklore, Theory and Practice*, Lewes, Falmer Press.

STENHOUSE, L. (1983) *Authority, Education and Emancipation*, London, Heinemann Educational.

YOUNG, R.E. (1983) 'Towards a critical theory of education', University of Sydney, nimeo.

Notes on Contributors

Herbert Altrichter is lecturer at the Department of Education of Klagenfurt University, Austria. At present his main academic interest is the methodology of teacher research.

Kate Ashcroft is Principal Lecturer at Oxford Polytechnic responsible for the BEd Honours programme and the development of the course.

Gordon Bell has been involved for a number of years in various approaches to collaborative school improvement. Formerly Principal Lecturer in Education (Research) at Sheffield City Polytechnic, he is presently Professor of Primary Education and Head of Department Designate at Trent Polytechnic, Nottingham.

Colin Biott is Principal Lecturer in Educational Development and Enquiry at Newcastle Polytechnic, UK.

David Burrell is Reader in Education at the University of Sussex and acted as evaluator for the Worcester review.

Doug Dennis is Director of Studies for BEd In-Service programmes at Worcester College of Higher Education.

Susan Groundwater-Smith is a senior lecturer in the School of Teaching and Curriculum Studies at the University of Sydney. She teaches courses in Curriculum and Evaluation and undertakes educational evaluation work for both national and state level sponsors.

John Isaac After experience teaching in both primary and secondary schools he has worked in teacher education on experientially based courses in two polytechnics.

Hugo Letiche lectures in Knowledge Management and Management Education, in the Department of Qualitative Information Sciences, Rotterdam School of Management, Erasmus University, Rotterdam. His current research interests include self-evaluation and corporate anthropology.

Ian Lewis was Senior Lecturer in the Education Department at the University of York at the time of writing. He is now Reader in Education at Westminster College, Oxford and beginning to develop school-based research in conjunction with a number of LEAs in the region.

Jennifer Nias is Tutor in Curriculum Studies, 3–13, at the Cambridge Institute of Education. Her current work is with experienced teachers on in-service courses, but she has also worked in pre-service education (BEd and PGCE).

Margaret Preedy is a lecturer in the School of Education, The Open University. She is chair of OU Course EP851, *Applied Studies in Educational Management*.

Colin Riches is a lecturer in the School of Education, The Open University. He is chair of OU course E325, *Managing Schools*.

Ian Robottom is senior lecturer in the School of Education at Deakin University, Geelong, Australia. He has interests in participant enquiry in teacher education.

Stephen Rowland works, mainly in the field of in-service education, at Sheffield University.

Judyth Sachs is senior lecturer at the Gold Coast College of Advanced Education, Australia. She teaches in the teacher education programme and has research interests in pre- and in-service teacher education.

Richard Smith is a reader in Sociology of Education at the University of Queensland, Australia with interests in teacher education, policy and cultural studies.

Bridget Somekh was a tutor on part-time courses for the Advanced Diploma at the Cambridge Institute of Education from 1979 to 1986. She is currently co-ordinator of the Classroom Action Research Network and from September 1988 will be leading an action research project based at the University of East Anglia (Developing Pupil Autonomy in Learning with Microcomputers (PALM).

M.E. Stevens has worked since 1962 as a teacher and counsellor with pupils and students in comprehensive schools in the Midlands and at Manchester University, and in Clwyd since 1980. He is currently involved in professional and curriculum development at NEWI, Plas Coch, Wrexham.

Jean Whittaker is an Honorary Fellow of the University of Hull. She was formerly Head of Education at Bishop Grosseteste College, Lincoln, co-ordinator of the DES Teacher Training Project at Charlotte Mason College and Research Officer at the Schools Council. Through these she has developed her interests in evaluation and in-service education.

Richard Winter is a Course Tutor for the MEd in Educational Research and Evaluation at the Essex Institute of Higher Education, Sawyers Hall Lane, Brentwood, Essex.

Index